Body Talk

to Sandy —

Here's to getting
together and
[illegible] —

Love
Jane

Body Talk

LOOKING AND BEING LOOKED AT IN PSYCHOTHERAPY

Janice S. Lieberman, Ph.D.

JASON ARONSON INC.

Northvale, New Jersey
London

Production Editor: Elaine Lindenblatt

This book was set in 12 pt. Bembo by Pageworks of Old Saybrook and Lyme, CT, and printed and bound by Book-mart Press, Inc. of North Bergen, NJ.

Library of Congress Cataloging-in-Publication Data

Lieberman, Janice S.
    Body talk : looking and being looked at in psychotherapy / Janice S. Lieberman.
      p. cm.
    Includes bibliographical references.
    ISBN 0-7657-0258-4
    1. Narcissism. 2. Psychotherapist and patient. 3. Body image. 4. Gaze—Psychological aspects. 5. Self.   I. Title.
RC533.N36L54 2000
616.89'14—dc21   99-088327

Printed in the United States of America on acid-free paper. For information and catalog write to Jason Aronson Inc., 230 Livingston Street, Northvale, NJ 07647-1726, or visit our website: www.aronson.com

To my mother,
Arline Wiegan Sternheim,
who taught me about
looking and being looked at

Contents

IV. APPLIED PSYCHOANALYSIS

Preface

Freud and his disciples wrote about visual symptoms—hysterical blindness, voyeurism, exhibitionism—and attributed their genesis to regression induced by unconscious conflict. They thought that their patients suffered from what they had "seen" as children. Today's patients seem, on the other hand, to suffer from "not being seen" or being "incorrectly seen" or "falsely mirrored."

Many of today's patients suffer from profound to moderate narcissistic disturbances and ask their therapists overtly or covertly: "How do I look?" "What do I look like?" "Do you like the way I look?" Their love objects are loved for their good looks or rejected for their bad looks. Those who cannot find someone to love are often all too aware of others' search for someone with ideal looks, compensating perhaps for the looks they do not have themselves. I have found these issues to be prominent in my work with both male and female narcissistic patients. Our culture's emphasis on having lean and muscular bodies as representing perfection, and the promotion by the media of such ideals, have had a significant impact on all of our patients and ourselves as well.

Despite the prevalence in clinical practice of such issues, few studies exist in the literature on the role of looking and being looked at, or about patients' feelings about their own looks or others' looks. When it has been mentioned, it has been dealt with as a derivative of a drive-related fantasy, as a vicissitude of voyeurism and/or exhibitionism, rather than in the form of an examinination of the important narcissistic function served by looking and being looked at.

Psychotherapists have long been struggling with the treatment of narcissistic issues. I believe that our focus has been an incorrect one. To the Freudian analyst, the "body" usually has meant the biological drives and the wishes emanating from them that are directed toward objects. When Freud (1923) wrote that the first ego is the body ego, he meant an *inner experience* of the body, the body imago. Today, when patients refer to their bodies and to their dissatisfaction with their bodies, they usually mean their *external* bodies as seen (1) from the outside by themselves in the mirror or by others—the body's size, shape, and muscle tone; and (2) from the inside, by their own all-too-critical internalizations.

Narcissistic patients make use of the therapist as a spectator (often a reluctant one) rather than as a voyeur. The therapist's focus on their bodies enables them to supplement its insufficient cathexis. The therapist should state quite concretely his or her awareness of patients' bodily changes or changes in clothing, that is, of what is on the surface rather than within the psyche. The therapist should address what is seen, not just what is heard. Seemingly mundane statements have a mutative influence. The therapist must stay linguistically attuned with the concrete language used by the patient, rather than rush to metaphor. This book also addresses the considerable countertransference difficulties the therapist experiences when working with narcissistic patients who are preoccupied with the appearances of their own bodies and those of others.

The development of language and thought, from concreteness to symbolization and metaphor, is linked to thoughts about the body and body narcissism. The language these patients use is concrete, stemming from the time in their development in which the integration of body narcissism was an important task. Review of the developmental literature shows that there is an historic link between the development of language and that of body narcissism.

The book is organized as follows: Part I discusses the power of looks. The visual ego and body narcissism are defined and elaborated and the psychoanalytic and social-historical and cultural backgrounds of these topics are presented in Chapters 1 and 2.

Part II deals with developmental issues. Chapters 3 and 4 review the relevant developmental literature on vision; the gaze and mutual gaze between infant and mother in the dyad; the intertwined development of language and body narcissism; the role of the mirror in the development of the body image.

Part III focuses on looking and being looked at in the clinical process, and presents clinical work with body narcissism. Chapter 5 introduces techniques for working with these patients, particularly with respect to their use of concrete language, and this subject is expanded upon in Chapter 6, which discusses working with women who are obsessed with thinness. Chapter 7 probes clinical material pertaining to the use of the couch or chair from the point of view of the visual aspects referred to in earlier chapters. Chapter 8 covers my own countertransference reactions and personal thoughts about our culture's focus on the "perfect body."

Part IV is devoted to applied psychoanalysis. In Chapter 9, I venture into the field of contemporary art and in Chapter 10, film and literature, applying the concepts discussed in the book and broadening the clinical perspective on these issues.

The clinical case illustrations are disguised amalgamations drawn from my own clinical experience and that of my students and colleagues.

Acknowledgments

I am deeply grateful to a number of gifted colleagues whom I am most fortunate to be able to count among my closest friends. Over the past several years, they have given me loving support and encouragement as I developed the body of work about the body that has become this book. Their painstaking reading of an early draft resulted in wise commentary that has enriched and deepened my work. I alone am responsible for any errors or misconceptions or omissions. I want to thank, in alphabetical order, Linda Futterman, Daniele Knafo, Judith Levitan, Steven Levitan, Arlene Kramer Richards, Barbara Stimmel, and Isaac Tylim.

Jason Aronson, my publisher, encouraged me to start this project and gave me support and wise counsel throughout. Norma Pomerantz provided much sustaining humor as she saw me though various editorial tasks. Production editor Elaine Lindenblatt carefully monitored all the steps of production with warmth and clear, precise direction. Acquisitions editor Anne Marie Dooley assisted in the final stages. I was greatly helped by the skills of Leslie Shaw, Barbara Frank, and Tamar Richards, and by the instruction of a computer expert, John Ammirati.

Many groups have heard presentations of the papers whose substance formed the core of this book. I would like to thank particularly several discussants and panel moderators who shed useful light on many of my ideas and enabled me to develop and refine them: Maria Bergmann, Mark Stevens, Sharon Zalusky, Linda Gunsberg, and Susannah Falk-Shopsin. I have learned much from the members of my RAPS group on female gender, and from discussions with Richard Reichbart, Carol Chinn, Rena Greenblatt, and Dana Dorfman.

Finally, this work would not have been realized in its final form without the assistance of the keen mind, sharp wit, and challenging editorial style of Eve Golden.

I

THE POWER OF LOOKS

1

The Visual Ego

Like a latter day Tiresias, Freud in effect sacrificed sight to insight. He turned away from the symptom toward the association, from the theatrical appearance to the psychological meaning, from the dream's manifest content—a theatrical symptom—toward its latent content. The symptom is visible to the naked eye, the association is visible to the mind's eye—reason's eye.... The visible symptom is not there to be mirrored ... but to be understood.

Kuspit (1998, p. 12)

This book considers the meanings of looking and being looked at, of seeing and being seen, in the human psyche. We possess at birth a highly complex visual apparatus, which is fundamental in our adaptation to the world around us. Vision helps us first to recognize our caregivers, and then to "read" them in order to figure out the best ways of convincing them to attend to us. Vision shows us what we look like, both to ourselves and to others. Mirrors, the evaluative gaze, the gleam in the eye, and the averted glance all inform us further about who we are. We learn at an early age to attach positive and negative values to our looks and the looks of others, and to the way we look *at* others and they at us. In short, we develop over time a complicated set of psychological and cognitive habits that has been called "the visual ego" (Weissman 1977). According to Weissman:

> The discriminating smiling response between mother and child is the nucleus of the early visual ego. As mother and child gaze at each other, they interact with increasing social nuance. The child learns to make his eyes and their gaze complex social instruments. He also learns to discriminate and rely on his perceptions of the face, eyes, and gaze of others. We learn to use our eyes to read emotions in others, to express emotions of our own, and to communicate with others. [p. 447]

Weissman noted that although these issues have received attention in the areas of infant observation and child analysis, a resistance to these issues in the analysis of adults still exists.

We also develop over time a more or less healthy "body narcissism," a complicated physical sense of ourselves that is in many ways dependent on early visual experience. Body narcissism is a complex and multifaceted construction that also includes experiences of touch and the internal kinesthetic sense of the body. But I want to explore rather exclusively the neglected connection between the visual and the sense of self. Therefore, this discussion is limited to a study of positive and negative feelings about the external body, as they develop from experiences of being looked at by others and by one's own experiences of looking.

The visual ego, like its generic counterpart, is not immune to intrapsychic conflict or any other psychological strain, so our feelings about how we look and what we see can develop in normal or in conflicted ways—they can, for example, become hypercathected in neurosis, or split off in perversion. By the same token, the development of healthy body narcissism can be disrupted by the same developmental stressors that influence the other aspects of narcissistic development.

Vision impacts upon all aspects of life including psychotherapy, although this has not always been adequately accounted for in discussions of theory and technique. There are reasons for this, some of which are historical. My training in social psychology prior to my becoming a psychoanalyst gave me a respect for the role of social context in the development of theory and some understanding of the cultural and intellectual heritage in which psychoanalysis developed. For example, it is held that highly intellectual and sexually repressed late-nineteenth-century Vienna tolerated Freud's ideas about sex and the body more readily in the context of fantasies and metaphors than as concrete realities (Gilman 1998).

This book is a product of the culture and thought of the late 1990s, and I think that these times demand a return to the concrete realities of the body that have been neglected in favor of more abstract approaches. Time and place influence psychoanalytic theory.

Articles written just twenty-five years ago already seem out of date. When film and art critics in the 1970s wrote that "the gaze" was "masculine"—that "looking" was the domain of men and "being looked at" the domain of women (Berger 1972, Mulvey 1975), their assertions appeared to be valid, and in fact they elucidated a phenomenon that many of us had not considered; it raised our consciousness. Today, due in part perhaps to the efforts of those same writers, it is becoming clear that women are socialized differently, and they do actively look at men and at other women, just as men actively look at other men as well as at women, and seek to be looked at by them as well.

It is true also that the very phenomena of looking and being looked at have new constellations of meaning at the dawn of the twenty-first century. Our patients today were raised in the age of television. Many of them can be considered to be *visuels*, a French term I have borrowed from Jay (1993), who used it to describe those who are visually oriented, or "ocularcentric," people who use their eyes to process experience more than they do their ears or their other senses. (Freud labeled Charcot, who observed hysterics' physical characteristics in his amphitheater and photo studio, a *visuel*.) Many people now spend their working days staring at computer screens, their evenings watching television, and their social lives on the Internet. Spectatorship, voyeurism, and exhibitionism have assumed extraordinary prominence in our culture. Technological advances such as communication satellites, cable TV, and portable video cameras have made all of us, willing or not, witness to the private lives of the famous and infamous. Coupled with this enforced emphasis on looking is a corresponding emphasis on being looked at and therefore on looking good. Good looks, perfect bodies, and ultimate fitness are no longer the exclusive domain of movie stars and models, but are goals considered both attainable and obligatory by many. Some of these people, male and female both, become psychotherapy patients, and some of them judge themselves (and others) almost exclusively on the basis of what they see. Many have grown up in families that characterize people (including themselves) in judgmental and binary fashion: thin or fat, tall or short, small-nosed or large-nosed—in short, as good or bad.

The patients I have treated over the last decade lead very different lives from the people I saw in my training and they present with very different issues. In the 1970s, my women patients were involved in battles, at least on a manifest level, for equality with husbands and lovers. They wanted a say in what happened during sexual relations; they wanted their husbands involved with their children and with the running of the household as they struggled to have careers rather than be housewives. They had to work through underlying conflicts about what it meant to be female. My male patients were trying to hold onto their marriages, and had to work through their own conflicts about being male and feeling castrated in the new roles cast upon them. Today I hear less about sex or sex roles. I hear more about the difficulties of maintaining body tone and a desirable weight. Child-care professionals and higher incomes have taken some of the pressure off the sex-role debate, and provided leisure time that increasingly seems to be devoted to working out. Many of my patients, both men and women, spend their free time in health clubs, taking advantage of the day-care facilities provided for babies and children. The babies have their own exercise classes and gyms when they are not out being pushed around in jogging strollers. I see patients now who embark upon the psychotherapeutic journey with the goal, explicitly or implicitly stated, of finding the way to a perfect body or finding a "perfect 10" to love. Are these patients' presenting issues really "old wine in new bottles"—have these problems always been there, but gone unrecognized? Or are we dealing with a new kind of psyche? I think the latter, and I think that new psychotherapeutic techniques are needed to analyze it. Thompson and colleagues (1999), in the preface to their exhaustive review of the theory, assessment, and treatment of body image disturbances, remarked that "the toll of trying to meet increasingly unrealistic models of beauty has never been more exacting" (p. xi).

Up to the 1970s, clinical reports on body issues based on psychoanalytic theory tended to be organized around issues of gender. They focused on clinical observations that women envy men their penises, and that men envy women their wombs and their breasts. The theory has changed, but it seems to me that despite the changes, the focus is still on the metaphoric body rather than the concrete one (see, for example, Bach 1994 and Aron and Anderson 1998). In my clinical work, many patients, especially those who present with issues around body narcissism, are developmentally located or fixated much less in issues of gender identity than in issues of identity per se; like children fascinated by their images in mirrors, these patients are attempting to find out who they are in some very basic way. These patients seem fragmented; they speak with desperation about their bodies, trying to get the therapist quite literally to look at them as if that would help them hold themselves together. When such patients find themselves envious of others, and many *are* envious, the envy is quite concrete. These times require us to differentiate between the wish for a "concrete" penis and the wish for a penis "as metaphor" that represents the power and status afforded men in our culture. This distinction has been made by Laplanche and Pontalis (1973) (who use "phallus" to describe the symbolic aspect, while "penis" denotes the bodily male organ), as well as by many feminist psychoanalytic writers. (Freud himself was referring to the actual penis in his writings.)

Little attention has been given in published clinical reports or in theory to problems in the development of body narcissism, to the fantasies related to it, and to the types of transferences manifested in psychoanalytic treatment by patients who present with such issues. The metaphoric bias in psychoanalysis has led us to listen for fantasies about the body as symbol, metaphorically reflecting conflicts about gender and genitalia, rather than for material about the "real" body—we listen *for* the latent, rather than *to* the manifest. In this age of the image, we need to learn how to use our technical tools to deal with these manifest issues when they emerge.

When Freud began his psychoanalytic explorations, he wrote about actual bodies—their instincts and their needs. The physical body at that time was widely understood to be relevant to psychiatric illness. Freud's teacher Ernest Brücke published a handbook on the beauty of the body, illustrating the perfect female breast and male torso, and Charcot published photographs of the hysterics at his clinic at Salpetrière. Early on, in *The Psychopathology of Everyday Life*, Freud (1901b) advised psychoanalysts to note people's postures, movements, and gestures as revealing communications. In his analysis of Dora (1905a), he noted her fingering of her reticule, and in this context made his famous remark that "If his [the analysand's] lips are silent, he chatters with his fingertips: betrayal oozes out of him at every pore" (pp. 77–78). Nevertheless, as Gilman (1995) noted, "Freud's intellectual as well as analytic development in the 1890s was a movement away from the 'meaning' of visual signs . . . to verbal signs, from the crudity of seeing to the subtlety of hearing" (p. 22). Gilman (1998) observed about Freud:

> After 1896, he no longer believed that one could alter the psyche by operating on the body. Freud stopped seeing the outside to [*sic*] the body as a means of judging the internal workings of the psyche and began to focus on the invisible and unseeable aspects of the psyche. He now saw the fantasy as the source for the types of physical ailments that manifested themselves in sexual dysfunction and hysteria. [p. 93]

According to his daughter Anna, Freud did not like his looks; he did not like to be photographed and he made faces when he was. On the other hand (or perhaps on the same hand!) his mother was quite vain. She was concerned with looking good and not looking too old, even in home movies taken when she was in her nineties (Yorke, home video, Freud Museum, London). It is tempting to speculate that her vanity, and by extension his, might have influenced his neglect of such issues in his theories.

As Boxer (1998) has said, Freud championed a "talking cure" rather than a "looking cure." Kuspit (1998) suggests an aspect of Freud's personality that might have contributed to this development: "[Freud] wanted intellectual pleasure from art, not sensuous pleasure . . . he could not enjoy beauty unless he could intellectually dissect it" (p. 3). He preferred to turn visual experience into words. A. D. Richards (personal communication, 1998) has argued that since dreams are visual phenomena, Freud was visually oriented. Freud (1900) wrote that "in a dream an idea is turned back into the sensory image from which it was originally derived" (p. 543). (See also Schust-Briat 1996 for a discussion in which she takes the same position.) I would argue, though, that putting dream images into words that are then soon treated as symbol and metaphor can be a way of distancing the images from their origins.

As accustomed as we therapists are to reflecting back to patients what we hear, we are often very inhibited, for reasons I will discuss later, about reflecting back to them what we *see*. We may consciously refrain from such commentary to avoid making our patients feel seduced, self-conscious, or ashamed, but in so doing we may miss the opportunity to increase self-awareness in areas where self-consciousness and shame play a part. When patients try in various ways to get us to look at them, we often feel like reluctant spectators. Angry countertransference feelings can emerge and negatively influence the treatment. We are at times praised or attacked by our patients for our own appearance, for aspects of our facial features, body type, or clothing. In this book I attempt to understand such transference–countertransference developments, and to suggest ways of dealing with them.

Today, many psychotherapy patients have issues about body

narcissism, and think and talk about them in *concrete terms*. They have not yet made the progression from concrete to symbolic and metaphoric thinking, at least when they think about their own bodies and other people's. Psychoanalysts, on the other hand, usually think and speak in symbol and metaphor. Arlow (1979) believed that psychoanalysis is "essentially a metaphorical exercise," and that "metaphor is the analysand's indirect expression of an unconscious fantasy and in the transference as a transfer of meaning from a childhood to an adult situation" (p. 373). Levin (1979) noted that "metaphors will resonate with the highest and deepest layers of the patient's functional hierarchy of experience" (p. 241). More recently Borbely (1998) said: "In psychoanalysis we use metaphors for effecting change and observe metaphors *in statu nascendi*" (p. 924).

When patients think and speak concretely, however, stalemates can occur because the patient and the therapist are speaking in two different modes, the therapist favoring and promoting metaphors that are beyond the patient's grasp or interest. It is important in these cases to avoid what I think of as the therapist's characteristic rush to metaphor. Although the literature addresses the fact that some patients cannot make use of metaphor, specific recommendations are lacking for how to communicate with such patients in other ways, how to get through to them, so that deeper layers of the psyche can eventually be analyzed. I will address this question.

Freud and his disciples wrote about visual symptoms—hysterical blindness, voyeurism, and exhibitionism, for example—and attributed their genesis to regression induced by unconscious conflict. They thought originally that their patients suffered from what they had *seen* as children. Today's patients seem, on the other hand, to suffer from *being* seen—incorrectly perceived or falsely mirrored—and in some cases from not having been seen at all.

So in this book, while ranging over a wide variety of topics having to do with the intrapsychic uses of sight, I will keep returning to considerations of people whose problems are rooted in *narcissistic deficit*. These problems present not as hysterical symptoms, but as an enhanced *narcissistic body awareness*, accompanied by enhanced shame and self-consciousness and a profound need for attention. I will show how such problems can manifest themselves in the psychotherapeutic situation, and how I have learned to deal with them.

Pluralism now rules the field of psychotherapy. I have not always taken well to the pluralistic zeitgeist. I find the pluralistic zeitgeist confusing, and I have tried as much as possible to hold on to the classical stance in my work, both as a discipline and as a compass. Still, I am influenced, if not converted, by object relations theory, attachment theory, and self psychology. Out of sheer frustration with some analytic stalemates, I have explored certain modifications of standard technique that I have found to be consistently useful and helpful. When I discuss such interventions with colleagues, I hear not infrequently that others have been working in similar ways. These technical innovations, however, do not find their way into the literature, and so they tend to retain a slight tinge of illegitimacy. I hope this book helps to change that connotation.

My interests and my data are not merely clinical. I believe that we add to and deepen our understanding of psychotherapeutic concepts when we examine them in many contexts. Psychology, neurobiology, sociology, politics, art, literature, and film all can contribute to our understanding. Multidisciplinary thinking tests, expands, and consolidates our theory.

Although I have surveyed and will touch upon many works in the areas of psychotherapy, child development, art, literature, and film, this book is not intended to be an exhaustive or a comprehensive survey. I have selected for discussion those works that have especially intrigued me; undoubtedly some will find my choices highly idiosyncratic. I have deliberately chosen to concentrate on vision alone, teasing it out as much as I could from the other senses with which it interacts—hearing, touch, proprioception, taste, and smell. Such interactions are beyond the scope of one book. I have provided reviews where necessary of representative portions of the literature on vision and on the developing psyche in an attempt to bring together these disparate topics.

Vision, language development, and the development of body narcissism are intimately connected, and this books shows how this connection can manifest itself clinically. This book also speculates about how the link between the concrete and the visible develops. I will make technical recommendations and give specific examples about working with patients who use concrete language to express their preoccupations with what can be concretely seen, and who are primarily concerned with issues about their own or others' appearance. I will thus demonstrate that there can be an important mutative function in seemingly mundane interventions and in simple language that is close to that of the patient, rather than a translation of it into more abstract metaphoric terms. The *linguistic* attunement of therapist with patient, parallel to the better-recognized *affective* attunement, is equally necessary for optimal therapeutic work.

It is also necessary to raise some questions about the use of the couch with those who present with issues around body narcissism. We are accustomed to traditional psychoanalysts being heard but not seen. But certain kinds of information are not, and cannot be, received either by a therapist sitting behind the patient, or by a patient with the therapist behind him. When issues of seeing and being seen do not predominate for a particular patient, then the use of the couch is indicated. But there are some issues that cannot be dealt with unless patient and therapist can see each other. Psychotherapists must learn the art of looking as well as of listening; they must learn not only to listen with the "third ear" (Reik 1948),

but also to "hear with eyes" (Khan 1971), and to speak "body language" as a native tongue (Paniagua 1998).

It is time for the therapeutic lens to focus on the important but
neglected role of vision—of looking and being looked at, of seeing and being seen—in the development of self and self-esteem, in
object awareness and object interaction, and in the psychotherapeutic situation itself. Traditionally, analysis has placed great emphasis on the role of words—the verbalization of repressed affects,
fantasies, and memories—as the patient speaks and the analyst lis-
tens. But it sometimes neglects the important role of visual cues
and visual communications between patient and analyst. Sometimes
the avoidance is more active. Freud's discomfort with being stared
at all day led to his use of the couch in psychoanalytic treatment,
a practice followed by later generations of psychoanalysts. As Peter
Brooks (1993) has said, language substituting for the body and body
experience is now used by psychoanalysts to distance from the body.
To the extent that this is true, it is time to change it.

This book is a twenty-first-century update of the important work
on vision in psychoanalysis that began with some of Freud's early
writings, and was then pursued by Greenacre, Jacobson, Mahler,
Winnicott, Lacan, Stern, and Beebe and Lachmann. Greenacre's
work on vision and Jacobson's theory of the formation of self and
object representations, in which vision plays a primary role, have
influenced me profoundly, as have the writings of A. K. Richards
on myriad subjects related to female development. I also owe a
tremendous debt to the authors of the major summary papers on
psychoanalysis and vision that appeared in the 1970s and 1980s;
notably Riess (1978, 1988), Barglow and Sadow (1971), and Pines
(1984). I want to acknowledge Wright's (1991) *Vision and Separation: Between Mother and Baby,* and the contributors to two volumes
of *Psychoanalytic Inquiry*: 1985/2 on the mirror, and 1995/3 on the
use of the couch. Peter Brooks's (1993) *Body Work,* although a study
of literature, was more psychoanalytic in its approach than some

psychoanalytic works, and was a rich resource. So was the fascinating, dazzlingly scholarly work of historian Martin Jay. His *Downcast Eyes: The Denigration of Vision in Twentieth Century French Thought* (1993), carefully documents the history of thinking about vision in France from Descartes through Freud, Lacan, Merleau-Ponty, Bataille, Foucault, and others, and it provided me with excellent references and much food for thought. It was Jay who noted that "paranoia, narcissism and exhibitionism suggest how powerfully visual experience, both directed and received, can be tied to our psychological processes" (p. 11). Jay also noted that there is a close relationship between language and sight; that ocularity in fact permeates language, and that when people speak different tongues, they process visual experience in different ways.

2

On Looking and Being Looked At, Seeing and Being Seen

Psychoanalysis, unfortunately, has scarcely anything to say about beauty.

Freud (1930, p. 83)

$\mathcal{I}$t is not surprising that the theory of psychoanalytic technique developed with an injunction implicit within it against looking and being looked at, because something aggressive, taboo, or pathological has been ascribed to these phenomena since civilization began. Such sayings as "if looks could kill" and "dressed to kill" acknowledge the magical powers of the eye.

"Looking," for art historian James Elkins (1996), "activates desire, possession, violence, displeasure, pain, force, ambition, power, obligation, gratitude, longing. . . . There seems to be no end to what seeing is, to how it is tangled with living and acting. . . . There is no such thing as just looking" (p. 31).

Oedipus, the bedrock figure of psychoanalysis, incurred blindness as a punishment for his incestuous deed. Orpheus, seeking to rescue his beloved Eurydice from Hades, disobeyed the stipulation that he not look back to see if she was following him, and so lost her forever. Lot's wife was turned into a pillar of salt for looking back at the destruction of Sodom and Gomorrah. Odysseus blinded the Cyclops. Athena blinded the Theban seer Tiresias for watching her bathe. When she later relented, she gave him back not his eyesight, but the ambiguous gift of vision called prophecy.

Oscar Wilde's playlet *Salome* (1894) is filled with references to the dangers of looking: "You look at her too much. It is dangerous to look at people in such fashion. Something terrible may happen" (p. 13); "Those men are mad. They have looked too long on the moon" (p. 41); "One should not look at anything. Neither a thing nor at people should one look at. Only in mirrors is it well to look, for mirrors do but show us masks" (p. 56).

The power of looking is intrinsically tied to the power of "looks." Those endowed with special attributes of appearance have always been felt to have special powers. Helen of Troy's beautiful face launched a thousand ships; Medusa's ugliness was so destructive that it turned those who saw it to stone. Perseus used his shield as a deflecting mirror against Medusa's power, and once he had killed her, he used her severed head as a weapon that petrified his enemies. Circe's beauty was such that, by unlocking men's baser natures, it turned them into swine. Narcissus, a more recent pillar of psychoanalysis, fell in love with his own image and perished while transfixed by his reflection in a pool of water. In the Bible, the first mention of a sorrowful woman is Leah, in the book of Genesis. Although we are told nothing specific about her appearance, "lack of looks seems to be the aspersion cast upon this older sister over time, as if the only explanation for her depression or downward spirits was a failure to attract suitors—as if unhappiness were an affliction of the unbeautiful" (Wurtzel 1998, p. 173).

Looking has also to do with eyes. Superstitions about the "evil eye" (Reiss 1988) abound in most cultures. They warn those that visible success—riches, beauty, achievement—attracts the eye of the less fortunate person, and therefore possibly his destructive envy as well. In Greece, blue beads hang from the fenders of tractors, and those who fear catching "the eye" wear blue plastic eyes next to their crosses, for blue is supposed to repel danger. In Eastern European cultures, a red ribbon is tied to the crib (and sometimes to the pregnant mother's underwear) when a baby is born to ward off envious eyes. Freud (1919) wrote about the dread of the evil eye: "There never seems to have been any doubt about the source of this dread. Whoever possesses something that is at once valuable and fragile is afraid of other people's envy, in so far as he projects on to them the envy he would have felt in their place" (p. 240).

Many cultures have outright prohibitions about the making of graven images, and the dangers of looking upon the face of gods. Ivan the Terrible, after he saw the glorious sight of the completed St. Basil's Cathedral in Moscow, ordered the architects' eyes cut out so that they could never again perform such a feat for anyone else.

In our culture, a bride prepares for many months for the moment when she will walk down the aisle to her groom, a vision for all to see. It is considered unlucky for the groom to see the bride in her gown prior to that moment, although this superstition has been recently defied for the convenience of wedding photographers! In Moslem countries, women veil themselves in public so that no one may see their faces but their husbands. Similarly, Orthodox Jewish women shave their heads, wear wigs in public, and sit, unseen, in the balconies of synagogues. These restrictions are a response to fear of the sexuality that the sight of a woman's beauty can arouse. In India today, where arranged marriages are still the custom, some couples are now allowed to receive photographs of one another before any deal is made between the parents, another acknowledgment of the important role and power of looks.

Many cultural rituals around death also involve vision and visual taboos. When Jews sit *shiva* to mourn the dead they cover all mirrors in the home to deny themselves the pleasure of looking at themselves, of being vain. Rules about looking or not looking at the dead and about open or closed caskets exist in most cultures. Those who do look often comment about how the dead appear— "beautiful" or "peaceful"—and the dead are dressed and made up for the occasion.

Cultures institutionalize the pleasures as well as the dangers of looking in such popular pastimes as going to the movies and theater, watching television, attending spectator sports, star gazing, bird watching, and people watching. Foreigners flock to Italy and France to sit for hours in cafés, where there is absolute permission to sit and to stare at those who pass by, over and over, in an exhibition-

istic *passaggiata* or "walk-around." On the other hand, in Japan it is
forbidden to stare, and foreigners there at times experience themselves to be invisible.

The eyes and their powers are not just the stuff of folklore and
superstition. They have been taken very seriously by intellectuals
and philosophers. According to Jay (1993), from the time of the
ancient Greeks to the age of Descartes, vision was always considered to be the noblest of senses, and the expression "seeing is believing" reveals the pairing of vision and truth. Jay carefully delineated a turning against the eye in the "anti-ocular" trend that began
to pervade French thought in the late nineteenth and twentieth
centuries. He traces the loss of confidence in this "noble sense" in
the works of such philosophers as Bergson, Merleau-Ponty, Lacan,
Barthes, Derrida, and others. According to Jay, Sartre, who believed
himself to be ugly, was especially hostile to "the look." For Sartre,
mirrors were fraught with danger; he escaped from sight into words,
and his denigration of vision especially influenced the thinking of
Lacan, Foucault, and Irigaray. "Sartre elevated his own experience
as the victim of the look . . . into something very much like a
universal human condition" (Jay 1993, p. 287). The body looked at
was to Sartre a fallen object subject to the mortifying gaze of the
other. And Lacan (whose "mirror stage" I discuss in Chapter 4)
preferred what he called "the Symbolic" to "the Imaginary." "Only
when the unconscious functions like a language and not like a
mirror can the mature subject, split and introjecting the other rather
than projecting itself onto it, be achieved" (Jay 1993, p. 352). Lacan
believed psychosis to be rooted in a disturbance of sight—a
scotomatization, a "blind spot" related to the sight of the mother's
apparent castration, the rejection of that image, the resulting inability to symbolize, and the eventual production of a substitute,
the hallucination. Merleau-Ponty explored "the madness of vision,"
dethroning the observing subject, but he preserved the value of
the mutual regard.

The optical metaphors of the nineteenth century (for instance, Helmholz's views on distortions of perception) provided Freud with a basis for thinking about transference distortions (Makari 1994), although a number of philosophers curiously considered Freud, an atheist, to be an "anti-visuel" because Jews forbade graven images (Jay 1993).

THE VICISSITUDES OF VOYEURISM AND EXHIBITIONISM

Freud provided us with some basis for thinking psychoanalytically about the important role of vision in the normal gratification of the drives in psychosexual development, but he wrote more extensively about deviations from, and perversions of, normal drive development. In the cases from which he derived his theories, the patients suffered from overstimulation of the visual sense. Little Hans (Freud 1909) witnessed his parents' intercourse; Schreber (Freud 1911) believed that he could safely look at the sun; the Wolf-Man (Freud 1918) saw his parents as well as dogs copulating. They were exposed too early to sights that overwhelmed the infantile ego— the primal scene and the naked genitals of adults—resulting in a hypercathexis of looking, excessive castration anxiety, and fantasies about damaged genitals.

Freud (1905b) saw voyeurism and exhibitionism as perversions relating to the castration complex. Perversions result from the nonintegration of the component instincts, of which *scopophilia* (pleasure in looking) is one. There is a split in the ego. Pleasure in looking becomes a perversion (a) if it is restricted exclusively to the genitals, or (b) if it is connected with the overriding of disgust (as in the case of *voyeurs* or people who look on at excretory functions), or (c) if, instead of being *preparatory* to the normal sexual aim, it supplants it (p. 157).

In "The Psycho-Analytic View of Psychogenic Disturbance of Vision," Freud (1910) postulated a split between unconscious and conscious processes in the act of seeing. The eyes perceive not only alterations in the external world important for the preservation of life, he thought, but also characteristics of objects that lead to their being chosen as objects of love. The hysterical patient becomes blind because of a disassociation between conscious and unconscious processes in the act of seeing. The lusty eye becomes eroticized and acts like an active genital. The eyes see the charms of the object chosen for love, but the ego represses this and refuses to see as a form of self-punishment for the fantasy of incestuous pleasure received from a talion (retaliatory) object.

In 1915, in "Instincts and Their Vicissitudes," Freud differentiated active from passive scopophilia, the former being transformed into a need to know, and the latter, the result of overstimulation, resulting in an autoerotic fixation of an oral incorporative nature. In voyeurism there is a loss of the active external function of the eye and actual seeing, and as a result, reality knowledge, one of the functions of the ego, is impaired.

In "The Uncanny" (1919), Freud analyzed childhood fantasies about the "Sand-Man," from Offenbach's opera *Tales of Hoffman.* Who is this Sand-Man, who tears out children's eyes? The Nurse tells little Nathaniel:

> He's a wicked man who comes when children won't go to bed, and throws handfuls of sand in their eyes so that they jump out of their heads all bleeding. Then he puts the eyes in a sack and carries them off to the half-moon to feed his children. They sit up there in their nest, and their beaks are hooked like owl's beaks, and they use them to pick up naughty boys' and girls' eyes with. [p. 228]

There is also a "demon optician" in this tale. The Sand-Man spoils love, and represents the dreaded father at whose hand castration is expected. Similarly, Freud analyzed the myth of Medusa (1922) as arising from castration anxiety and the sight of the female genital, usually that of the mother.

Abraham (1913) wrote that both the instinctual pleasures of looking and of exhibiting the body are allowed free expression in childhood, and then are subjected to repression and sublimation. In neurosis, where they have been directed onto forbidden, incestuous objects, they are inhibited and transferred. Abraham cited many aberrations of the eye—blurry vision, twitching eyelids—and presented fascinating cases of photophobia in which patients experienced all light as disagreeable. These people had witnessed parental intercourse, had been seen masturbating, or experienced a wish to return to the womb. One lived in a room with three layers of curtains over the windows and the keyhole stuffed in order to keep light out. He was preoccupied with the idea of being blind in one eye, and had an obsessive notion that a relative might lose an eye. Abraham related these symptoms to the patient's death wishes toward his father, whose watchful eye and superiority were compared with the sun. He could not look at his mother when she was in any way uncovered. The sun was a bisexual symbol representing the incestuous wish to look at his mother naked, and the wrath of his father that such behavior would provoke. Abraham saw the eye as a displacement upward from the genital, usually female, but at times male.

Fenichel (1945) provided the most comprehensive summary of psychoanalytic thinking about the range of exhibitionism and voyeurism, from the normal to the abnormal:

> In exhibitionism a denial of castration is attempted by a simple overcathexis of a partial instinct. Exhibitionism in children certainly has the character of a partial instinct; any child derives pleasure from the display of his genitals and, in pregenital times, of the other erogenous zones and their functions. Perverts regress to this infan-

tile aim because the stressing of this aim can be used for denial of
a danger that is believed to be connected with normal sexuality.
[p. 345]

An exhibitionistic man, a "flasher," Fenichel continues, says (unconsciously) to his audience (little girls): "Reassure me that I have
a penis by reacting to the sight of it" (p. 345). He asks for reassurance both that they are afraid of his penis and that he is not afraid.
His flashing is a magical gesture: "I show you what I wish you
could show me"— a mask for scopophilia and a wish that the little
girls could show him *their* penises.

Fenichel did not believe that women were exhibitionists per se,
but that when they were their exhibitionism was a displacement.
Two ideas are involved: The woman lacks a penis; the woman's
genital is ugly. Fenichel cited a 1924 paper by Harnik:

"Men's exhibitionism remains genital and may develop into a
perversion; that is, men show their potency; women's exhibitionism is displaced away from the genitals; that is, women show their
attractiveness" (p. 346).[1]

Fenichel addressed the voyeur's dilemma:

The fact that no sight can actually bring about the reassurance for
which the patients are striving has several consequences for the
structure of voyeurs: they either develop an attitude of insatiabil-
ity—they have to look again and again, and to see more and more,
with an ever increasing intensity—or they displace their interest
from the genitals either to forepleasure activities and pregenitality
or generally to scenes that may better serve as reassurances than
does actual genital observation. [p. 348]

---

[1] I disagree with Fenichel that women do not "flash" their genitals; see Ruth in
Chapter 9 and reference to A. K. Richards (1998a) in Chapter 10.

Very often, Fenichel adds, "sadistic impulses are tied up with scopophilia: the individual wants to see something in order to destroy it (or to gain reassurance that the object is not yet destroyed). Often, looking itself is unconsciously thought of as a substitute for destroying ('I did not destroy it; I merely looked at it.')" (p. 71). Therefore, it is subject to repression and a fear of looking may result. "There are specific fears that are dreaded by inhibited voyeurs as a talion punishment. The 'evil eye' and 'being turned to stone' are examples" (p. 72). Both exhibitionism and scopophilia appear together as a common precursor of the sexual aim of looking at oneself.

It is impossible to do justice in a summary to the many studies of the perversions of looking and being looked at. Ostow (1974) found that many who suffered from perversions "demonstrated an unusual sensitivity to visual stimulation" (p. 36). This permitted "a visual incorporative identification—a 'merging'—with the desired object. . . . By looking at an athletic man, for example, one patient felt that he became like that man—virile, lithe, similarly endowed with a 'magnificent' penis" (p. 37). Ostow noted a lack of abstract thought in such patients, who used concrete "looks" as compensation. These findings foreshadow the important connection between sensitivity to visual stimulation and concrete thought, a theme that I will take up later.

In recent years, few cases have been reported that focus on clear-cut visual symptoms. One exception is that of Traub-Werner (1998), who explored the vicissitudes of scopophilia in the analysis of a 38-year-old man presenting with a voyeuristic perversion. At a family gathering, he tried to videotape a child whose skirt was partly lifted. When she cried out "Camera!," thus exposing his perversion, which had hitherto been kept separate from the rest of his life, he felt as if the world were falling apart. Traub-Werner felt his perversion rested "on a three-pronged perverse structure that organized itself around inordinate castration anxiety, scopophilia and fetishism" (p. 35). As a child he had been traumatized by visual overexposure—to extremes of maternal seductiveness, to primal scenes, and to family violence.

Today, character neuroses and character disorders are the most prevalent disorders seen in psychoanalytic treatment. Fogel (1991), like many others, prefers the terms *perversity* and *the perverse* for this psychopathology. He defines the perverse as "that which is turned away from what is right, reasonable or good" (p. 3), using the common connotation of the term implying moral valuation.

> It is often useful to view perverse fantasies and enactments as complex adaptive and defensive compromise formations that serve some multiple functions over a wide range of diagnoses and degrees of psychopathology, just as any character trait or neurotic symptom may do. . . . [Many] of the so-called character perversions can now be readily defined in terms of a pathognomonic underlying personality structure than the presence or absence of sexual symptoms. [pp. 2–3]

Kaplan (1991a) wrote that "perversions, insofar as they derive a great deal of their emotional force from social gender stereotypes, are as much pathologies of gender identification as they are pathologies of sexuality" (p. 128). She noted the importance in perversion of relationship to others: "In a perversion there is always an extensive enactment and always a fantasized or real audience" (p. 131).

I define *voyeurism* as a driven and repetitive sexualized looking at some bodily aspect or function of another person that is ordinarily that person's private matter (the genitals, sexual activity, bathroom functions). It is important to remember that the parameters that define voyeurism vary from subculture to subculture and from time to time. "Normal" voyeurism today might include the viewing of X-rated movies or its more socially acceptable derivative, people-watching in cafés. (I do not know how "normal" is the current practice of watching porn on the Internet. There are Web sites, for example, devoted to the viewing of plastic surgery, or of college women dressing and undressing in their off-campus house.) Conducting psychoanalytic treatment is sometimes considered a sublimation of voyeurism. Pathological voyeurism characterizes the "peeping Tom" who obsessively peers through the windows of nonconsenting others, masturbating while he watches them undress or have intercourse.

I define *exhibitionism* as the driven and repetitive need to show to others things about oneself that are ordinarily not shown to others in public (again, the genitals, sexual activity, bathroom functions). Here, too, the parameters of permissible public behavior vary. A woman going topless on the French Riviera is normal, while one who leaves her head uncovered in Iraq is "abnormal." Men who urinate in urinals are exposing themselves normally. When they urinate along the side of the road where anyone can see, they are "flashers."

Stannard (1971) made the following astute observations at a time when feminist writers were deftly describing the different deals society offered men and women:

Because women are narcissists, they are also exhibitionists whose exhibitionism like their narcissism is approved by the culture. The male exhibitionist who thrusts his penis at a female is put in jail, but the female who thrusts her bosoms, behind and legs at a male is admired. Female exhibitionism is socially approved because the culture wants to keep woman infantile, to keep her identity focused on her physical person, not on her accomplishments. The culture therefore compels a woman to show off her body, makes her feel unfeminine unless she does so, and makes the woman who accomplishes something feel unsexed. The accomplished woman feels unsexed because she has achieved identity the way a man is supposed to—indirectly, through the active use of his abilities. The male exhibitionist is put in jail for trying to achieve his identity the way women and infants do directly by sheer physicality. He wants to prove his masculinity simply by exposing his penis. He does not want to have to prove it indirectly through accomplishment. [p. 129]

THE IMPORTANCE OF APPEARANCE

The vicissitudes of drive development in passive and active scopophilia may account to some extent for an emphasis on appearance, but not entirely. Freud and Abraham's patients suffered from overstimulation; they hypercathected looking, due to what they had seen. Many of the patients I have treated, however, have suffered from deficiencies in being looked at, or in being spoken to, in ways that enabled them to know what they looked like and, especially, to like what they looked like. Body narcissism, like voyeurism and exhibitionism as discussed above, is expressed by a broad range of behaviors, and societies and cultures vary as to the parts of the range they accept as normal or reject as pathological. The assessment of pathology also takes into account considerations of intensity and the extent to which behavior may interfere with other aspects of life. For example, a woman who spends ten minutes getting dressed in the morning may well be considered normal. If she spent just ten minutes getting dressed for a formal wedding, I might wonder about it.

Freud occasionally addressed the issue of appearance. He often wrote about men who fell in love with beautiful, narcissistic women, who were a mystery to him. However, he did not write about women who fell in love with handsome, narcissistic men, commonly found or described in clinical practice today, although he did admit that such men existed. But he did allude to the issue of beauty:

The progressive concealment of the body which goes along with civilization keeps sexual curiosity awake. This curiosity seeks to complete the sexual object by revealing its hidden parts. It can, however, be diverted ('sublimated') in the direction of art, if its interest can be shifted away from the genitals on to the shape of the body as a whole. [1905b, p. 156]

In a footnote to this paper he added:

There is to my mind no doubt that the concept of "beautiful" has its roots in sexual excitation and that its original meaning was 'sexually stimulating'. . . . This is related to the fact that we never regard the genitals themselves, which produce the strongest sexual excitation, as really "beautiful." [p. 156]

In "On Narcissism," Freud (1914) described beautiful, narcissistic women as loving only themselves. Nevertheless, he said,

The importance of this type of woman for the erotic life of mankind is to be rated very high. Such women have the greatest fascnation for men, not only for aesthetic reasons, since as a rule they are the most beautiful, but also because of a combination of interesting psychological factors. [p. 89]

He meant by these, as I take it, that beautiful women are unable to love, and they torment men by withholding love.

There is some evidence that Freud did not like what he looked like (see Chapter 4), and some evidence, too, that he did not deal with his patients' complaints around body image; at least he did not mention them in his published case histories. Gilman (1998) in a chapter entitled "Freud's Nose Job" in his book on aesthetic surgery, suggests that some of the surgery performed by Fliess on Freud's nose was for cosmetic purposes. Phillips (1996) believed that the Wolf-Man suffered from body dysmorphic disorder (BDD), which Freud never mentioned in his case history. She cited Brunswick (1928), the Wolf-Man's second analyst, as noting that he "neglected his daily life because he was so engrossed, to the exclusion of all else, in the state of his nose," its supposed scars, holes, and swelling: "His life centered on the little mirror in his pocket, and his fate depended on what it revealed or was about to reveal" (p. 19).

Freud saw the longing for a beautiful woman to be normal, albeit painful and frustrating, and he regarded being fashionable and enjoying clothes to be normal as well. (The psychology of clothing is a fascinating topic well covered in a paper by A. K. Richards [1996].) Winnicott (1971), on the other hand, attributed the wish for a beautiful or handsome partner to the realm of the pathological:

> When girls and boys in their secondary narcissism look in order to see beauty and to fall in love, there is already evidence that doubt has crept in about their mother's continual love and care. So the man who falls in love with beauty is quite different from the man who loves a girl and feels that she is beautiful and can see what is beautiful about her. [p. 113]

Winnicott seemed to have concurred in the folk wisdom that "beauty is only skin deep" and that "you can't tell a book by its cover."

Patients increasingly present in my clinical practice with obsessive anxieties and concerns about looks: about feeling fat (when they are normal or underweight), with complaints about what their lovers look like, and so forth. Some female patients who complain about their bodies tend to idealize the men they are attached to and behave submissively in their relationships with them. On the other hand, some male patients who are not happy with their own looks tend to focus in treatment on their attempts to find women with ideal bodies, and to complain about the imperfect bodies of those women they are actually with. In our culture, a young, beautiful woman on the arm symbolizes status for men, compensating for whatever physical imperfections or perceived inadequacies they may feel in themselves.

In analytic work with such patients, I have found these concerns to have meanings over and above the more traditional interpretation of bodily dissatisfaction originating in fantasies about the genitals. Narcissistic issues of intactness versus deficit in self-image and body image are involved. Insufficient visual and other kinds of feedback about the body, its form, and its qualities are among the genetic factors. Family or peer-group teasing about some aspect of face or body during childhood is another. The tremendous value placed on being thin, young, and beautiful in our appearance-obsessed culture reinforces from the outside the internal narcissistic deficits such patients already experience.

Traditional theories about why women try to look beautiful have focused singularly on wishes to avoid the sight of the "ugly" female genital and the consequent castration fears such a sight evokes. The issue of looking good is therefore the female's burden and therefore a problem the female must fix for *both* sexes. When men have body image disorders, the theories would have us believe, it is because of the sight of the female genital, not their own!

Not only must women fix their "ugliness," they must also renounce their intellectual pursuits. Riviere (1929) has been widely quoted as seeing womanliness, the donning of feminine clothes and adhering to canons of beauty, as a masquerade, a reaction formation countering masculine wishes to steal the phallus.

Edith Jacobson (1964) attempted to explain women's investment in looking beautiful as stemming from both sexes' seeing the female genital as damaged, coupled with a prohibition against looking at it: "As a further result of this prohibition, the sexual interest is displaced from the 'ugly genital' to the 'pretty body' and especially to facial appearance. In women this commonly leads to an intense narcissistic investment in their faces and figures" (p. 71).

Jacobson pointed out the girl's tremendous need for narcissistic supplies from men, a need caused by the narcissistic injury of the past.

Lachmann (1982) echoed Jacobson:

> The little girl's development is . . . understood as essentially compensatory and therefore quite vulnerable to fluctuations and depletions. . . . The little girl's comparison between her "inadequate" clitoris and the male organ served to explain her sense of inferiority and humiliation, the presence of penis envy, and hence, a compensatory investment in bodily appearance. [pp. 228–229]

Men are considered to be attractive as a result of their activity, action, and dominance: "Handsome is as handsome does." They are evaluated by their income and professional status. Physical beauty, defined as the capacity to attract, is considered to be a female trait (Etcoff 1999). Regardless of the uncomfortable sexual politics of the above, so unfavorable to women, most psychological studies have concluded consistently that many women simply do not like their own appearance. This conclusion was drawn by Rodin and his colleagues (1985), who coined the term *normative discontent* to describe the norm, if not the normal.

In her autobiographical account, Barbara Grizzuti Harrison (1996) addressed this normative discontent and purported to speak for all women:

> I don't think I know a single woman who knows what she looks like. . . . Mirrors notwithstanding, and in spite of the fact that we're invited, from the time we approach puberty, to take stock of our physical assets (and maximize them), and of our deficiencies (so as to minimize or mask them), I can't think of anybody who sees her body in a clear and dispassionate light, of anyone who doesn't center her anguished attention on an imperceptible flaw, or, on the other hand, perversely see as lovely that which others perceive to

be flawed and love herself exactly for those physical attributes others have chosen tactfully to overlook. [p. 16] . . . When I walk into a room I absolutely know that the first thing anybody will think about me is: she is fat, how fat she is, yuck. This may not be true. I KNOW it nonetheless. [p. 39]

A number of writers have attempted to document a virtual war against women, who despite their advances in becoming educated and in entering the professions, are still plagued by the conviction that they must devote time and money to looking beautiful or they will be scorned by others and certainly will not attract husbands. Or, if they have husbands, they will eventually lose them to someone younger and slimmer, very often tall with long blonde hair. These are not just fantasies. Terms such as *arm candy* and *trophy wives* are now part of everyday parlance. Faludi (1991) has described this "backlash" against women, and Wolf (1991) has tried to deconstruct the "beauty myth" that has kept the cosmetic, health club, diet pill, and cosmetic surgery industries afloat.

According to Thompson and colleagues (1999), "One thing is certain: cosmetic approaches to modify appearance continue to push the envelope" (p. 70). In their study, they published a report of cosmetic procedures performed in the United States in 1996. Almost 70,000 procedures were reported, 11 percent having been done on men, and 89 percent on women! They noted that this gender imbalance is shifting, as more men with male pattern hair loss undertake procedures to replace their hair. They thoroughly documented the culture of thinness that has plagued women and some men since the 1960s, an albatross for the women who wish to succeed with men in the workplace while balancing family obligations.

Davis (1995) contended that the prevalence of cosmetic procedures relates to a search not so much for beauty as for a new identity that agrees with a person's image of him- or herself—it relates to gaining power when one feels powerless. I agree that such behavior may have to do with identity, but it seems to me that it occurs more often in the context of getting recognition from others in the form of attention: being noticed by the plastic surgeon and his staff, having permission to look in the mirror, getting compliments from others, and so forth.

In *The Body Project*, Brumberg (1997), who found that contemporary adolescent girls' diaries were filled with the phrase "I'm so ugly," compared nineteenth-century young women, who valued "good works," with twentieth-century women, who value "good looks":

> Before World War I, girls rarely mentioned their bodies in terms of strategies for self-improvement or struggles for personal identity. Becoming a better person meant paying *less* attention to the self, giving more assistance to others, and putting more effort into instructive reading or lessons at school. . . . At the end of the twentieth century, the body is regarded as something to be managed and maintained, usually through expenditures on clothes and personal grooming items, with special attention to exterior surfaces— skin, hair and contours. [p. xxi]

Good looks are culturally defined, as are clothing styles. College professors and psychoanalysts, for example, can wear clothing that the rest of the world regards as dowdy, avoid cosmetics and cosmetic procedures, and still be held in high esteem and considered good looking by their colleagues. It is important to know the values of any patient's subculture when working with him or her on these issues. Models and actors and actresses are held to a different standard and their bodily complaints may relate more to reality demands than to narcissistic deficit, although their very choice of profession might indicate issues around body narcissism.

Hersey (1996), in his study of culturally defined mate choice over the centuries, documented body types in both sexes. He noted a Western canon of human features or proportions that may have influenced the evolution in the human species of hyperdevelopment in both sexes of breasts and muscles, since sexual selection has been based on these factors. In the late twentieth century men work on developing muscles that resemble breasts. Women work on developing muscles that give them a masculine appearance and try to reduce their breasts—a new canon of beauty. I have observed that women who are overweight often seek breast reduction, while those who are fashionably thin seek breast *implants*, which may be more fashionable these days than real breasts!

Whether we like what is going on or not, whether or not it feels like a "war against women" (Faludi 1991), in our culture today women are expected to be beautiful, vain, and *looked at*. Berger (1972) saw the essence of woman as *surveyed*:

> To be born a woman has been to be born, within an allotted and confined space, into the keeping of men. . . . A woman must continually watch herself. . . . She has to survey everything she is and everything she does because how she appears to others, and ultimately how she appears to men, is of crucial importance for what is normally thought of as the success of her life. Her own sense of being in herself is supplanted by a sense of being appreciated as herself by another. [p. 46]

Some women view this "condition" positively; in her novel *Spending*, Mary Gordon (1998) described the experience of her middle-aged heroine, who was walking down the street with a man who had selected her:

> You're walking as a chosen woman. You watch yourself being watched, you're being watched by him, yet already chosen, so you don't need to watch him at all. You can't possibly lose. . . . What an odd thing it is, this business of looking and being looked at. Being

looked at is a bit like being tasted. It doesn't have to feel a bit like being eaten up, so there's nothing left of you. . . . I've been added to by being looked at by men, also subtracted from. [pp. 18–19]

Not to be seen can be painful, as the novelist Anne Tyler indicated in *Ladder of Years* (1995). Her heroine was a married woman who ran away from her husband and three adolescent children:

Delaware State Police announced early today that Cordelia F. Grinstead, 40, wife of a Roland Park physician, has been reported missing while on holiday with her family in Bethany Beach. . . . A slender, small-boned woman with curly fair or light-brown hair, Mrs. Grinstead stands 5'2" or possibly 5'5" and weighs either 90 or 110 pounds. Her eyes are blue or gray or perhaps green, and her nose is mildly sunburned in addition to being freckled. Presumably, she was carrying a large straw tote trimmed with a pink bow, but family members could not agree upon her clothing. [p. 3]

Winnicott (1971), whom I regard as a *visuel*, sensitively picked up on this issue of not being looked at in his case vignette of an attractive woman patient who went out to a coffee bar. He asked her: "Did anyone look at you?" The patient thought she had "drawn some fire" but that people were really looking at the man she was with. They went over her history "in terms of being seen in a way that would make her feel she existed" (p. 115). Winnicott thought her history to be "deplorable" in this respect.

Nancy Friday (1996a) views the wish to be appreciated as a beauty as quite basic: "I am a woman who needs to be seen. I need it in a basic way as in to breathe, to eat" (p. 1). She says to her disapproving reader, "Perhaps you ducked out of the competition over looks so many years ago that you can't remember, but you did want to be seen, taken in and loved. If you don't today, consider that it might be that you tried and lost" (p. 2).

Germaine Greer (1991) would not agree. She stares out at the reader from her book jacket—black, circled eyes and less-than-firm chin are her badges of honor. Writing about aging and the menopause, she complains: "A grown woman should not have to masquerade as a girl in order to remain in the land of the living" (p. 4). She has documented the change in others' attitudes toward her as she aged and could no longer trade on her appearance, and has reported enviously watching men her age woo younger women.

Lois Gould (1996), novelist and daughter of dress designer Jo Copeland, provided a poignant description of the role appearance can take, in this vignette:

> My father was often told he looked like Cary Grant which he pretended not to like hearing. After the flatterer had gone, he would wink and strike his chin with his fingers massed like a blade, to encourage the cleft that wasn't there. He would say, "Let's go handsome up the joint," when he came to take me to a movie. My mother made it clear that she wouldn't have married anyone who couldn't handsome up the joint. In her value system, a man, like anything else a woman was to be seen with, ought to enhance the ensemble. . . . She rarely wore trousers because good legs were meant to be shown. Looking at these photographs, you would think this woman was a flirt: this woman enjoyed sex. You would be half right. She did flirt —with mirrors, with cameras, with the admiring glances of passers-by. Sexy was wonderful. Sex wasn't. [p. 68]

Yes, the beautiful get more approval and recognition (Etcoff 1999). Nevertheless, in spite of all that has been said about the search for beauty, it is also true, as the conventional wisdom goes, that beauty can be a curse. Beautiful people are exposed to extraordinary acts of envy and aggression. They often are unaware that they are mistreated by the envious because of their good looks, and make false connections to explain to themselves, and their therapists, what they could possibly have done to warrant such treatment.

By the same token, psychotherapists must be sensitive to the underlying low self-esteem of those who *are* unattractive, or who keep themselves unattractive by poor grooming or clothing choice. Such patients are usually well defended against such topics and it takes much tact to address them. It is important, too, to be aware of the particular demands of any subculture on the subject of beauty, grooming, or style.

Finally, therapists must keep in mind the considerable potential for countertransference acting out with especially good-looking patients—therapists, too, can feel sexual stimulation and envy in the presence of the beautiful, and avoidance and rejection toward the physically unattractive.

Thus, it is obvious that there is no simple answer as to what constitutes normal or pathological in this search for beauty in oneself or in another. What is important is that when these issues emerge in the psychotherapy consulting room, they must be addressed.

II

DEVELOPMENTAL ISSUES

3

Gaze and the Development of Body Narcissism

It seems to me that vision is not only an adjunct but an indispensable one in establishing the confluence of the body surface and promoting awareness of delimitation of the self from the nonself. "Touching" and taking in of the various body parts with the eyes (vision) helps in drawing the body together, into a central image beyond the level of mere immediate sensory awareness.

Greenacre (1960, p. 208)

$\mathcal{P}$hyllis Greenacre was a pioneer in understanding the role played by vision in the development of the emotions, the self, language, and object relations. She regarded vision as the "nucleus of ego development," and described the reciprocal and mutually reinforcing cooperative work of eye and mouth (1958, 1960). She recognized how the eyes, which are quickly able to focus, take the exploratory lead early in infancy, and how soon they control the movements of hands and arms. She also pointed out that eye and mouth, having learned to cooperate early, tend to serve as substitutes for one another. This phenomenon is of considerable importance for the disposition of defensive displacements later in life. Greenacre also noted that "the body areas which are . . . most significant in comparing and contrasting and establishing individuation, recognition of the body self and that of others, are the *face* and the *genitals*" (1958, p. 117, Greenacre's emphasis) and she described how body image is consolidated by touch, by reflection, and by making comparisons between one's own body and the bodies of others.

The forty years that have passed since Greenacre's work was published have seen the evolution and integration into psychotherapy of theories of attachment, of object relations and of the self, and of relational and intersubjective theories, all of which have changed the nature of what therapists regard as significant data. The study of the infant's solitary development, with the slow mastery of ego over drive and of reality over fantasy, has been supplemented, not replaced, by the study of what goes on in the mother–infant dyad, and visually, a great deal goes on. The infant tracks his mother and she tracks him as well. Through the dynamics of this mutual looking—who looks at whom first, who gets the other to look or to stop looking—the seeds of the power and dominance dynamics between the two are established early on. The experience of this "mutual gaze," therefore, is a foundation of the later behavior of the adult. Any mother whose baby refuses to look at her after she has been away for a while can attest to the fact that an infant is no stranger to vision as an instrument of control! The mother is instrumental too in the regulation of visual stimulation, and in the matching of visual stimuli with words, as in such familiar utterances as "See the doggie." (What pertains to the mother also applies to any adult who serves as primary caregiver to the infant, whether it be the father, grandparent, nanny, or someone else.)

One can say that the development of the infant's visual ego is mediated by the mother. Although the visual apparatus matures very rapidly, because of the infant's physical and psychological dependency, the mother is for a long time the "gatekeeper" of sensory experience, and controls what the infant sees and touches. Her affects and her language convey to the infant essential information about himself, his body, and the outside world, and therefore influence how and how well his own affects and language develop, and what degree of complexity they reach. All of these in turn profoundly influence his inner life, including the life of fantasy, as the drive-related phases of development progress. The mother's gatekeeping will affect the growing child's feelings about his own body and how it looks and feels, about others' bodies and how they look, and about the look of the inanimate world; more, it will affect his potential for curiosity and aesthetic appreciation in general.

The way in which the mother/caregiver elicits her infant's smile response and the way she responds to it (Spitz 1965), the toys she puts in the infant's crib and how she arranges them, what she lets the baby see from the crib or carriage or baby-carrier, how she plays peek-a-boo (Kleeman 1967); the degree of self-locomotion she permits as the infant begins to explore the world—all of these factors will eventually help to determine the range and the strength of the developing visual ego. In conjunction with such behavior, the words she uses to structure, differentiate, and describe the world for her baby; the way she responds as he begins to structure and differentiate independently; the way she seeks out sights to show him and talk about; the way she does or doesn't let him touch or mouth what he sees; the way she connects seeing and naming and touching and exploring—all of these help to integrate the visual apparatus with proprioception, language, attachment, and self-esteem. They will structure the way the child thinks about the world, including his or her own body, and the bodies of others. What she does not notice, does not see, does not describe, and does not talk about is also significant.[1]

Take again, for example, the reciprocity between eye and mouth noted by Greenacre. The mouth at first can explore only what is offered to it, but the eye can roam at will, and so the eyes are first to achieve active exploration of, and attempts to influence, the environment. As they learn to direct and motivate the movements of the hands and the arms, they increase greatly the possibilities for oral exploration. As eye and mouth tend to serve as substitutes for

---

[1] The observations and experimental research that I consider here are specific to Western cultural patterns of child rearing, and conclusions drawn from them may not be universal. Argyle and Cook in *Gaze and Mutual Gaze* (1976) have cited a number of cross-cultural differences and suggested, for example, that because Japanese mothers tend to carry their infants on their backs, their culture is less dependent on mutual gaze. Japanese people tend to look away or look down rather than look another person in the eye, and this gaze aversion must be understood as meaning something different from the gaze aversion of a person raised in a Western society.

one another (for example, the sight of food becoming associated with its taste), they serve each other as channels for defensive displacements later in life. And as the infant grows older, an increasing and ever more complex interplay comes into being between what the eye sees and what the mouth describes.

This chapter discusses the current research relevant to the development of the visual ego and body narcissism. There have been many studies of development of the visual self in infancy and childhood, and of the visual experience of the other. Researchers in the fields of perception, neurology, psycholinguistics, and ophthalmology, as well as psychologists and psychoanalysts, have contributed to this work, which is still in too early a stage to yield clear conclusions. Most of the studies include other senses along with vision. But I am focusing on vision without these interactions, to highlight the visual ego as a separate entity and demonstrate its influence upon the development of body narcissism. Thus, I have chosen only the studies that most pertain to these issues, but they cannot prove the points I am making. Therefore, I will describe the relevant studies, but not try to integrate or synthesize their findings. My main point is to raise psychotherapists' consciousness about visual matters. More definitive conclusions will have to wait.

I have organized this chapter along a continuum from the biological through the individual to the social and interpersonal. I begin with studies that address the functioning of the innate biological apparatus from which the visual ego develops. Then I consider the work on how drives and their vicissitudes influence the processing of visual information and the nature of individual fantasies. I then proceed to the social gaze of the infant, as he looks to the outside world and attempts to track and then to interact with his mother. These three areas all have significance for the central issue of this book: the development of the complex triad of body narcissism, vision, and language.

The research suggests many intricate parallels between the verbal and nonverbal communications that take place in the psychotherapeutic situation, but it is too soon to extrapolate from infant to adult behavior in this area. Instead, we can use this research to broaden the context in which therapists understand what is happening clinically, and to increase our awareness of issues having to do with looking and being looked at, and with feelings about one's looks and the looks of others. I have found these studies useful in informing my own work with patients. Increasing the scope of our observation increases our powers to ask appropriate questions, make educated reconstructions, and give appropriate interpretations.

Many experiences of looking and being looked at are essential to a healthy psyche. The normal infant's visual capabilities are present at birth and mature rapidly thereafter. But it takes a mother to regulate and interpret what the infant sees, and to provide the infant with feedback in the form of return looks, affects, and words linked to the visual experiences of both infant and mother. The variants that occur in these categories reflect the wide variations we see clinically in the capacity for social interaction and healthy body narcissism.

BIOLOGICAL CAPACITIES OF
THE VISUAL EGO

Vision plays a central role in the infant's "imprinting" of his mother on the way to establishing an attachment to her (Bowlby 1969). It is not known to what extent this is biological and to what extent social, but from the beginning infants choose preferentially to look at faces (Fantz 1961), and they construct very early a concept that Stern (1985) has called "face-ness," which becomes the first step in the intricate affective give and take between baby and caregiver.

Werner (1948) described the tendency of infants to perceive faces as a whole and to perceive categories of affects rather than individual perceptual qualities such as shape, intensity, or number; he called this tendency "physiognomic perception." He found that affect acts as a universal currency into which stimuli of any modality (voice, expression, feeling) can be translated. In other words, infants read their mothers' faces (as they read their voices and their touch) for feelings.

Beebe and Lachmann (1988) found that an infant from early on makes comparisons of visual stimuli, and uses them to make order of the world. He can abstract information quite early, and can remember how interactions go and what he has successfully made the environment do. The innately programmed smiling response, for example, produces affect in the caregiver (Stern 1985). Beebe and Lachmann (1998) cite studies showing that infants as young as 42 minutes old can imitate an adult model's facial expression, and others indicating that by 10 months infants watching videos of laughing actresses show brain patterns of positive affect themselves.

Lichtenberg (1983), one of the pioneers of the new "attachment theory," has reviewed recent evidence from neonate research and found that it challenged some basic assumptions of classical drive-reduction theory. He believes that infants seek stimulation and novelty rather than drive reduction. He cites studies indicating that infants are able to fix their gaze and pursue an object visually earlier than believed. For example, they will drop the breast to see something and, when held over the shoulder where they can see, will often stop crying. He noted the importance of the interaction of mother and baby: "Even though adultomorphized, the mother's often-stated conviction that her baby is looking at her connotes the remarkably rapid appearance of a recognition response" (p. 50).

Demos (1992) focused on issues of organization and integration in her description of how early infant development unfolds. She characterized the relationship between visual perception and experiences as one of *decontextualization*: "The more experience an infant has with an object, e.g., a cup, and the more that experience consists of small variations on a theme, the more rapidly the infant will construct a distilled image of the object, an image that is continually becoming more independent of context and therefore more easily evoked in an increasingly wide variety of contexts" (p. 224). She went on to say that there must be "an optimal balance between redundancy and variation, both in internal affective states and the external events" (p. 224).

Similarly, Greenspan (1992) spent many years studying how difficult it is for some infants to balance everything that comes in through their senses. Some cannot use all the information, while some are easily overstimulated. Infants differ in what they need to be soothed. Greenspan has been interested in how infants organize experience. Because the ego organizes, integrates, differentiates, elaborates, and transfers experience, these activities promote ego development, and, ultimately, increase ego complexity from phase to phase.

Trevarthan (1993), measuring brain function itself, has studied the complex interactions between mother and infant: eye to eye communication, auditory vocalization (what he calls "motherese"), as well as touch and bodily gestures. He concluded that these interactions are needed for even the physical growth of the infant's brain.

All of this being so, the mother/caregiver's attunement to the infant in regulating the amount of stimulation (too little, too much, just right, too simple, too complex) is important. Emde (1991), who has looked at the biological preparedness of the infant for visual stimulation of the brain, wrote also about "social fittedness," the mutual adaptation between mother and infant. If there is too much stimulation, infants do not remember.

This delicate balance is helped along by the fact that infant and mother both possess powers to titrate the amount of stimulation the infant receives. Even the youngest infant wields some influ-

ence over what he does and does not take in, and can both seek
stimulation out and avoid it very actively:

> Up to three months of life (and longer) a nursing baby will not
> look at the breast but at the mother's face. This is an observational
> fact. He does not look at the breast when the mother approaches
> him, he looks at her face; he continues looking at her face while
> he has her nipple in his mouth and is manipulating the breast. From
> the moment mother comes into the room he stares at his mother's
> face. [Spitz 1965, p. 81]

In their discussion of the special conditions some infants require
during social engagement, Beebe and Lachmann (1998) cited a
study by Koulomzin and colleagues (1993), in which the researchers used videotape microanalysis of mother–infant face-to-face play
at 4 months, and coded certain variables second by second—for
instance, infant gaze, orientation, self-touching, and facial behavior. They reported that "secure infants at 4 months tend to look at
the mother while holding their heads in a stable en face orientation. The avoidant infant looks to the mother less, while holding
his or her head at a slight angle as if 'cocked for escape'" (p. 497).
Beebe and Lachmann are attempting to trace these behaviors
through toddlerhood and then into adulthood, when relational
difficulties really become manifest.

Schore (1997), whose primary interest is affect regulation, also
emphasizes the importance of visual experiences for optimal social
and emotional development: the infant needs to see the mother's
face and eyes and to experience a mutual "looking at" one another
(see his article for a thorough review of the research in this area).
He has confirmed in neurobiological research that the "gleam in
the mother's eye," a phrase to which Kohut (1971) gave currency,
is more than just a metaphor. He suggests that

the infant's right hemisphere, which is dominant for the child's processing of visual and prosodic emotional information and for the infant's recognition of maternal facial affective expressions, is psychobiologically attuned to the output of the mother's right hemisphere. . . . The child is using the output of the mother's right cortex as a template for the imprinting, the hard wiring of circuits in his own right cortex, that will come to mediate his expanding affective capacities. [pp. 19–20]

I understand Schore to mean that there is brain-to-brain communication (what psychoanalysts usually describe as unconscious-to-unconscious communication) as well as communication from eye to eye. Schore believes that this research enables us to understand the mechanism Kohut called "mirroring." He believes that early preverbal (including visual) mother–infant communications are recorded on the right side of the brain prior to the elaboration of the left brain's linguistic capacities. It is from research like this that I hope eventually to support my clinical observations about the linguistic symptoms manifested by patients with issues of body narcissism.

DRIVE THEORY, UNCONSCIOUS CONFLICT, FANTASY, AND SYMPTOM FORMATION

There is also a small body of traditional psychoanalytic literature on vision in the developing psyche. In their comprehensive and invaluable 1971 review, Barglow and Sadow organized what was then known about visual perception along a developmental time line, and integrated Freud's theories about the perceptual apparatus and ego development with the findings of some of the most important experimental researchers in visual psychology to that date.

Writing about the first three months of life, Barglow and Sadow (1971) concluded that "the capacity of the eye to function as a receptor organ for external stimuli presupposes a low level of oral tension or a state of relative gratification. Experiments suggest that the success rate in visual following is significantly diminished by frustration of the sucking needs of infants" (p. 438, citing Wolff 1965). This conjunction sets the stage for and explains the instinctualization of perception that may occur in later regressions—neurotic blindness, for example (Freud 1910, and see below); hysteria commonly manifests itself in symptoms and disorders of sight and bodily awareness. In infants between 3 and 6 months of age, the sight of the breast or bottle as well as the touch of it elicits sucking. The sight of the mother's face elicits a smile. Barglow and Sadow point out that when vision is not possible, oral channels are chosen for discharge. They cite as examples congenitally blind children, in whom the mouth is a primary organ of perception. At the age of 6 to 12 months, the eye slowly becomes independent of the mouth, acquiring the capacity to explore the world autonomously, and to distinguish visually the love object from all others (the simultaneous development of stranger anxiety is the proof of this).

Barglow and Sadow (1971) reviewed a variety of symptoms (such as visual distortions) of adult patients that originated in this early phase of development. These symptoms were all linked to sights: the sight of the phallus, the sight of feces lost in the toilet, the sight of the primal scene. They observed that vision can defensively reassure one against castration fear. The disguised or displaced content of what is looked for may be more crucial than the activity of looking. The fetishist, for instance, sees the hair or the shoe and in so doing avoids the sight of the genital, enabling him to deny the possibility of castration.

After the age of 5, language and symbols become ever more abstract and further removed from organ pleasures and drive, although "the earlier libidinal and aggressive pleasures of vision persist in the phenomena of sexual forepleasure and are subsumed under genital primacy" (p. 445). Vision is also implicated in obtaining continual superego approval; one example that Barglow and Sadow give is the positive value put upon bodily appearance and attractive clothing. "Perception contributes to the acquisition of the sophisticated, abstract, and symbolic methods of maintaining the object's love and admiration" (pp. 445–446). They concluded:

> Visual functioning at the beginning of life utilizes neutral energy. Visual perception may continue to use neutral energy late, or it may become instinctualized. Visual perception may then subserve sequentially the libidinal and aggressive drives of the oral, anal and phallic phases. Visual activities brought within the nexus of infantile conflict can become by a "change of function" secondarily autonomous, utilizing neutral energy. However, there is always the possibility of regression with the consequence of re-instinctualization. [p. 448]

Their review supports the supposition that the visual apparatus, like the other senses, may be experienced and employed in normal, neurotic, and perverse ways.

Freud (1905b) theorized about the origins of exhibitionism and voyeurism as well as of normal curiosity:

> Small children are essentially without shame, and at some periods of their earliest years show an unmistakable satisfaction in exposing their bodies, with especially emphasis on the sexual parts. . . . Under the influence of seduction the scopophilic perversion can attain great importance in the sexual life of a child. . . . [S]copophilia can also appear in children as a spontaneous manifestation. Small children whose attention has once been drawn—as a rule by masturbation—to their own genitals usually take the further step without help from outside and develop a lively interest in the genitals of their play-

mates. Since opportunities for satisfying curiosity of this kind usually occur only in the course of satisfying the two kinds of need for excretion, children of this kind turn into *voyeurs*, eager spectators on the processes of micturition and defecation. [p. 192]

Later theorists, on the other hand, attributed preoedipal origins to *voyeurism*. Kris (1956) thought that some defect in the nursing situation led to a displacement of the oral drive to the eye. Almansi (1979) reported a number of cases suggesting that early object loss resulted in voyeurism; the hypercathexis of vision developed from a need to maintain visual contact with the object so as to incorporate it.

Almansi (1960, 1979) observed preoedipal regression in children whose aggression had been excessive after watching younger siblings nurse, and thought that there was an unconscious equation of eyes with nipples.

Greenacre (1947) wrote about the effect on certain young boys of watching their older brothers show off by masturbating to ejaculation. She felt that the younger boys defensively withdrew, in some cases to the point of later developing homosexual tendencies. She also thought that both sexes suffer shock upon observing the birth of a child. She also wrote about "penis awe" and "penis envy" (1953). One or the other developed, she thought, depending on the timing of the visual experience of the little girl, who has seen her father's penis, or the primal scene, or an exhibitionist: "The full effect of the observation can be felt by the girl only after there is some sense of separateness of the self, some definite appreciation of her own body—that is, not before the last half of the second year" (p. 34). The girl who is awestruck may as an adult only be able to become erotically attached to a man she perceives of as God-like or who has an exceptionally large penis.

Observations like these indirectly illustrate the point I made above, of the importance of mother and father as "gatekeepers" who permit or forbid the possibility of such looking for the developing child. There are vast differences from family to family and from culture to culture in how much children are allowed to see of parental nudity, and equal differences in how long parents are permitted to see their children nude.

THE GAZE

Mahler and colleagues (1975) described the developmental timetable like this: At 6 to 7 months of age the peak of manual, tactile, and visual exploration of the mother's face and body occurs. The infant discovers the brooch and the eyeglasses, and delights in peekaboo games. At 7 to 8 months a "visual checking back to mother" emerges, a comparative scanning of mother and other, and then eventual recognition of the parents' faces. With this comes the corresponding recognition that some faces belong to strangers, and also the characteristic 8-month-old stranger anxiety. During what Mahler and colleagues call the "practicing subphase proper," which extends very roughly from 10 to 18 months, the child achieves uprightness, and the scope and angle of his vision change, allowing him to find "changing perspectives, pleasures and frustrations. There is a new visual level that the upright bipedal position affords" (p. 71). During the early rapprochement phase, if the mother waits outside the room, the child goes to see her periodically and then goes back to play. In the rapprochement phase proper (15 to 24 months), which Mahler and colleagues call "refueling," there exist at the same time an intense interest in the extremes of bodily contact (both deliberate searching for it, and deliberate avoidance of it), and a new integration of the mother–toddler interaction on a higher level, that of symbolic language. The child at times follows the mother's every move, "shadows" her, literally cannot let her out of his sight. At other times he darts away and waits for the mother to chase him and undo the separateness. At every phase of development the child gazes at the mother and has some degree of control over that gaze, but it is important to recognize that the child begins to relinquish the gaze only as the alternative possibilities of long-distance (that is, verbal) contact increase.

MUTUAL GAZE

Kaplan (1978) stated, "Eye-to-eye contact is an important component of human contact. What we do with our eyes becomes a measure of how friendly or close we feel toward another human being—turning the eyes away, averting the gaze, looking directly in the eyes, or closing the eyes altogether in order to maintain a state of intense intimacy" (p. 78). She describes the search for eye-to-eye contact as the infant evolves from "looking right through" the mother to recognizing her. The smile is no longer automatic. "The baby appears to be looking for something—and he will not smile until he finds it." Nothing arouses him like the contour of the face: "It is as though the baby had been searching for something he knew would be there" (p. 78).

In "The Mother's Eye—For Better and for Worse," Riess (1978) reviewed the existing child development studies of early mother-child eye-to-eye contact, and considered its potential for later psychopathology. She concluded, "Mutual gazing between infant and mother has been found to elucidate increasingly the important contribution of the visual mode of communication to . . . preverbal affective ties. *The mother's wish for eye contact is determined by her own emotional state and this is influenced by how responsive the infant is to her*" (p. 382, my emphasis). According to Riess, the eye is a window onto the mother's feeling states, and, in particular, onto how she feels about her child. "Reading" the mother's face for affect begins toward the end of the first year or the beginning of the second, at about the time the infant begins to locomote. Some mothers express approval or disapproval facially more than others, influencing in this way as well as more concrete ones (words and gestures) what their babies do and where they go. In fact, Riess thinks, visual prohibitions signaled to very young children may have more profound and/or disturbing effects than verbal ones. The visual experience precedes the verbal one developmentally, and therefore reaches a less mature and more vulnerable organism, with fewer means of impulse and anxiety control. She noted that the absolute helplessness of the baby at that time may make these the most poignant of all prohibitions, and they may be very difficult to discern later, by the grown person or by his therapist, precisely because they were never put into words or otherwise made concretely manifest. Riess described two adult patients who had had frightening eye-to-eye contact with their mothers. She concluded, "The mother's angry expression in early pre-verbal eye-to-eye contact with her child may be a source of severe anxiety to the infant and contribute significantly to the development of superego forerunners by its frightening and forbidding qualities" (p. 407).

It is worth noting that "dirty looks" are not trivial communications. Freud (1900) wrote about the angry Brücke's "terrible blue eyes" reducing him to "nothing" in his dream. Goldberger (1995b) discussed facial expressions in dreams, and memories and fantasies about prohibitions from "looks" that were never verbalized. (See also Chapter 2 on the "evil eye.") This is one reason why certain kinds of false connections are so common and so difficult to deal with in the clinical situation: Mother's tense face may have been due to Grandfather's death and not Johnnie's bad behavior, but this kind of reality testing is impossible for young children. By the same token, angry looks in the absence of angry words may cause confusion.

In the conclusion of Riess's comprehensive survey of the power of the eye a decade later, Riess (1988) wrote, "Mutual gaze is a universal form of communication among all humans everywhere and at all times. It has its ancestry in the animal world and has, as is known now, an innate biological component" (p. 416).

Beebe and Lachmann (1988) studied the interrelatedness between mother and infant in the early months, particularly in terms of how it produces structures that the infant learns to remember and expect. In a complex and highly sophisticated study, they found that aspects of the relationship are remembered in presymbolic form in the first year and provide the basis for emerging symbolic forms of self and object representation. They also believe that they found evidence for memory in utero, infant pattern-recognition memory, face memory, and memory of context, and they noted that "a number of capacities underlie an early general representational ability" (p. 308).

I find it interesting that infants can reject visual contact as well as solicit it. Moreover, they learn very quickly to communicate through gestures their mothers can see: saying "no" by turning their heads away or "yes" by watching what is going on. Although in many ways helpless, they are not passive, and they both have and exercise some degree of control over what happens to them and (especially) over how much stimulation they receive. They, as well as their mothers, can disrupt contact, keep it disrupted, or repair it.

In this context I recall a very needy and disturbed adult patient who would look at me intensively for a few sessions and then disappear for a few sessions without calling to cancel. By so doing she put me into the position of having to call her to find out why she was not coming to her sessions and when she was planning to return. Since she had caller I.D. on her phone, she would respond to my call only when she was ready to return. I reconstructed that her "turning me off" was a repetition of what she had done with her mother as an infant, but her mother had allowed her to disconnect for longer than was good for her.

Stern (1985) summarized research findings that demonstrate the infant's control over mutual gazing with the mother as he or she looks away. He described the infant as "a remarkably interactive partner" (p. 21) who self-regulates stimulation through the gaze:

> Infants exert major control over the initiation, maintenance, termination and avoidance of social contact with mother; in other words, they help to *regulate engagement*. Furthermore, by controlling their own direction of gaze, they self-regulate the level and amount of social stimulation to which they are subject. They can avert their gaze, shut their eyes, stare past, become glassy-eyed. And through the decisive use of such gaze behaviors, they can be seen to reject, distance themselves, or defend themselves against mother. . . . They can also reinitiate engagement and contact when they desire, through gazing, smiling and vocalizing. [pp. 21–22, my emphasis]

Beebe and Lachmann (1988) videotaped mother–infant pairs when the baby was between 3 and 4 months old, and then viewed the tapes in slow motion, coding degrees of affective involvement. The highest level was called the "gape smile"— open mouth, head forward, prolonged gaze and delight. They observed that infants are able to communicate slight changes in affect. The lowest level showed, among other things, looking away, and inhibited responsiveness. Three patterns of interactive regulation—facial mirroring, matching of timing, and derailment—were found, all showing mutual influence between mother and infant. They also speculated about the outcomes of various interaction patterns:

> The kinds of withdrawal responses the infant shows and the interactive regulation of these withdrawal responses may affect later adaptations, defenses, representations and subjective experiences. If the infant characteristically must resort to increasingly severe and prolonged withdrawal status in order to accomplish "time-out" and a re-regulation of arousal, his or her attention and information pro-

cessing may be compromised. For example, an infant who typically must use inhibition of responsivity (playing possum) or seems to stare right through his partner ("glazing over") alters his capacity to stay alert and to be fully attentive and responsive to the environment. [p. 329]

Here too there are analogies that can be drawn to adult treatment. Beebe and Lachmann (1998) asked: "What self-regulatory range do the patients bring, and what capacity do this particular therapist and patient together generate to gain access to the patient's self-regulatory range and to expand it?" (p. 494). They go on to describe various therapist styles that address these issues.

On the other hand, the mother can actively offer visual stimulation to the infant (deliberately moving her face into his line of sight, making faces, talking). In their study of infant and child development, Mahler and colleagues (1975) found that "all other conditions being equal, symbiosis was optimal when the mother naturally permitted the young infant to face her—that is permitted and promoted eye contact, especially while nursing (or bottle-feeding) the infant, or talking or singing to him" (p. 45). However, not all mothers do permit this. According to Riess (1978), while mothers are generally pleased when their newborns gaze at them, and at times infer that more is going on than the infant is in fact yet capable of, some mothers, out of their own pathological needs, withdraw at times from eye-to-eye contact with their children. In those cases, Riess says, "The children in need of acknowledgment, approval or disapproval are then left bewildered and frightened, their world depleted of the life-giving force of the mother's eye and of her emotional availability" (pp. 386–387).

These phenomena have been described and studied experimentally by Beebe and colleagues; their studies are so important that I will describe them here in some detail.

Beebe and Stern (1977) conducted an initial experiment in which the mother fixed her face directly above the infant's eyes.

They found that the infant attempted to meet her eyes, then withdrew. They called these interactions "games of chase and dodge." In subsequent work on the "chase and dodge" interaction Beebe and Lachmann (1988) then studied a scenario in which the mother did not permit the baby's withdrawal. The mother began trying to engage her baby by rapidly looming toward his face. The infant responded by moving his head back and away, breaking eye contact. In this experiment, once the infant had turned away from her, the mother responded by pulling his arm toward her. He then pulled his hand right out of hers with such force that he repeatedly lost his balance. With each increased attempt to engage him, the infant moved farther away from the mother, exercising a seeming "veto power" over her efforts. Finally, the infant became limp and unresponsive, as if saying: "'When I stay close to you, I feel overaroused and inundated. I feel you are moving in on me. No matter where I move in relation to you, I cannot find a way to feel comfortable. I can neither engage with you nor disengage from you'" (p. 329).

In the clinical situation patients often describe their own difficulties, or those of their lovers, in love relationships in such terms. Adult patients sometimes manifest this kind of behavior in the transference, leaving the therapist wondering what stimulated the derailment. When such material emerges in sessions, I have found that it is more useful to speak of concrete actions ("You have closed your eyes and moved away. Did you feel I was moving my head too much or speaking too much?") than to speak to the patient metaphorically using terms such as *closeness* or *engulfment*. (See Chapter 5 for more on the limitations of metaphor in patients with such issues.)

Beebe and Lachmann (1988) also studied the effects of other derailments or "misattunements" in the mother–infant dyad, and found that patterns of face-to-face exchange in the first 6 months predicted cognitive and social development at 1 year. (Their work on face-to-face play is predicated on a visual system that is "highly functional at birth and by approximately 3 months, achieves adult maturational status" [p. 313].) In healthy interactions, they found, the patterns recalled Stern's (1977) observation that "mothers tend to gaze steadily; it is the infant who 'makes' and 'breaks' the visual contact, regulating social contact" (p. 313).[2] All of these findings indicate that lack of visual engagement, or even lack of attention to visual phenomena, implies a real loss for normally sighted infants and children.

Wright (1991) made another effort to characterize the importance of mutual gaze, based on different theoretical underpinnings. Using the theoretical models and language of Bowlby, Winnicott, and Lacan, he made a case for the importance of the face-to-face experience for the infant. For Wright, the early face-to-face interaction helps to facilitate the infant's separation from the mother as well as his attachment to her. It also facilitates language development and symbol formation. He described shame as "originally founded in the experience of being looked at by the Other and in the realization that the Other can see things about oneself that are not available to one's own vision" (p. 30).

Wright contrasts the breast (touched, incorporated) with the face (not incorporated) and with the smile (not incorporated, and evanescent): "There is *an essential distance* in relation to the smile that cannot be overcome" (p. 108, emphasis Wright's). The smile, according to Wright, is the first object that is not an object. The mother's smile occupies a special place. It is not tactile or primitive. It points to the space where communication can develop. It is a precondition of symbol formation. Wright also tied the visual

---

[2]In thinking about adults and how they developed, Gedo (1996) instructed psychoanalysts to pay attention to these early preverbal modes of perceiving and communicating. These "earliest basic skills," he says, "are never lost, even after they have been for most purposes superseded by more sophisticated analogues" (p. 118).

apparatus to language, putting the most concrete perception—
breast—on a continuum from *face* to *smile* to *metaphor.*

> As development proceeds, the space of separation from the object
> becomes the space of symbols whose function may be anywhere
> between a re-creating of the object and a representing of it. The
> more complete the infant's tolerance of separation, the more rep-
> resentable the symbol can be; until with the development and even-
> tual resolution of the 3-person Oedipal situation, the representa-
> tional space is freed from the object sufficiently to become a place
> of pure representation. [p. 133]

I will discuss aspects of vision, concreteness, and metaphor further in Chapter 5.

Mahler and colleagues (1975) reported a case of a little girl,
Wendy, who used the gaze and her smile to stay attached to her
mother, who tended to relate to her symbiotically. This highly
cathected visual mode cost her some opportunity for locomotive
functioning and the tactile exploration of objects, as she preferred
to sit still and passively take in her environment. She had difficulty
internalizing an image of her mother when her mother was not
visually present. The authors noted further that "Wendy's language
development was rather delayed. She never seemed to get much
pleasure from talking and communicating with words and seemed
to prefer bodily language, which she used very expressively" (pp.
167–168).

THE DEVELOPMENT OF BODY NARCISSISM

Language

Mahler and colleagues (1975) described a 3-year-old boy who,
when asked who he was in the mirror, could only point to body

parts—eyes, nose, or mouth—rather than to his whole body, his self. They felt that this uneven body-image integration was due to a deficit in eye contact with his mother during the symbiotic phase.

Body narcissism, vision, and language develop concurrently and interconnect. Early body awareness and the differentiation of body parts and facial features are accompanied by the beginnings of word recognition. I see this process occurring as follows: Typically the mother/caregiver points to or touches in sequence the infant's and her own nose, eyes, lips, hands, hair, toes, and names them each carefully and repeatedly, teaching at once the rudiments of language and a conceptualization of the body. Accompanying this naming are the affective voice and touch intonations that convey to the infant messages of good or bad, for by 10 months of age, the infant's mind can classify information in binary form (Davidson and Fox 1982). The infant in time learns to imitate the mother— gestures, words, and intonations alike.

Mothers differ in their own use, and in the uses they will permit their infants, of these three modalities—vision, bodily touch, and language—that they share with their babies, particularly in the kinds of touching they will allow. Vision is constrained at first by the infant's lack of mobility, and may be further constrained later by more active prohibitions. Language, too, is limited by parental interest and psychological comfort, and for that reason the genitals have traditionally been exempt from the touching and naming that all the other body parts undergo. This is one reason they are usually less consolidated in the total body image (Lerner 1976). Similarly, the negative affect and words that accompany the child's failed efforts at toilet training may affect his developing feelings about his body, which he may describe later on as "shitty" or "smelly." There are great variations in the capacity for verbal differentiation of the body and its parts; the results of these variations and constraints may show up in the uneven use of language in psychoanalytic patients, as I will discuss at length in Chapter 5.

The mother's words offer different levels of complexity in this conjoint task of labeling, exploring, and reflecting the body, and demonstrate different levels of tolerance toward bodily activities. "No!" is different from "No, don't touch the stove," and different again from "No, don't touch the stove, it's hot!" Similarly, "Face!" "Nice face!" and "Nice face, soft!" provide different levels of information about bodily experience, and about where the body can go, what it can do, and why. Some mothers/caregivers fail their infants at this very early level of concrete naming, which is an important act of caregiving in itself, and one that gives most, but not all, adults a great deal of pleasure. Dutiful naming—where the mother feels she *must* label body parts as a pedagogical obligation— is different from naming as a game. I believe that children who do not master this very first level of language—the description of their own body parts and those of others—along with its necessary intrinsic connections with body awareness, vision, and mother herself, are likely to suffer as adults from deficits in the consolidation of the body image. The words by themselves are not enough. Such children may use symbol and metaphor as they get older and increasingly higher levels of language are demanded of them, but in this area of language and thinking about the body, the language is in some ways false, that is, it is not connected adequately with all of its necessary referents. A kind of pseudo-language develops, and may be lost under sufficient psychological stress. Mothers/caregivers who are narcissistic, schizoid, or depressed, or preoccupied, those who are unable to regress enough to play, and those who expect their children to be precocious and therefore beyond baby talk may not take the time to engage with them in this way. This lack of engagement may manifest itself later in sight-related symptomatology, or in the strikingly concrete use of language when speaking about the body.

There is some recent neurobiological confirmation of these empirical findings. Schore's (1997) overview of the genesis of emotional dysregulation makes reference to studies that suggest that visual and egocentric representations are stored in the brain's right hemisphere, inaccessible to the language centers in the left. This supports my thesis that the early baby talk involved in the naming of body parts could serve a bridge function connecting right brain to left brain, connecting visual to higher levels of thinking and language.

The developmental conjunction of vision, language, and touch has also received some indirect experimental support from Stern (1985), who has studied how infants take in information in one sensory modality and transfer it into another; for example, the breast is sucked and then seen, the one experience becoming connected one with the other so that eventually each internally evokes the other. His experiments deal with what infants like to look at (and what other senses are being used at the same time, as in the recognition of audiovisual correspondences): "Infants . . . appear to have an innate general capacity, which can be called *amodal perception,* to take information received in one sensory modality and somehow translate it into another sensory modality. We do not know how they accomplish that task" (p. 51). In this context it is worth recalling that babies watch people speak to them before they understand their words, and they reach out to touch moving faces— yet another connection between vision, speech, and touch.

It is beyond the scope of this volume to review the wealth of contemporary theories about language development (for review see Aragno 1997), but I will note some especially relevant of language as it pertains to the experience of "the body as looked at." As Rivlin and Gravelle (1984) have noted, "The ability to visualize something internally is closely linked with the ability to describe it verbally. Verbal and written descriptions create highly specific mental images. . . . The link between vision, visual memory, and verbalization can be quite startling" (pp. 88–89). In their 1971 review of the state of the developmental literature, Barglow and

Sadow observed that "lack of vision interferes with the ability to acquire language and to make use of words as symbols" (p. 444). They report that blind children concretize ideas.

The work of Melanie Klein (1930) and her disciples, especially Segal (1978, 1991), is noteworthy here, particularly their writings on symbol formation and its origins in the infant's experience with the mother's body and breasts, the first objects of curiosity. To the Kleinians, body parts and sensations are the building blocks of a symbolic order. The infant who has a good experience at the breast will go on to symbolize and to use metaphor. If he does not, "symbols formed are excessively concrete, empty of meaning or bizarre. If the projection (from projective identification) is not excessively envious or narcissistic and if the mother's response is not mutilating, the infant introjects a breast and a mother capable of the symbolic function" (Segal 1978, p. 319).

Contemporary linguists such as Lakoff and Johnson (1980, 1999) have confirmed the link between the development of metaphor and bodily experience. Much of our thought and perception depends on mostly unconscious metaphors drawn from bodily experience and on how we try to understand nonbodily experience in terms of bodily experience. For example, the concept of inside/outside refers back to the body; having a "close" friend who is physically close, one of the earliest sensations of the developing body, becomes associated with intimacy. Lakoff and Johnson cite the expression "life is a box of chocolates" as pertaining to a bodily experience—the taste of the chocolates producing a state of inner satisfaction akin to life itself.

Vygotsky (1988) wrote about the interpersonal use of language, and thought that speech originates socially and then goes "inside," becoming internalized in what he called "inner speech." He postulated a vital state, the "zone of proximal development" (ZPD), to describe how the more developed and sophisticated member of the dyad can provide cognitive and emotional growth to the other—

another analogue of the therapeutic situation. The ZPD acts as a scaffold that serves for the transmission of the culture at large. Wilson and Weinstein (1992) understand Vygotsky to mean that "the earliest communication climates between infant and caregiver become ground into the composition of the word itself" (p. 736); this is an example of my assertion that the child learns touch and intonation along with "nose" and "cheeks." Wilson and Weinstein (1996) see pathology as related to "the ways in which object use influences speech acquisition" (p. 168). For them, "the expansion of the child's mind depends on the mother's intuitive understanding that the infant requires the stresses and strains that accompany being introduced to what lies ahead, in order to form categories, ask questions, acquire new syntactical rules, and to obtain new and necessary ways of apprehending the world" (p. 193). The mother gives an upward push.

In a somewhat different but relevant vein is Fonagy and Target's (1996) research on what they call "mentalisation," which refers to the developing child's self-concept as dependent on the mother's view of the child as well as the child's appreciation of others as dependent on the self-reflective capacities of the mother. Lecours and Bouchard (1997) found that what they called insufficiently "mentalised" substrata, for example, primitive affects, "tend to retain their concrete and interpersonally oriented quality" (p. 873). These affects lead to acting out and to enactments. Affects that are "mentalised," internally represented, are better tolerated, and their abstract and symbolic features facilitate their becoming organized intrapsychically. Lecours and Bouchard present a number of examples illustrating clinically observable differences in the use of language. They reinforce their clinical findings with a more metalinguistic approach, describing what they call "dimensions of mentalisation," a supraordinate concept that encompasses representation, symbolization, and abstraction—an ego function (preconscious) that transforms somatic sensations and motor patterns into higher level language (see also Melnick 1997).

Sense of Identity

Greenacre's (1958) paper on the development of the sense of identity is critical to an understanding of the development of body narcissism. She noted that, although the face and the genitals are the most common body areas used for comparisons with others,

> at the same time they are the areas which are least easily visible to the individual himself. As no one ever sees his own face, the nearest he approaches this is the reflection of his face in the water or a mirror. Further, no one ever sees his own genitals as fully or in the same way that he sees those of another individual. While vision offers in many ways a seemingly more precise and comprehensive image than that assembled from touch, still it is indirect and subject to distortion by different perspectives, according to whether the report is on the body or that of another. While most of the back is not visible to the individual, this less differentiated area does not show great variations among the many others observed, which is not true with the face or genitals, and is more readily assumed on the self. . . . The reinforcement of the sense of the own body by the constant association with others of predominantly similar appearance is apparent throughout life. Appearance remains exceedingly important even in a very primitive way and spreads its influence into emotional and supposedly intellectual attitudes. [pp. 117–118]

I believe that one of the most important determinants of the positive or negative valence we ascribe to our bodies has to do with how much or how little we resemble those around us, particularly those who are held in high esteem by others. Those who are different, whether the difference is one of skin color, height, weight, or facial feature (type of nose or eye color), often regard themselves negatively, even when those traits that make them different might be highly regarded in other cultures.

Gender Identity

The explosion of attention to female psychology over the past thirty years has brought with it a great deal of discussion and criticism of Freud's (1931) basic pronouncement that "at some time or other, the little girl makes the discovery of her organ inferiority" (p. 232). Greenacre (1958) observed that since girls cannot see their genitals, they are prone to disturbances in the sense of identity per se. Boys, on the other hand, see and touch their penises regularly when they urinate, which consolidates the male organ into the total body image. They can also see the penises of other boys at urinals, and those of men as well, especially their fathers. Lerner (1976) has ascribed girls' difficulties in establishing clear gender identity to parental reluctance to name their important body parts, not just the vagina, but also the vulva, labia, and especially the clitoris. These are all names seldom used, and of which some parents themselves are ignorant. Since it is difficult to name what one cannot see, Bernstein (1990) called for a "concrete, visible, boundaried word concept" (p. 154) to describe the female genitalia as an essential for female ego development. Studies such as these further corroborate the interrelatedness of body narcissism, vision, and language.

Dio Bleichmar (1995), who has theoretical roots in Lacan and Laplanche, wrote, "The most common instance of infantile seduction between father-adult and girl goes on at the level of looking and being looked at. The male adult's seductive gaze falls upon the girl's developing body and carries a certain intensity that has sexual meaning for both adult and child" (p. 335). The father is in most cases not part of the child's physical care, as is the mother:

> The girl's realization of her [imagined] provocativeness creates a conflict of public versus private on the one hand, and exhibitionism versus voyeurism on the other. . . . When the woman looks in the mirror, when she bathes, there is always another detached pair of eyes looking at her body through her own "sexualized eyes." [pp. 336–337]

There are important links between feelings about the genitals and feelings about the body in general. Edith Jacobson (1964) described a tendency to see the female genital as damaged, coupled with a prohibition against looking at it, as I pointed out in a previous chapter:

> As a further result of this prohibition, the sexual interest is displaced from the "ugly" genital to the "pretty" body, and especially to facial appearance. In women, this commonly leads to an intense narcissistic investment in their faces and figures. But we likewise observe in boys' attitudes toward girls a shift of interest from the "castrated" genital to the pretty facial and body appearance, an interest which may assume exaggerated focus. [p. 71]

Jacobson noted "the girl's tremendous need for narcissistic supplies from men, a need caused by the narcissistic injuries of the past" (p. 168).

Lachmann (1982) provided a poignant case illustration of this. His patient, Jane, was sent to ballet class to cure her weight problem and give her grace. After she had danced for her father, he commented: "Nothing helps." This triggered social withdrawal, defensive trancelike states, the repression of grandiose expectations, and a strengthening of the regressive tie to the mother. She made a silent pact with her father that if she suppressed all displeasure with him, he would no longer express how disappointed he was with her appearance.

McGihan (1996), writing about the body's contribution to the female sense of self, described

> an attractive young woman who had an extremely negative sense of her own body. She was a large baby at birth and was delivered by forceps. She was a disappointment to her parents, both in her size and in her sex. Her father had wanted a boy. She had come to see her body as gross in the aversive responses of her petite mother to her in infancy. This was compounded by her father's teasing and labeling of her as an "eightseps" rather than a "fourceps" baby. [pp. 58–59]

In general, however, psychoanalysts have not paid much attention to the importance of appearance in the developing psyche. In a comprehensive survey of contemporary thinking on the psychology of women, the 1996 supplement to the *Journal of the American Psychoanalytic Association* on Female Psychology, only one author referred to the external body! In her paper on the pregnant mother and her daughter's body image, Balsam (1996) suggested that "the whole exterior of the body of the female is as important to her as the outer and inner genitals, and makes a vital contribution to the final shape of her gender role identity" (p. 401). She noted that the literature stops with genital comparisons: "None of these . . . studies has been attentive to female-to-female body comparisons. Yet obviously, a pregnant mother is inescapable to the eye, to the touch and to the imagination of her daughter" (p. 405).

In contrast to the psychoanalytic literature's cataloging of the so-called normal female sense of inadequacy, I find a regrettable paucity of recent studies of normal male development. Little boys go through stages of running around the house naked, "flashing" for all to see. They try to peek under girls' skirts and "play doctor" (as do girls). They enjoy dressing up in their father's clothing and shocking everyone when they dress up as women in their play. They, too, need to be told by their mothers that they look handsome in new clothing. My clinical work with men has led me to conclude that extreme parental responses, from overattentiveness to the complete ignoring of any of these normal behaviors can tip the boy in a pathological direction.

Being Looked At and Praised

I believe too much emphasis has been placed on feelings about genital differences in the development of body narcissism. Other factors have been omitted. Stern, Beebe and Lachmann, and others have recorded mothers' affective attunement with their infants. But not much has been written by psychoanalysts about such attunement as related to how the mothers experienced their infants' looks and how that affected their behavior toward them. Etcoff (1999), in *Survival of the Prettiest*, has documented the fact that mothers of attractive newborns spend more time exclaiming and cooing over their babies, whereas a disproportionate number of abused children are unattractive. Mothers' differences in verbal behavior, for example, "What a beautiful baby you are," "You look so cute today," "What a lady-killer you are going to be—a real hunk," are affective statements that provide the feedback that seeds self-esteem in both sexes.

The mother's verbal feedback, her gaze, the affective expression on her face, the quality of her touch, and her general care of her baby can be optimal during one phase and neglectful or destructive during another—for instance when a beautiful cherubic baby turns into a thin, wiry, sallow-skinned child. A patient of mine claimed to have been dropped like a hot potato by her mother after she became ill and lost her looks. Some parents re-create with their children their own unfortunate histories in this area as in others. When a sibling is born and an older child rejected, or a child has to wear glasses that the parents dislike, or an illness or death occurs in the family and the response to the child changes— all these reasons can cause a decathexis of the child, leaving him without positive feedback for and mirroring of his physical self.

Some children evolve into appearance-obsessed adults and others do not. Some parts of the body and/or face are chosen by child and/or parent for particular valuing or devaluing. This is due in part to the so-called Barbie-Ken phenomenon in which stereotypical good looks are used as yardsticks, and in part to changing cultural norms of beauty as seen on television and in the movies, and as learned in social relationships. Children's fairy tales emphasize appearance: Cinderella won the prince because of her tiny feet; Rapunzel gained power through her long hair; Sleeping Beauty had white skin and ruby lips.

Tyson (1986) has sketched out the developmental course of the little girl's gender identification. Her exhibitionism becomes prominent during the early part of the first genital (phallic) phase. She adorns herself like her mother and dances around showing off her body:

> Ann, age five . . . delighted in wearing her mother's nail polish, with mother's support chose a "sexy" bikini for the summer, and declared unashamedly, shortly after her mother had given birth to a baby girl, that she dreamed that her daddy had given her five Barbie dolls. Her play with the Barbie dolls often revolved around beauty contests between Barbie and the adolescent doll Skipper where Ken was the judge. She was empathically concerned, however, that neither should have her feelings hurt, and so she often staged family outings in which Ken's time was equally shared between the two females. Of course the main difference in these two

dolls is in the size of the breasts, and Ann's narcissistic vulnerability focused around her realistic realization that she did not have a mature female body necessary to win her father for herself. Although she felt herself to be his princess, mother remained his queen. [p. 364]

Today's more educated and enlightened parents do not support the stereotypical and sexist Barbie-Ken differentiation with its concentration on superficial appearance— at least not consciously. The authors (Thompson et al. 1999) of *Exacting Beauty* indicated that one of their reasons for writing the book was the reply of one author's 2-year-old daughter to the question (p. xi) "When your hair grows out, do you want it to be like your mother's hair?": "Want hair like Barbie."

Thompson and colleagues (1999) emphasize the pathological effects of familial and peer group teasing of children who do not meet ideal notions of good looks. The experience of the preadolescent and adolescent of his or her looks and those of peers are critical during these very important and narcissistically vulnerable years when the psyche is breaking apart and reorganizing. This period—replete with worries about whether one will ever be loved by another or even attract a boyfriend or girlfriend; when the body is changing; when many young faces sprout acne; when there is heightened physiological activation, sexual arousal, and sweating; when some parents defend against counteroedipal arousal by actively and tactlessly expressing negative opinions about their children's attractiveness—is ripe for the reactivation of long-repressed pathological fantasies and intrapsychic conflicts. Those branded at school as nerds, pinned like butterflies to that image, often withdraw into depression or become suicidal.

Wright (1991) offered a personal experience: "When I was an adolescent, I often felt awkward and self-conscious. I would feel that I was being looked at; this feeling inhibited my spontaneity and created a sense of no longer being in touch with myself. I had become a spectacle. I can remember walking down the long aisle in the school chapel feeling that all eyes were on me" (p. 22). Similarly, Nancy Friday (1996a) described poignantly how the line between childhood and adolescence was marked for her by one horrible dress she wore at a party:

> I stood in my horrible dress, shoulder blades pressing into the wall, watching my dear friends dance by in the arms of handsome boys, with a frozen, ghastly smile on my face, denying I needed to be rescued. Why, even the girl who couldn't hit a ball danced by. Though they all whispered for me to hide in the ladies' room I stood my ground. . . . By morning I had buried and mourned my 11-year-old self, the leader, the actress, the tree climber, and had become an ardent beauty student. From now on I would ape my beautiful friends, smile the group smile, walk the group walk, and, what with hanging my head and bending my knees, approximate as best I could the group look. [p. 82]

This appears to have been an adaptive solution for an 11-year-old. Some girls, faced with such strong feelings, take the opposite path, refuse to fix themselves up, and find themselves facing rejection and humiliation on an ongoing basis. Tactless mishandling of adolescents with regard to their appearance has gone on from time immemorial. One patient reported telling her mother when she was 13 that she didn't think she was pretty. Her mother responded: "Well, you could be rearranged somehow!" This comment haunted her all her adult life.

Blos (1962) described the challenge to the adolescent ego: "Component instincts come blatantly to the fore, the attempt to control them is evidenced in typical adolescent reactions. Scopophilia leads to shyness, embarrassment, or blushing, exhibitionism to modesty and self-consciousness" (p. 173). But the importance of current cultural mores in the characterization of developmental stages is important; note how outdated the following statement of Blos's seems today:

> In contrast to the girl, any boy who attempts to call attention to his beauty or who parades it with exhibitionistic pleasure is always considered effeminate. It is the prerogative of the female to display her physical charm—indeed to emphasize and enhance it through the use of cosmetics, adornments, and dress. Her need is to be loved. The boy is permitted only to display what he can do; he therefore focuses his pride on prowess and accomplishment. [p. 167]

Today many adolescent boys pride themselves on wearing whatever is "in," the "cool" sunglasses, sneakers, sweatshirts. They are less afraid of seeming effeminate when they concern themselves with such matters, which pertain to male group bonding. Our consumer culture now includes boys as well as girls. There is considerable evidence that today's boys are becoming as obsessed about appearance as girls. In an article in *The New York Times Magazine*, Hall (1999) interviewed a 16-year-old boy, Alexander, bright, articulate, and funny, who made a conscious decision that these were not the qualities he wanted people to recognize in him, at least not first. He wanted them to see his muscles and massive shoulders first. The writer noted that boys were catching up to girls in body-image disturbances. Whereas the girls were preoccupied with being thin, the boys were concerned with size and muscles. The boys were concerned about the cruelty of other boys. Adolescent body image problems can last a lifetime. The boys described in this article were using anabolic steroids even though they were aware that prolonged use might result in their testicles shrinking.

Concern about looks and clothing is connected with the wish to attract sexual partners as well as with basic identity and identifications with parents and peers. From early on, alert girls and boys look at their peers and compare themselves as to looks, clothing, and accessories. Today's young girls feel bad about themselves if they are not reed thin, and scorn their developing breasts if they seem large. Some are taken *by their parents* for breast reduction. The flat-chested, on the other hand, seek implants. Parents can be instrumental in mediating misconceptions and in helping their adolescents to adjust to physical anomalies. Parents' empathy and willingness to work sensitively with their children about perceptions of or denial of body problems can prevent the development of pathological body images.

Knafo (in press b) wrote about the analysis of a young woman who personified what she called "the Barbie syndrome." Issues of thinness, and competition with her mother about it, predominated, on both oedipal and preoedipal levels. She came to analysis "to get skinny and find a man." She needed to look and be looked at by the analyst. She felt cast away by her mother like a cat thrown off a bed. As an adolescent she felt pressed into watching and admiring her mother get dressed and made up. When she sought such looking and admiration herself, it was coupled with criticism. Her neurotic solution was not to compete with her mother, to become "the chubbo" and allow her mother to be "the belle of the ball." In her fantasy she could not be pretty and smart at the same time. She experienced Knafo as pretty, but was certain that she began to look good only after getting her degree. She had the not-uncommon fantasy that "pretty" and "smart" could not coexist.

Family photographs and home movies and videos play an important role in the genesis of children's theories about how they look. Those whose parents do not carry their photos or display them in frames or photo albums sometimes develop the belief that they are not good-looking. Some adult patients who are doubtful about being good-looking bring in to their therapy sessions photos of themselves as children and quite vigilantly note the therapist's immediate facial response to their images. Maintaining analytic neutrality without inflicting narcissistic wounds is quite a challenge in these cases. Refusal to look at the photos, even when the therapist asks the patient to hold onto them and to speak about the wish that the therapist see them, and/or a lack of verbal or facial responsiveness can be experienced as hurtful (and may be doubly problematic when the patient is unable to speak about the perceived hurt). On the other hand, the normal tactful social response of a smile and a statement like "What a lovely child you were" interferes with whatever transference is in place or could emerge in the future. This is a Scylla-and-Charybdis dilemma that the sensitive therapist must muddle through.

Concerns about appearance exist throughout life. As people age, their appearance changes while vitality and physical strength decline. Pre- and postmenopausal women suffer from lack of sleep, hot flashes, and night sweats that result in their looking older and tired. Some passively accept these changes. Others work at it and quip about "maintenance" taking up all their time. On the pathological end are those who become obsessed with reversing the ravages of time to the detriment of all else in their lives. In our culture, those in the latter category often get positive feedback and the curious envy of those who take a more normal approach. Women are not alone in this; men may similarly go through stages of trying to look and dress younger and deal with hair loss and other visible signs of aging. Some resort to divorcing their wives and marrying younger women to "mirror and match" with, in an effort to ensure their narcissistic equilibrium.

No part of the human life span is exempt from challenges to the consolidation of a positive body image. A person's physical sense of self and of self-image is influenced throughout life by verbal feedback from others, in the form of compliments and criticism. There is no escaping it in life, and it must be part of any therapy.

4

A Developmental Perspective on the Mirror

If the mother's face is unresponsive, then a mirror is a thing to be looked at, but not to be looked into.

Winnicott (1971, p. 113)

$\mathcal{E}$xperiences with mirrors, both metaphorical and real, facilitate the development of healthy body narcissism in children, and are essential in establishing an image of what one looks like and how one feels about that image. The real mirror offers the opportunity to see oneself as a physical object—from the outside, as it were—and to correlate external appearance with the physical sensations of movement. Metaphorical mirrors of various kinds provide opportunities to acquire verbalized and symbolized intrapsychic images and feelings as one's body interacts with, and is reflected by, others. These two kinds of mirror experiences, alone and in combination, occur throughout life. Infants and young children develop and evaluate notions about what they look like by standing in front of mirrors with their parents and others. (Some lovers enjoy admiring themselves as a couple in a mirror; for some, mirror play is a prelude to, or a part of, intercourse.)

Theoretical, clinical, and research commentaries on mirroring tend to oscillate between the concepts of body image and the more amorphous self image, often with little differentiation made between them. I will focus on the examination of body image alone as it relates to mirror experiences. *Psychoanalytic Inquiry* (Bornstein and Silver 1985) devoted an issue to the psychology of mirrors. Pines gave a masterful overview of this subject in 1984, and Haglund (1996) and Lemche (1998) have made major contributions as well. These papers are exemplary guides to the extensive psychological and child development literature. I will limit my discussion to the psychoanalytic literature, and add to it some observations and thoughts of my own. This material is a subcategory of the literature on the development of the visual ego, which I reviewed more generally in the previous chapter, and is intimately connected with it.

Mirror theories reflect (the metaphor is a pervasive one in our speech) the theme of this book: healthy body narcissism is enhanced by positive interactions with real mirrors and with "mirroring individuals," and that from these experiences one internalizes a conceptual mirror as symbol and metaphor for psychic experience. But like other developmental experiences, the results of mirror experiences may vary widely among individuals. Just as real mirrors can be blurry and distorted, so can psychic reflections. Just as real mirrors can shatter and split upon impact, so too can self and object representations shatter or split under the impact of certain kinds of psychological stress.

Haglund (1996), considering the mirror in human development and in the psychotherapeutic relationship, wrote:

> To poets and social scientists over the centuries, the image of a surface on which we see our own reflection has provided a compelling metaphor. For some the mirror is a lure capturing viewers and isolating them from others. For others, the mirror image is an objective representation of who we are. In this view, in our reflection, we see ourselves the way we believe others see us. We measure ourselves against some social ideal in such a reflected image. For still others the metaphor for mirror reflection is part of what favors the self. How others *mirror* back what they see in us contributes to the self we become subjectively and objectively. [p. 226]

Haglund thought that mirroring evolved out of the developmental milestone of self-recognition into the more diffuse incorporation of others' responses into the subjective experience of oneself. Oliner (1996) noted the discontinuity of the self that can occur during the mourning process, as reflected literally and figuratively in the Jewish tradition of covering mirrors during *shiva*.

She had a patient who reported shock at seeing herself in a mirror when for a time after her mother's death she had not looked at herself. I would regard this as a temporary regression to an early stage in which self-recognition in the mirror has not yet been achieved.

Freud considered the subject of mirrors on a number of occasions. In the Rat Man case (1909), for example, he reported that as a prelude to masturbation his patient would open the door of his apartment as if his dead father were alive and about to return. He would then take off his clothes and look at his erect penis in the mirror, reassuring himself thus that it was not too small. He would sometimes put a mirror between his legs. Underlying the masturbation was a reenactment of primal scene fantasies (see also Bradlow and Coen 1984).

In "Beyond the Pleasure Principle" (1920), Freud described his grandson's attempt to master object loss in the form of his mother's absence. He noted that the child would first look at himself in the mirror and then crouch beneath it, trying to hold onto the stability of his own image as a substitute for that of his mother. In a footnote to his paper on "The Uncanny" (1919), he revealed his dislike of his own image and the probability that he did not spend too much time in front of mirrors familiarizing himself with what he looked like:

> I was sitting alone in my wagon-lit compartment when a more than usually violent jolt of the train swung back the door of the adjoining washing-closet and an elderly man in a dressing gown and a travelling cap came in. I assumed that in leaving the washing-cabinet, which lay between the two compartments, he had taken the wrong direction and had come into my compartment by mistake. Jumping up with the intention of putting him right, I at once realized to my dismay that the intruder was nothing more than my own reflection in the looking-glass on the open door. I can still recollect that I thoroughly disliked his appearance. [p. 248]

Freud, an "anti-visuel," was more comfortable with mirror as metaphor than he was with the real thing, as when he advised that the beginning analyst should "be opaque to his patients and, like a mirror, should show them nothing but what is shown to him" (1912a, p. 112).

Just as the eyes have been invested by fantasy with magical and evil powers, mirrors have also been endowed with moment beyond their physical capacity as objects. Elkisch (1957) conducted anthropological studies of primitive beliefs about mirrors; she found that primitives experienced seeing their own images as dangerous, and considered this experience a harbinger of death, for the image seen in the mirror was supposedly the soul. She contrasted these beliefs with those of psychotics she studied, who looked into mirrors in order to deal with their fears of disintegration, to reassure themselves that they were not falling apart. Such disparate notions about how mirrors function permeate the literature on mirror theory (Priel 1985).

According to Shengold (1974), "The mirror's magic, good and bad, stems from its linkage with the narcissistic period when identity and mind are formed through contact with the mother; the *power* of mirror magic is a continuation of parental and narcissistic omnipotence" (p. 114). He described a young woman patient, plain, without makeup, and wearing ill-fitting clothes, who would stare at herself in the mirror in her analyst's waiting room. "How ugly you are," she would think. She had been seduced and traumatized as a child and wanted to break mirrors. Her identifications and introjects were organized around the internalization of a displeased mother transferred onto the analyst: "The image of the analyst was also lurking in the mirror—he owned the mirror and was the chief object of the patient's projections" (p. 98). According to Shengold, "The optimal mirroring situation involves the acceptance of the child's separate identity by a loving mother. The child gazing into the fond and accepting mother's eyes makes possible the secondary identifications with parental figures" (p. 99).

I wondered, reading about Shengold's patient, about the role of mirrors in therapists' waiting rooms, offices, bathrooms, lobbies, and elevators. There is a particularly harsh light in the elevator in my apartment building. Women patients sometimes report consternation at what they see in that mirror prior to their sessions. How much is this a displacement from the anticipation of *my* negative regard? Some patients spend much time with the bathroom mirror before or after sessions repairing their makeup. What does this mean? Conversely, what does it mean when a patient does *not* fix up her face, and goes out into the street streaked with tears for all to see? Waiting-room behavior, whether acting in or acting out, is difficult to address tactfully unless the patient brings it up in the session. We do not inquire as a matter of course about the number and placement of mirrors in the homes of our patients, either as children or as adults. I wonder if the availability or lack of a mirror in a therapist's waiting room predicts anything about the development of the therapy. Certainly the presence or absence of mirrors in the therapist's terrain reflects at least the therapist's views on the morality of mirrors. Is trying to fix one's hair and look neat before or after a session considered a sign of healthy narcissism or unhealthy vanity?

A patient of mine once said that she had no idea of what her back or the back of her head looked like. I asked her why she did not use a mirror to look. She replied that she did not own a hand mirror. Not owning a hand mirror served as a way for her to not see something threatening. In analysis she found that this fear was related to her wish not to look "behind her" into her troubled childhood, as well as to not see her genitals.

In *The Broken Mirror*, Phillips (1996) chronicled the plight of patients who feel tortured by their relationships with mirrors, feeling stuck to them for hours, compelled to stand there and look. One such patient found it hard to function because of her need to comb and recomb her hair. It was difficult for her to perform her work in a hospital because the patients' rooms had mirrors. She tried to conquer this problem by getting dressed without her contact lenses, so that she could not see. She eventually resorted to mirror avoidance to cope with this severe dysfunction.

DEVELOPMENTAL RESEARCH ON MIRRORS AND MIRRORING

Mahler and colleagues (1975) reported the following observations of infants and toddlers:

> Mirror reactions are most relevant for following the process of building self-representation and differentiating these from object representation. Put on the mattress before the floor length mirror when the baby first shows an interest in the image, he becomes excited and flails his arms in discharge movement. Later, at four to eight months, his movements slow down and he appears to become thoughtful as he seems to relate his own body movements to the movement of the image in the mirror. (The children who did not respond motorically at this age would look at the image with some perplexity.) At a still later age, nine or ten months, the child makes deliberate movements while observing his image seemingly experimenting and sorting out and clarifying for himself the relationship between himself and the image. [p. 223]

These researchers observed that immature narcissistic mothers would rock their babies in "unrelated" ways, such as holding them in awkward positions. In one case, to compensate, the child took on the rocking herself "for self-comforting and for auto-erotic self stimulation, as if the child were playing mother to herself. During the sub-phase of differentiation, this little girl would try to augment the pleasure of rocking herself by rocking in front of a mirror, thereby adding a visual feedback to the kinesthetic pleasure" (p. 151).

According to Lichtenberg's 1985 summary of many related experiments, infants between 9 and 12 months of age when placed before a mirror would laugh, coo, and jiggle their bodies with excitement, but could not recognize themselves, whereas infants 13 to 15 months of age reacted more soberly and less actively. If a smudge was put on their faces, they might reach for it in the mirror, but did not touch their own faces, somehow seeming to know that their own actions were determining what was being seen. Between 15 and 21 months, they reached up to touch the smudge seen in the mirror. Lichtenberg postulated an "imaging capacity," by means of which an infant creates a relatively objectified perceptual world "out there" (p. 201); the mirror told these babies something "out there" about themselves. During the first half of the second year, this imaging capacity bridges the learning by action that is characteristic of the first year and the learning through increasingly verbal symbolic representation that is characteristic of the second half of the second year. Imaging capacity sets up boundaries. Signs, for instance of parental moment-to-moment responsiveness, can be read. "This in turn helps to establish a discrete sense of self, one property of which is physical experience" (p. 205).

Similarly, Priel (1985) reviewed the gist of the conclusions drawn from experiments on the development of self-recognition in the mirror. At first there is social, joyful recognition (4 to 5 months); then the infant concentrates on comparisons between body parts as reflected in the mirror (8 to 10 months). He is comfortable at first because he is usually with his mother and/or held by his mother in the mirror. By 15 to 18 months he exhibits withdrawal and concern, followed by self-recognition according to objective criteria (20 to 22 months). Priel studied Bedouin children in the Negev desert who never had mirrors; these children avoided them and showed withdrawal reactions at an earlier age than her usual subjects. She concluded that children familiar with mirrors were able to mask what could be the more natural response, a special variety of "stranger anxiety" (at 8 months and up) when the child sees himself as a stranger in the mirror. This image has an uncanny quality and gives the child strange me/non-me cues; "mirror-image anxiety" is related to the constancy of the body and its boundaries.

Summarizing her own ongoing research, Kernberg (1984) attributed some of the anxiety of the 14- to 24-month-old child alone in front of a mirror to the fact that the reflection is *not* mother. His image alone reflects the still unstable sense of self. By 24 to 36 months, however, the child is more secure with his image as seen in the mirror alone.

The eye itself can serve as a mirror. Papousek and Papousek (1974, 1977) found that parents intuitively interact with their infants by staying centered in the infant's visual field. These experimenters videotaped and photographed infants' corneas, which acted as mirrors in which the infants saw themselves reflected in the mother's eyes. There was an interaction between both, a mutual learning experience about what each could do, a phenomenon they observed to occur cross-culturally.

Pines (1985) discussed mirroring as a dialogue between mother and baby in the context of the nonvisual senses, such as the mother imitating a baby's noises: "By reflecting back imitatively, mother is acting as a psycho-biological mirror, an active partner in the infant's developing capacity for social relations and the beginning awareness of self-representation" (p. 215).

Lewis and Brooks-Gunn (1979) related their experiments with mirrors and videotaping to the knowledge of one's identity. Recognizing oneself in a picture or in a mirror involves knowing that one cannot be in two places at the same time, and that one is continuous through space and time.

Weissman's (1977) work on the visual and observing egos, and their origins in observing and being observed, deserves more attention than it has received. The "visual ego," according to him, develops from pleasurable gazing along with the nonverbal mirroring of a variety of feelings between mother and infant. Permanent memory traces of the mother's face become linked to the infant's own facial expressions. Weissman postulated the development of organized units that contain affect, motoric memory of facial expressions, and memory of mother's face:

> The earliest transitions which form these units consist of a mutual mirror. The mirror could be initiated by either party. Mother may mirror and imitate the child and vice versa. At first only the crude expressions of pleasurable and unpleasurable emotions are mirrored. Gradually, the process becomes more artful and refined as the kid's communicative potential to act and be acted upon by facial expression becomes more subtle. Mother and child enter into increasingly elaborate visual conversations. This ability for visual communication permits the refinement of emotions in the infant. In time, he or she develops a wider range and repertoire of emotional responses which are stored in organized units. [p. 448]

As adults, we use this experience of our infancy to observe ourselves and to look after ourselves—to decide, for example, when to approach and when to avoid our employers depending upon their facial expressions. We gauge whom to approach and whom not to approach at cocktail parties. Those who are not able to make these refined social discriminations often have difficulty both personally and professionally.

LACAN'S MIRROR

The authors I have cited so far understand the mirror as furthering healthy psychic growth and identity. Lacan (1977) disagreed with this belief. His compelling but difficult (at times impossible!) to understand ideas have had many explicators, but it is not clear how well these explicators in fact mirror him (Barzilai 1995, Hamburg 1991, Jay 1993, Laplanche and Pontalis 1973, Muller 1985,

Muller and Richardson 1982, Pines 1984). I will cite a number of explications of Lacan because, although his writings have been so mysterious, his influence has been widespread.

Lacan began early in his career studying criminal cases in which vision was linked to aggression. He studied disturbed people who took their eyes out. He was what Jay (1993) called an "anti-visuel." He based his theory of the "mirror stage" on Wallon's (1921, 1931) experiments comparing the mirror behaviors of infants and animals. (Barzilai [1995] has demonstrated that Lacan did not really acknowledge the extent of his debt to Wallon.) Wallon found that animals failed to see their reflections as their selves, whereas infants were able to do this. He observed the over–18-month-old infant as "jubilant" in response to his own image in the mirror, the earlier period between 8 and 18 months being just a period of getting ready to perceive and identify with the human face. Children of 6 months of age placed before a mirror with a parent recognized the parent before recognizing themselves, smiling at the parent's face in the mirror. If the "real" parent spoke, the child turned to him in surprise, but by 8 months he showed surprise at his *own* mirror image. The mirror image or specular image of one's body develops later than the image of another, since the visual image in the mirror is the only image the child has of his own body, whereas when he looks in the mirror, he has two images of the other person: the direct image and the one in the mirror.

In my opinion, Lacan's most useful contribution to psychoanalytic thought was his theory of the mirror stage (1936, 1953, 1953–1954, 1977). He hypothesized that the primary experience of the self takes place in relation to the (m)other. At first the infant is in a state of "postnatal fetalization," which I understand to be an undifferentiated state. As he separates from his mother, at 6 to 18 months, the infant recognizes his image in the mirror and in a compensatory way identifies with it as an imaginary (nonverbal, nonlanguaged, presymbolic) bodily unity (see Muller and Richardson [1982] for further explication). This narcissistic experience of the self as a specular, or mirror, reflection, however, is a *mis*recognition, a false recognition—what Lacan calls a *méconnaissance*. The infant's self is in fragments, yet he sees himself as a whole in the mirror. The infant (subject) identifies with the image as the form (gestalt) of the ego in a way that conceals what it really looks like. The infant therefore overextends himself, taking an illusion for reality. The mirror image is whole; the infant's ego is not. This leads, retroactively, to a fantasy of "body-in-pieces." In adulthood this is represented in the experience of the fragile body and the danger to that body of a fragmentation that replicates the original infantile experience.

Acting as the arcane Lacan's "mirror," Muller and Richardson (1982) explained Lacan's (1936) landmark essay, "The Mirror Stage as Formation of the Function of the I as Revealed in Psychoanalytic Theory." They understood it as structured by the polarization of two themes: (1) the role of the image in the development of the subject, and (2) the manner in which social experience evolves. In their reading of Lacan's notion of the "mirror stage," the 6- to 18-month-old child first sees his self as a unity by experiencing some reflection of himself in the mirror. This serves as the "form that informs the subject and guides its development" (p. 29). Prior to this, chaos and fragmentation have reigned, but then "this totality becomes idealized into a model for eventual integration and as such is the infant's primary identification, the basis for all subsequent secondary identification" (p. 30).

However, once stable and fixed, it can also be rigid, and therefore can lead to the child's taking on the armor of an alienating identity with the external world and to an experience of the self seeming inverted and therefore somewhat awry. Muller and Richardson observed, "There is a primitive distortion in the ego's experience of reality that accounts for the miscognitions (*méconnaissances*) that for Lacan characterized the ego in all its structures. . . . [The mirror creates a confusion not only about the self but others as well] . . . The mirror stage comes to an end in this 'paranoiac alienation' which dates from the deflection of the specular into the social" (pp. 31–33). "Paranoiac alienation" is the misidentification of the subject himself with his own reflection, and the misidentification of this reflected image with the image of the other. Lacan called this distorted reality "paranoic knowledge."

Lacan's theory of the mirror has been embraced by the film and art worlds. Critics use his theory to explain the identifications audiences make with the figures on screen or canvas. The viewer sees the actor or actress on the screen and (falsely) experiences him or herself as the one being viewed. Feminist theorists have commented on Lacan's theories as well. Gamman and Makinen (1994) noted, "It is interesting that the Lacanian concept of 'misrecognition' bears such a strong similarity to most Western women's experience of not being able to recognize their actual body shape (even when they are looking at themselves in the mirror)" (p. 166).

Laplanche and Pontalis (1973) characterized the mirror phase as follows:

> As far as the structure of the subject is concerned, the mirror phase is said to represent a "genetic moment": the setting up of the first rough cast of the ego. What happens is that the infant perceives in the image of its counterpart or in its own mirror image, a form, a *Gestalt*, in which it anticipates a bodily unity which it still objectively lacks (whence its jubilation), in other words it identifies with this image. [p. 251]

Muller and Richardson (1982) saw, as a consequence of the mirror stage, that

> the anxiety of the fragmented body experience provokes aggressivity in response to the threat posed by the image of the other. Through "an appeal to the power of the image in which the honeymoon of the mirror so delighted" . . . the anxiety is quelled, i.e., through the pseudo-unification of the ego. The model of this synthesizing func-

tion of the ego is the notary or functionary mastering reality by treating objects as functional images of himself. [p. 136]

Muller (1985) further explained: "To identify with the whole human form thus has a defensive function in concealing helplessness and fragmentation under the cover of perceived coherent unity and mastery" (p. 237). The ego has a defensive function. The body is constructed from the elaboration of the body image.

Barzilai (1995) believed that for Lacan, the crucial image in the mirror was not the mother, but resided somewhere between the self and the mirror image. Both Wallon and Lacan agreed that the unity, the gestalt in the mirror, was not the mother, but was indispensible to maturation. But still a sense of fragmentation is never overcome. The "good-enough gestalt" is a mirror mirage: "In Lacan's view, the mirror is the mother of the ego. But the mother is not in the mirror" (p. 380).

Lacan actually was not very interested in the mirror function. For him, it was a way station on the path to symbolization, the symbolic relation that results from the intrusion of the father into the close unity between mother and child. I find a real irony in Lacan's emphasis upon the superiority of language, since his own writings are so poorly understood. The "mirror stage" was, for him, a series of encounters between the infant and a physical object, the mirror.

WINNICOTT'S MIRROR

Lacan was not referring to the mirroring mother of Kohut or of Winnicott. According to Winnicott (1971), who was influenced by Lacan, the first mirror is the mother's face. This is concrete.

Now, at some point the baby takes a look round. Perhaps a baby at the breast does not look at the breast. Looking at the face is more likely to be a feature. . . . What does the baby see when he or she looks at the mother's face? I'm suggesting that, ordinarily, what the baby sees is himself or herself. In other words, the mother is looking at the baby and *what she looks like is related to what she sees there.* [p. 112; emphasis Winnicott's]

The mother whose face reflects her own mood and the rigidity of her defenses cannot respond in a mirroring way, and, Winnicott believed, "There are consequences" (p. 112). He speculated that in such a case creativity would be diminished. The infant would become an overly vigilant being, watching the mother's face to see when it was safe to be himself, and making attempts to engage the mother. Winnicott thought actual mirrors in the home to be useful, but that "the actual mirror has significance mainly in its figurative sense" (p. 118). Eventually its reflecting back becomes part of what he called "the inner reserve," what I understand to mean a grounded, stable sense of self.

KOHUT'S MIRROR

By now contemporary psychotherapists tend to associate the term *mirror* with Kohut (1971) and his concept of the "mirror transference," in which the patient feels completely understood and reflected by the analyst. Kohut differentiates this sharply from the "twinship transference," in which the patient experiences himself as *like* the analyst, and the "idealizing transference," in which the patient experiences the analyst as someone who embodies the patient's archaic grandiose strivings. Kohut's writings are replete with references to mirror as metaphor, and in my opinion deficient in concrete references to real mirrors and what is seen in them! Since the term *narcissistic* came from the myth about Narcissus, who fell in love with his image in a real pool of water, it is another irony that the "father of narcissism" did not discuss in his writings what his patients looked like, or what they said and felt about their own looks or his.

Kohut (1971) did write about the "gleam in the mother's eye" as she responds to the infant's exhibitionistic displays. His narcissistic patients presented in treatment with issues around grandiosity and unrealistic notions of their abilities and accomplishments, and wanted him to mirror these views of themselves. Kohut did not suggest either that therapists provide this kind of "mirroring," nor that they display their own actual reactions to the patient. Instead, he felt that their empathy toward the *need* for mirroring would provide a safe container that would permit interpretations to take place. He wanted to remobilize the patient's need for a mirroring self-object, and through interpretation of empathic failures build more mature structure. The therapist's reflecting back to the patient the validity of his perceptions of the therapist's "misses" was seen by him as reparative and as serving as a catalyst for psychological growth.

Kohut's views on mirroring are often misunderstood, and do not include such examples of so-called positive feedback, as the mother of a patient of Lax (1997) provided. Rodney, charmless and unattractive, presented himself in his sessions with a grandiose opinion of himself as a painter. Lax wrote, "In mother's eyes Rodney was a 'genius' and she assured him of that. She narcissistically overfed him. Rodney basked in mother's praise and admiration, which contributed to his grandiose fantasies" (p. 843). Kohut's mirroring referred to the mother's pleasure in the child and the reinforcement of her recognition of him. Even so, I have difficulty with the nonchallenging, nonconfrontational technique of self psychology, which does not in my opinion sufficiently "mirror" the patient's aggression and negative behavior.

Hamburg (1991) provided a brilliant comparison of Lacan's and Kohut's notions of the mirror:

> For self psychology, the recapture of perfect mirroring became the Holy Grail in the analytic quest, melding nostalgia with perceptual hopefulness. For Lacan, the mirror stage was a developmental throw-

back confined to an atavistic place before and beyond adult discourse and subtly trivialized. It has no place in analytic practice.
[p. 357]

She felt that Lacan's theory "emerged from the impossibility of
absolute empathy within a therapy room where language was the
medium of discourse" (p. 349).

Pines (1985), on the other hand, found

a remarkable strength and even majesty in Lacan's thesis. However,
it is based on an intoxicating mixture of sensitive observation and
speculation and I'm not aware of a systematic attempt to integrate
his theories with the observation and theories of other more recent
psychoanalytic observations of infant behaviors toward the mirror
image. Lacan's thesis that mirroring is essentially an alienating experience of aloneness with the self contrasts with Winnicott's that the
child *finds* himself in the mirror of the mother's face. [p. 220]

THE MIRROR AS A FACILITATOR
OF IDENTITY

Mirrors can be used for psychological purposes by adults as well.
A. K. Richards (1998b) discussed a case in which the patient, an
identical twin, practiced for years in front of a mirror making her
facial expression hard rather than soft, to conceal her soft feelings.
She told the analyst that while masturbating in a mirror, she looked
at her facial expression at the moment of reaching orgasm. Being
a twin had made the psychological task of separation difficult for
her, in that it was difficult for her to see her twin experiencing
emotions that differed from her own. The mirror acted as a facili-
tator of individuation.

Another such use was reported by Malcolm (1988), a Kleinian, who elaborately described the function of a mirror fantasy in a perversion that served as a defense against psychosis, or breaking into pieces. Her patient, whom she saw as suffering from an encapsulated psychosis, told her about the fantasy with which she masturbated. It consisted of a one-way mirror inside of which violent, sadistic activity took place. Incestuous couples experienced humiliation and were barely satisfied. Outside the mirror were onlookers excited by what they saw. If they succumbed to the excitement, they would be pulled in.

According to Malcolm, the fantasy was an attempt by the patient to reconstruct the parental couple, the patient's own ego being in bits like the destroyed parental intercourse she contained in her fantasy of fragmentation. She used the fantasy to contain her destructiveness, and to protect the healthy parts of her psyche. Malcolm noted the importance of eyes in the sessions, and the patient's long, penetrating looks, which she interpreted as the patient's way of getting into her. The eyes were used as organs of projection and introjection and played a unifying role, by attempting to keep things together and by creating the mirror. In the transference, the therapist was an onlooker outside the mirror, whom the patient tried to drag inside. Malcolm concluded:

The mirror, as a concrete image within which the encapsulation takes place, provides her with borders firmly delineated and stable. [The mirror could only reflect her image and was ideal for her to control dangerous, threatening internal objects.] The mirror represents a breast, but a dead breast whose only function is to act as a concrete container, with solid borders, but nothing more. [p. 134]

I would understand this as having to do with Malcolm's patient's need for constancy as well as her intolerance of stimulation. She must have experienced the maternal breast as hard, cold, and mechanical. The only positive aspect of the mirror-breast was the stability of the fantasized mirror's frame.

I will not discuss here the considerable body image issues of those who have been born with disfigurements or have become disfigured by trauma or illness; these are beyond the scope of this book. Gunsberg and Rose (1998) have most sensitively written about the psychological effects of facial disfigurement in their work with children whose faces had to be surgically restored. The image of the face in the mirror and the mirroring response of the mother to the face are critical to the condition and the sense of constancy of the self.

THE MIRROR AND GENDER IDENTITY

Bradlow and Coen (1984) reported a case of a man who as an adolescent and young adult engaged in mirror masturbation, and who had to struggle for psychic differentiation and separation from his mother. They used this case to theorize about the function of the mirror:

> The person before the mirror, by his impersonation and magical gestures, creates an image in the mirror which can be transformed and altered at will to represent a multitude of objects. . . . The masturbator can be whatever he wants to be, of whatever sex, in a place safe for aggressive confrontations with others. [pp. 281–282]

Similarly, Chused (1997) has noted that "almost every male, regardless of his psychology, sex role or sexual object choice, has, in either childhood or adolescence, stood naked in front of a mirror with his penis hidden between his legs" (p.1). She presented three cases of male gender confusion. Each had the memory of pushing his penis between his legs and of looking at himself naked in a mirror, the accompanying fantasy revealing a "creative solution" to inner conflict. The first subject, a boy, wanted to look like a girl when he tucked his penis between his legs in the mirror so that he could believe that he could become one. The second, an adolescent, engaged in elaborate mirror play, in which he was both performer and audience, taking his mother's role as aggressor in his fantasy in order to have her be the one tormented, competed with, and possessed, instead of himself. The third, an adult, remembered standing in front of a mirror as a boy and then as an adolescent, in his fantasy hiding his penis from his mother so that she couldn't take it and it could not hurt her.

Chused's cases remind me of a cross-dressing heterosexual patient, who donned female clothing in secret and masturbated in front of a mirror to rock music. At times he would photograph himself, going back and forth in his fantasy from being a man making love to a woman to being a woman making love to a man. Periodically he would put all his paraphernalia into the garbage— the clothes, the wigs, the makeup, the false nails, and the photos— thereby destroying all evidence of his masturbatory activity. Powerful shame reactions followed upon these cross-dressing episodes, which were encapsulated and kept separate from the rest of his life as a married accountant with four children.

In spite of the many ways in which men affirm themselves in the mirror, it seems to me that women in our culture spend more time in the mirror than do men, and that mirror manufacturers usually have women in mind rather than men when they make and market mirrors. In *The Narcissist* de Beauvoir (1952) quite poetically embraced the function of the mirror for the woman, who must:

find the magic of the mirror a tremendous help in her effort to project herself and then attain self-identification. . . . Handsome appearance in the male suggests transcendence, in the female the passivity of innocence. Only the second is intended to arrest the gaze and hence be captured in the motionless silvered trap. Man, feeling and wishing himself active subject, does not see himself in his fixed image. It has little attraction for him since man's body does not seem to him an object of desire, while woman knowing and making herself object believes she really sees herself in the glass. A passive and given fact, the reflection is like herself a thing and as she does covet female flesh, her flesh, she gives life through her admiration and desire to the imagined qualities she sees. [p. 594]

I think it is important to mention here the use by feminists in the 1970s of the speculum in assisting women to look at their genitals and, by so doing, to develop a stronger sense of their female identity.

MIRROR DREAMS

Many studies of dreams in which the symbol of the mirror appears have been reported in the literature. I will cite just two examples. Silver (1985) noted that "in dreams, the mirror, which actually hearkens back to the mother's face as the reflecting mirror of selfhood, frequently symbolizes stages or gradations of crises in self-awareness." He went on to describe a patient whose mother had died when he was a child and this patient's dream: "'I am in a hall of mirrors in a palace like Versailles. I look out the window and over a balcony down on the street one floor below'" (p. 254). From his patient's associations, Silver concluded that he wished to have his mother back, as symbolized by the mirrors, and to repair a sense of inferiority stemming from having lost her.

Berman (1985), in his paper on rearview mirror dreams, reviewed studies of the meanings of mirror dreams having to do with identity and defense. In comparison with dreams in which the dreamer looks directly into a mirror, the latent content of rearview mirror dreams is "less narcissistically oriented and more object oriented. Furthermore, the element of 'behindness,' the view to or of the rear, seems of particular importance in these dreams and can represent anality, the analyst and the past looking backward" (p. 259). It can also represent primal scene fantasies and fantasies about the analyst sitting behind the couch. He discussed the human belief that the rear is less recognizable than the front, paralleling the difference of familiarity between the genitals and the anus, and the tendency to associate with untrustworthiness the parts we do not see.

THE MIRROR IN PSYCHOTHERAPEUTIC TECHNIQUE

When I trained as a "classical" analyst in the 1970s, many alternative therapies were in vogue, and from time to time I would hear stories about therapists who presented their patients with mirrors during their sessions and asked them to describe what they saw. I heard about one therapist who gave his patient a tape measure to measure her waist and hips before and after her meals in front of a mirror, the purpose being to test the reality of her contention that she grew excessively after every meal. Today these techniques do not seem to be as "far out" as they did then. Although I would not use such concrete techniques, I would and do *speak* concretely about such issues with my patients, as I will describe in Chapters 5 and 6.

Haglund (1996) did a conceptual overview of the richness and the inevitable elusiveness of the mirror concept and attempted to clarify "how psychotherapy facilitates movement beyond dyadic mirroring relationships by promoting the capacity for objective self-reflection" (p. 227). She concluded that patients who suffered from disorders of the self might need face-to-face sessions, eye contact, vocal matching, or other ways of confirming the self.

Pines (1984) described group psychoanalysis as a "mirroring process" in which different aspects of the person's self are reflected by the different group members, which enhances ego functioning and allows the patient eventually to see himself objectively. "In the psychotherapy group, the human mirrors offer us multiple perspectives on ourselves, on how we are seen by others and let us see the many facets of human development, our conflicts and attempts to color them. In the group I can see that only in this way I am like another but in this way I am not" (p. 30).

In individual analysis, there's one mirror; in the group, there are multiple perspectives. Pines wrote about *benign mirroring*: "This is me that I see in you, that I can reflect on or share with you or take back into myself and integrate with my already existing sense of self" (p. 36). This can be creative. There can also be *an absence of mirroring*: some patients are deficient in mirroring and only interested in themselves. Pines also wrote about *negative mirroring*: "Instead of mirroring its reflection, the one person regards the other person's vision as persecutory, defamatory and false, as if it were a searchlight trying to bring the person down and that has to be countered by an aggressive and retaliatory mirroring or trying to invalidate the vision. The other person is thus declared to be totally wrong in his perceptions or to be projecting aspects of himself into the other or is treated with contempt or devaluation" (p. 38).

But I myself like best Winnicott's (1971) metaphor of psychotherapy as mirror:

> Psychotherapy is not making clever and apt interpretations; by and large it is a long-term giving the patient back what the patient brings. It is a complex derivative of the face that reflects what is to be seen. I like to think of my work this way, to think that if I do this the patient will find his or her own self, and will be able to exist and to feel real. [p. 117]

III

LOOKING AND BEING
LOOKED AT IN THE
CLINICAL PROCESS

5

The Therapist's Rush to Metaphor

To hear with eyes belongs to love's fine wit.

William Shakespeare, Twenty-third Sonnet

Sometimes it is superficial to look beneath the surface.

Oscar Wilde

$\mathcal{T}$his chapter discusses how language develops, and how it is used in therapy, particularly with regard to the capacity for symbolism and metaphor, and how it is linked to body narcissism. The most active period of language development coincides broadly with the original integration of body narcissism; this language and body narcissism are linked at the very least by synchronicity.

In my clinical practice I have observed increasing numbers of patients, male and female, who present initially or after some months of treatment with preoccupying concerns about bodily and or facial appearance. Some focus exclusively on their own looks, some focus with great intensity on the appearance of others, especially present or potential love objects, and some focus on both. These patients do not, in my experience, understand their anxiety about these issues to be symbolic of anything (although they may be able to understand other feelings about other issues in more abstract ways). Their worries and questions about the importance of looks are concrete, and so is the language they use to describe them.

About twenty years ago, before I had considered the technical issues I am writing about here, I saw a patient with a compulsive wish to have the darkest tan in New York. He spent summer days in the sun, and winter weekends jetting to Florida and Puerto Rico in this quest. He loved the compliments and attention he received from friends and strangers, and he called himself proudly "the man with the tan." Nevertheless, the strain of travel and the time devoted to the sun was wearing on him, and he came into therapy to deal with the resulting conflict. He quickly manifested an idealizing transference, and after a handful of sessions began to feel better. He attributed this to me, "the best therapist in New York," and he sang my praises to everyone around.

He began to arrive at sessions in his jogging clothes, and would sit before me deeply tanned, sweating, and half naked. His dreams indicated an intense erotic transference. Just out of training, I tried to interpret what I thought to be erotic wishes toward me, but my efforts fell on deaf ears. He terminated shortly afterward, in his opinion "cured." I did not have at that time the diagnostic and clinical tools that would have enabled me to address the true nature of his problem. I have since learned more about the origin of narcissistic deficits and the adjustment of thought and language, the *linguistic attunement*, that such patients require.

I believe that disturbances in body narcissism are often reflected in more-or-less temporary disturbances in the capacity for metaphoric language when speaking about the body, its appearance, and its maintenance. This is not surprising in view of the facts that they develop contemporaneously with each other, and that the developmental deprivations that may influence the one (such as insufficient maternal attention) are also known to influence the other (as discussed in Chapters 3 and 4). The earliest registration of form is visual form, and the first representations of self and other are registered nonverbally, by sight, smell, hearing, and touch. Mothers and other caregivers teach the beginnings of language by looking at, touching, and naming the infant's (and their own) various body and facial parts. Positive or negative affects connected with the body and its parts are communicated in these very basic exchanges. Children whose mothers are depressed, narcissistic, or otherwise unrelated may not experience this close connection between looking, naming, and caregiving, and the resulting deficits may manifest themselves across all three fields.

This correspondence makes for potential difficulties in the psychotherapeutic treatment of such common developmental disturbances. These difficulties are a result of the conflict between the concrete language of that developmental period and the established mores of psychotherapeutic communication. Contemporary psychotherapists value metaphor. "Where symbol was, there metaphor shall be" was the way Wright (1991, p. 165) put it. The capacity for higher-level abstract thought is so highly valued in our field that it has long been held as a criterion by which to select those suitable for analysis (Arlow 1979, Borbely 1998, Levin 1979).

One reason for this preference is the undoubtedly greater capacity of metaphoric language for grasping and conveying subtle and complicated psychological constellations. Our own analyses were conducted in the language of metaphor, and our training in highly conceptual language. We are used to metaphor as the vehicle for elaborating psychological experience, and our work feels more stimulating and meaningful when conducted in abstract discourse.

However, there are some dangers in this preference. The first is that abstraction can be used as a defense against more immediate kinds of experience. As Malcolm (1999) says, "Using symbolic language bypasses the depths of the transference experience. It destroys the live contact between analyst and patient and turns the analysis into *talking* about unconscious phantasies, rather than experiencing them in their crude impact" (p. 51).

A second danger is that metaphor, being multilayered and multifaceted, is also open to multiple interpretations, and is much more likely than a concrete statement to be understood differently by the patient and therapist—sometimes without the awareness that this has occurred. I will have more to say about this shortly.

The third and most serious danger is the dismissal of concrete speech as either irrelevant to therapy or incapable of communicating anything important. In fact, however, many therapists strongly believe that the use of concrete language may be an important part of the therapeutic process.

I caution therapists to not "rush to metaphor." Especially with educated patients, we tend to assume that they share with us a common language and common symbols. I have found that many times this is not so, especially when issues about body narcissism arise in the treatment.

Patients regress to troubled points in their development, and this sometimes means regressing to less mature forms of mental representation. Lecours and Bouchard (1997) noted that "clinical observation confirms that each patient displays certain specific emotional 'dark zones' that are less mentalised and others that are more mentally elaborated, partly independently of their character organization" (p. 871). They also observed that "the desired evolution in the levels and forms of mental elaboration during analysis seem to imply a prior necessary activation and working through of dynamically more regressed and often less mentalized drive–affect material" (p. 870). They were referring specifically to the acting out of borderline patients who cannot maintain stable mental images, but I believe this formulation to be true for narcissistic patients as well. In addition, Borbely (1998) has noted that trauma affects the capacity for metaphor; only people who can tolerate strong emotional experiences can use metaphor. "Trauma reduces the polysemy of experience due to overwhelming anxiety and leads to a fixed meaning of the experience. . . . During psychological trauma . . . the fabric of semantic relations gets skewed or torn apart" (p. 930). "Cure" results from letting the patient regain metaphorical potential. Prior to that, "the individual is forced to resort to idiomatic, rigid analogical thinking" (p. 930).

Busch (1997) has addressed this topic also; I find his work highly relevant. As the ego undergoes changes in the therapeutic process, he maintains, it becomes temporarily less available for abstract thinking. Concrete thinking may appear in the patient's area of conflict, and the therapist must wait until, with integration of the changes, the patient's ego becomes once again available for abstract thinking.

> In making my interpretations, I often repeat the patient's themes and sequencing. . . . The practice is based on my observation that in areas of conflict patients' ways of thinking are concrete and limited to a 'before the eye' reality, . . . similar to a type of thinking seen in children at an age when conflicts become formed (eighteen months to seven years). Thus my interpretations rely, wherever possible, on what is most tangible, concrete and observable—that is, the patient's own thoughts. [p. 413]

Busch has criticized any uses of metaphor that do not take into account the current state of the ego and its readiness at that time to work with metaphor.

If in fact, therefore, certain psychological situations tend to be characterized by concrete rather than abstract thought, the question arises of how the therapist should address them.

Over the past few decades, the American Psychotherapeutic Association has presented several panels devoted to language. The 1983 panel, according to psychoanalyst Theodore Shapiro, was on "aspects of how analysts make interpretations and how these interventions and the focus they take influence what goes on in the treatment process" (p. 687, quoted in Weich 1986). In the 1986 panel, also reported by Weich, Gedo stated:

> The kind of dialogue we must establish in the psychotherapeutic situation in order to enable patients to communicate about archaic aspects of their childhood experience is the therapeutic counterpart of the way in which a small child conveys his experiencing to his caregivers. The analyst must also understand the patient's non-verbal enactments within the transference as meaningful commu-

nications. The language he uses in his participation in such transactions must be penetrating, *concrete*, simple, affect-laden, and dra-
matic. [pp. 689–690, my emphasis]

Gedo (1979) has commented further that "the majority of psychotherapeutic clinicians probably have not experienced much
discomfort about the loose fit between their theoretical tools and
their *patients'* associations" (pp. 161–162). More recently (1996), he
wrote that "in regressive states, analysands often become unable to
process the intended meaning even of syntactically and lexically
clear messages—unless these meanings are amplified by paraverbal
indications of affect" (p. 14).

These things being so, it seems that a patient (temporarily) limited to concrete thought and speech, and a therapist operating on
his accustomed highly symbolic plane, may not always be understanding each other, however well they may communicate when
the patient is in comfortably metaphoric mode. They may not always recognize when misunderstanding occurs. Further, the therapist may misinterpret an actual misunderstanding as psychologically motivated resistance.

Levin (1979), for example, has a great interest in and appreciation of metaphoric language for psychotherapeutic communication. He takes pains to describe the complexity of metaphoric
language, which involves what he calls "switching" functions, as
well as ambiguity, multiple meanings, symbolism, and thinking by
means of similarities. He notes that metaphors manage both to
surprise us and to bridge experiences by their capacity to bind
unexpectedly conjoined concepts. However, I am not convinced
that we all agree on what constitutes a metaphor in clinical work.
I will use one of Levin's illustrations to exemplify the kind of
possible misunderstanding I am talking about. He offers the following example of what he considered to be a metaphoric communication. The patient, Mr. A. had lost father, grandfather, and

uncle while young. Levin is describing how the patient's mourning process continues:

> Having had some of his clothes stolen from a laundry, he spoke one day of his outraged embarrassment and his impulse to immediately replace the lost articles. Unfortunately, he would have to order new clothes in a slightly larger size since he felt he had gained weight. He mused about having someone assist him in relation to this loss. I suggested that he needed a tailor and asked him if he knew any way to mend the situation. This ambiguous metaphor was a reference to his major loss in childhood (father), who was a tailor; to his recent loss (of clothes); and to myself in the transference as one who mends or helps him to mend himself, etc. [p. 234]

My impression of this encounter is that his patient was thinking concretely, and that Levin himself was speaking in both concrete and metaphoric modes. I am not necessarily right, but this is a good example of a communication that is ambiguous as to its concrete or metaphorical nature.

My experience with patients like this leads me to think that the therapeutic gains that Levin reports could as well be attributed to the concrete statement that the patient needed a tailor as to a metaphorical connection between the lost father and "mending the situation." It is not always clear what is concrete and what is metaphor. There can be mixtures of both in the same phrase, and different people read the phrases differently.

Another example: Silverman's widely studied and discussed clinical report in *Psychotherapeutic Inquiry* (1987) is of a patient who, when Silverman spoke symbolically and metaphorically, would follow him cooperatively wherever he led her. But she was located in a different cognitive and linguistic world in which concrete reality dominated. When she spoke about a problem in tipping her hairdresser, Silverman told her that she was avoiding sexual excitement, that scissors and fingers in her hair sounds "sexual." She replied that she had "no problem tipping my manicurist." This kind of exchange is characteristic of concrete patients. (Silverman's patient, by the way, like many of the patients I discuss in this book, presented in her associations preoccupying concerns about her looks.)

Ogden is another analyst with a great interest in metaphor who has done us a service in studying its place in analytic thought. In a series of articles on the analyst's reveries (1997), he described reverie as a metaphoric expression of what unconscious experience is like, and of the way metaphor is created. He praises the use of metaphor: "Without metaphor, we are stuck in a world of surfaces with meanings that cannot be reflected upon" (p. 727). Ogden values the use of metaphor highly, but he also appears implicitly to devalue concrete language. He does not (at least in his clinical reports) apparently use concrete language himself in talking to his patients, and he presents material from several cases in which he and his patient worked very well with metaphor.

In one example, however, Ogden describes a failed attempt to elaborate upon a metaphor. It seems to me likely that this is another good example of a case in which the therapist was in one place and the patient in another, and where misunderstanding was misinterpreted as resistance.

> In a recent analytic session, the analysand, Mr. H., said, "Last evening I didn't leave the college [where he teaches] with anyone. While waiting for the bus I was completely alone with myself." I asked: "What was it like being alone with yourself? What kind of company were you for yourself?" The patient replied: "I don't know. I finished almost all of my Christmas shopping yesterday." [p. 723]

Ogden interprets this response as a defense, which he counters with another metaphor, that the patient regularly feels like an unwelcome guest of the therapist. The patient then remarks that he is not sleeping well because of mechanical noises—a response that a metaphor-using therapist, I think, would have to understand as a comment that these interpretations were experienced by him as just that, "noises." Rather than adjusting his language to that of his patient, he keeps pushing metaphors.

But Ogden is very interested in these matters, and he in fact provides an excellent description of concrete patients:

> The experience of attempting to work with patients who are very concrete in their thinking and use of language is an experience of communication (or lack of communication) characterized by a paucity of metaphorical language (or more accurately, an inability on the part of the patient to experience a metaphor as a metaphor). For such patients, people, events, feelings, perceptions are what they are: a session cancelled because of the analyst's illness is just that, a session cancelled because the analyst was ill, no more and no less. The event is an event; it is not even felt by the patient to be his experience of an event. [p. 725]

He also provides some useful references to other therapists' studies of the limitations of metaphor, and their admonitions that the therapist not surpass the patient, or steal or create metaphors or in an authoritarian way give the patient the "right way." Ogden does not, however, offer technical recommendations that might help therapists working with such patients. Although in speaking with clinicians it becomes clear that many do in fact use concrete language with concrete patients, this informal practice has apparently not been much reported upon in the literature, or studied systematically.

A further complication of the technical implications of concreteness is that although its presentation is easily recognized and its results widely discussed, there is no widespread agreement about its causes.

Some therapists consider concreteness a defense; for others it is a defect in a primitive ego that has not yet integrated the symbolic and the abstract. I understand concreteness as Giovacchini (1972) did when he referred to "a mind that is unwilling to deal with both inner and outer experiences in psychological terms" (p. 353). (However, Giovacchini himself views concreteness as a function of ego defects, and/or as controlling manipulations designed to sabotage the therapist.)

So the question remains: How do you increase the capacity for metaphor in patients with whom you can't talk metaphorically? Bass (1997) has directly addressed this dilemma of what he calls the "problem of concreteness." He feels that concrete patients "present derivatives of fantasy material, often in an apparent drive-defense configuration, but cannot make use of interpretation" (p. 642). He sees persistent concreteness as "a particularly inert form of wish and defense working together" (p. 649), and "a result of the process that produces the primary split in the ego, a split between any differentiation that has become too anxiety-provoking and the defensive use of hallucinatory wish fulfillment substitute for it altogether" (p. 659).

If one has to believe that one's perceptions provide indubitable knowledge of "reality," the possibility of intervention is pre-empted. To interpret always implies that one thing might mean another. The "concrete" patient paradoxically defends against just this possibility while remaining in analysis. [p. 645]

Bass discusses dreams as convincing visual experiences. For the dreamer, "seeing is believing." When it is too threatening to deal with the unseen, patients must stay with what they can see. The therapist of concrete patients must bear this in mind.

Lacan (1953–54), in the context of a distinction between full speech and empty speech, described empty speech as "caught up in the here and now with the analyst, where the subject wanders about in the machinations of the language system, in the labyrinth of a system of reference offered him by his cultural context" (p. 61).

If the task of the therapist is to help the patient achieve "full speech," the problem of technique, then, is how to conduct the therapy without it. A wall of so-called empty words must be penetrated. How can we talk to these patients?

It is my impression that the need for concreteness of language and thought coincides frequently with times of preoccupation with the external, physical body. The nature of these preoccupations may change. Gedo (1979) has observed that "in the aftermath of Victorian prudery, Freud taught the victims of the discontent produced by a civilization simultaneously moralistic and prurient that one must live one's life within the body" (p. 259).

Today issues other than the moral use of the body prevail among our patients. Freud's writings reflected his patients' concerns about the inner body and inner fantasies about the genitalia. Today's patients speak of their concerns about the external body, particularly how it looks to themselves and others. Many seem manifestly less concerned with issues of gender and sexuality than with the narcissistic cathexis of the body, and the search for ways to shore up a shaky body ego.

However, whatever the particular bodily concern, it seems to me that it is likely to be associated with a diminution of metaphoric thinking, which becomes profoundly irrelevant, at least temporarily, to the patient. In *The Broken Mirror*, Phillips (1996) deals with body dysmorphic disorder (BDD). She cites the complaint of such a concrete patient:

"Some of my therapists have tried to convince me that my appearance concerns are just a symptom of other problems—that they aren't my real problem. After years and years of trying to figure this out, I've finally come to the conclusion that they're wrong. My obsessions have a life of their own. They're a problem in their own right. They're not just a symptom of other problems." [p. 39]

The body is a concrete object with an actual concrete manifestation and actual physical feelings (as opposed, say, to an idea or a fantasy). Also, people have to begin to deal with their bodies well before the emergence of abstract thought. For both of these reasons, and perhaps others that will become clear over time, psychological issues about the body appear to require a concreteness of thought that other issues do not. Hinshelwood (1997) has presented some of Melanie Klein's unpublished writings. Klein described the "inner object" in its deepest sense to be a physical being, lodged inside the body with concomitant bodily feelings. In her technical recommendations about addressing such a concept to the patient, she wrote:

> In my experience the more concretely, the more specifically, I should say vividly if this did not have a flavour of dramatization which is unnecessary, we can convey to the patient the content of the unconscious phantasies we see in action, the more effective our interpretations will be. [p. 895]

I would add to this "the more visually."

I think that the contemporaneity of the development of language and the integration of body narcissism, and their joint dependency upon intense maternal involvement, both bodily and linguistic, gives them a sort of joint vulnerability. A deficiency in the caregiving environment that affects the one will be likely to affect the other; therefore, disturbances in bodily narcissism are likely to be accompanied by disturbances in higher-level thinking and speech. I have found that concrete thinking is often connected with problems in the development of the bodily self and its boundaries, and tends to be the result of deficits in attention to the body and its care and maintenance. Such problems intersect and interact with the development of internal fantasy, conflict, and defense from early childhood on.

I believe that in circumstances where a patient is dealing concretely with concrete preoccupations about looks, concrete responses from the therapist actually facilitate and promote the concrete patient's capacity for symbolic thinking, and that such responses can begin to repair the narcissistic deficit underlying the preoccupation, allowing the ego to grow and further develop. Just as Busch (1997) advocates speaking to the surface of the ego, I believe that in this area of body narcissism the therapist's comments to the patient must include concrete references to the therapist's observations of the patient's body, of what is revealed at the level of the skin and its covering, clothes. Only apparently superficial, this is very much a way "in," for the external body is the gatekeeper to the inner self and its thoughts and its fantasies.

The prevalence in some of our patients of thoughts and obsessions about their bodies is evident in the amount of time and effort many of them spend in exercise, on diet and nutrition, and on the selection of clothes. When they appear in our offices in scanty exercise garb, too quick an understanding of this as sexually seductive can lead us to overlook the more immediate therapeutic need to be looked at by us. Kohut (1971) referred to the "mirror transference," and he developed from it an analytic technique of reflecting back to the patient important aspects of self. On a concrete level, some of these phenomena may be understood as reflecting the more literal wish on the part of the patient for the therapist to be a mirror, telling the patient what the therapist quite literally sees.

For Lacan, symptoms are resolved through an analysis of language. An analysis of the language deficits manifested by patients preoccupied with appearance leads to the conclusion that the therapist must use concrete language to communicate with them until they are ready to use symbol and metaphor.

Before offering some extended clinical studies of patients in whom an upsurge of issues around body narcissism temporarily shut down the capacity for metaphoric work, I want to address the belief that concrete communication is necessarily simple and not psychological when it occurs in therapy.

When patients are dealing concretely with issues of body narcissism (as opposed to the times when they are using concern about their looks to symbolize something else, such as castration or oedipal victory), I think that they must be responded to directly and concretely in the here and now. This feedback about what the therapist sees provides them with confirmatory, empathic responses that demonstrate the therapist's awareness of their experience of and in their bodies in the moment. But such responses are not necessarily simple, psychologically uninformed or uninforming, or even untherapeutic, and they should not be devalued as part of an ongoing therapeutic process. I offer as illustration three exchanges from the therapy of one patient:

Patient: I never feel that I look that great. I never know what to wear. I am so uncomfortably warm today.

Analyst: It is 90 degrees out, yet you are wearing a wool cardigan and slacks. What about that?

P: (Complains that she has to go to a business lunch the next day in a fashionable restaurant and has no idea of what people would be wearing.)

A: Why not go over to that restaurant today and have a look?

P: (She is envious of me but not yet aware of that, and she always avoids looking at me when she comes into the office.) My rear end is so large. I am so out of fashion. I haven't the vaguest idea of what people are wearing this fall.

A: You have the option of looking at people when you are out in the street.

In the first example, I could (correctly) have interpreted the links between the patient's conscious discomfort with the unconscious discomfort of her sexual feelings toward me. I did not because this patient had demonstrated many times that she could not yet hear or process an interpretation like that, whereas she could easily comprehend and relate to my more concrete comment. But it is important to note that when I responded to what I saw, my response, although concrete, was not simple. It was informed by long and hard analytic work, in which I had come to the conclusion that there had been a profound lack of concrete maternal attention when this patient was a child. In light of this reconstruction, my concrete statement addressed the consequent deficits that I had observed in the patient's capacity to care for herself. My comments were available for understanding on two levels: the concrete one of which she was at that time capable, and the historical/metaphorical one in which I encoded my understanding of her childhood experience.

In the second and third examples, I spoke from another convincing reconstruction—that this patient's curiosity had been suppressed when she was a child. I did not interpret at that moment her envy of me or her not looking at me, but I did interpret what I had learned about her, in a displaced form.

A series of interventions such as these, in which looking and being looked at were facilitated, eventually enabled this patient to purchase a fashionable wardrobe, to feel good about her body, and more importantly for the therapy, to begin to work symbolically again to understand the genesis of her narcissistic problem. She was then able to proceed to talking about issues of envy and competitiveness with me.

Similarly, if the man with the tan (cited above) were my patient today, I would not try to interpret erotic transference at such a time of concrete narcissistic preoccupation. I would focus first on the narcissistic issues and speak to him about his tan, the perspiration I observed, and so on. That is, I would stay close to concrete bodily issues in my comments. I would say, for example, "You are sitting on the floor in the position you take in the sun."

When patients have regressed to concrete ways of thinking, it facilitates progress when the therapists report what they actually see (as opposed to interpreting what they think it means). However, the therapists will do this in the context of what they know about the patient's issues with seeing and being seen. Symbolizing therapists must give up symbolic speech in order to communicate with a nonsymbolizing patient, but they do not give up the capacity to think symbolically, or to be aware of the psychological context. (The temporary regression involved in relinquishing symbolic and metaphoric speech may of course have countertransference implications for the therapist.) The kind of consequent "narcissistic repair" demonstrated in the examples above stimulates the ego to grow. If all goes well, eventually the patient will become able once again to communicate in symbol and metaphor.

Many researchers and commentators have maintained that women suffer more about their bodies, and dislike them more, than men do theirs. In my clinical practice I have had a number of male patients, both heterosexual and homosexual, whose predominant concerns have centered around body narcissism. Men tend, however, to displace their insecurities about the appearance of their bodies onto women's bodies. (Since women have, since time began, been willing to accept such displacements, these practices continue!)

Male and female patients both report concerns about what they look like. Often their communications in therapy are aimed, consciously or unconsciously, at getting feedback about how they look to the therapist, how the therapist sees them, and whether or not the therapist likes their looks. I have had a number of male patients who were obsessed with the looks of the women they were trying to date, were dating, or were married to. They also spent much time in the mirror looking at themselves, trying to reassure themselves that they were physically acceptable, and they used women to buttress their own self-images.

CASE VIGNETTES

I want to illustrate now what has in my experience been the characteristic clinical presentation of these kinds of issues: the coincidence of a period of intense bodily preoccupation with the loss of a previously available capacity for metaphoric language. Most of these patients began treatment with language and associations that suggested an oedipal level of development. All of them were capable of symbolic thought and speech, all of them were psychologically minded, and all became quickly involved in the therapeutic process.

My first three illustrative patients are men. Initially, when they came to therapy, they all wondered whether they were good-looking or not, and reported feeling insecure with women. Each, however, somewhat paradoxically started out convinced that he was his mother's favorite: the oedipal winner (over father), the sibling winner (over brothers and sisters), or the only child in the family.

In the next phase of treatment, each of these men regressed to a completely syntonic, highly concrete phase in which he experienced himself as extremely attractive, and displayed an intense and very judgmental interest in the appearance of the women he encountered. During this period, not one of these men was able to search for the meanings of such an attitude in the way he had been able to do, and had been interested in doing, in the earlier phase. My purpose in these examples is less to illustrate the particulars of the verbal process (as I did with the patient above). Instead, I want to demonstrate what I consider the characteristic aspects of the clinical presentation, and the consistency of this type of presentation over a number of patients: a regression to an intense preoccupation with body narcissism, and at the same time a loss of the capacity for metaphoric thought and speech.

Mr. H., an attorney, was suicidally depressed when he came into treatment at the age of 37. At that time he undertook and completed several years of analytic work in which symbol and metaphor were used as a matter of course in the usual analytic way. Mr. H. had experienced himself to be the favored child of his mother, although he was the middle one of three boys, and his mother, a physician, was seldom home. However, his treatment focused predominantly on an intense rivalry with his successful, castrating, competitive father.

Mr. H. "took" to his analysis like the proverbial duck to water, and during it he progressed both in his legal career and in his social life. During the difficult times of working through his rage at his father, he had a number of brief homosexual encounters, but he thought these to be compulsive behaviors that he would some day be able to control—he considered himself straight, not gay or bisexual. He moved in with his girlfriend (despite my challenging this decision, for the relationship lacked passion) and he terminated his treatment believing that it was successful. He felt happy enough and was quite successful in his career.

But five years later, Mr. H. returned with an entirely different set of issues. His relationship was in trouble, and he was preoccupied with physical and sexual concerns. It was strikingly apparent to me that his manner of speaking had also changed. It was much simpler, and he no longer used abstract or symbolic language.

Mr. H. was in the middle of a passionate sexual affair with a woman named J. who lived in California and who shared his love of athletics and exhibiting the body. J. wore thong bathing suits and spandex shorts and tops, and could not possibly, said Mr. H., be more unlike his short, plump girlfriend. J. was "hot." He said to me with joy: "Imagine finding someone who looks just like myself!" He regarded the lean, long-legged J. as his female counterpart, and he gave both of them high ratings for beauty and firm skin-tone.

"Imagine having someone who looks just like you!" His excited tone indicated that he believed I shared this wish and valued it as highly as he did. He felt contemptuous of those who did not. Mr. H. was furious with his girlfriend for not working out and being toned. He was clearly turned on by the women in thong bathing suits he saw on the beaches in California and the ones who wore short shorts on the streets near his summer home. Being toned and fit had moral value for him.

But J. did not want to leave California, and she attempted to end their affair. Mr. H. decided to work on his official relationship, and he asked his girlfriend to work on her body so that she could please him more. She did not like this request, but she acquiesced. She did a several months' makeover, from which she emerged as quite a beauty. However, she was still short, and so her transformation did nothing to shift Mr. H.'s interest away from J., who, being tall, looked like him. He attempted to deal with his disappointment by trying to contact her, but she refused to see him. For weeks he fantasized revenge on her.

A suicidal depression then ensued. He threatened to kill himself by jumping from a bridge, and I was concerned enough that he might do it that I recommended that he take medication. He said that he had heard that Prozac caused weight gain, and he was afraid to gain weight. I responded: "You mean you don't want to be a fat corpse?" He began to laugh uncontrollably, and pulled somewhat out of his depression after that session. The

fact that he could laugh at himself indicated at least some degree of self-awareness and ego strength, and I became less concerned about his potential for suicide. For a brief time he did
take antidepressants, but what really seemed to affect him and
return him to his formerly positive ego state were the concrete
statements, like the "fat corpse" one, that I made to him about
his body, his attachment to J.'s body, his lack of interest in his
girlfriend's body, and most important, his concerns about how
he was going to meet women once he gave up J. and separated
from his girlfriend. We discussed concrete options, such as the
personal ads, parties, and blind dates. Mr. H. began an avid search
for a new woman with excellent body tone and fitness. We discussed together what he wanted in a woman in concrete terms.
He said that he did not care about anything beyond her having
a good body to match his own. I did not at this time challenge
him or ask him to think about why.

We stayed on this level for a long time, perhaps a year. It seemed
much longer to me, for I continually had to monitor and analyze my negative countertransference feelings about how completely Mr. H. experienced and treated women as objects (I will
discuss some aspects of this later on). I followed Mr. H. through
the dating and bedding of numbers of women, most of whom
were socially and intellectually incompatible with him, but who
met his physical criteria. His anger toward women showed in
his asking them what they weighed before he met them, or telling
them he would not see them again because they were not toned.
I did not address the shallowness of his connections, nor did I
ask him to understand his fear of fat. We had covered this ground
with little understanding or psychic change during the year he
was trying to work things out with his girlfriend. (I hypothesized privately that the fear of fat was rooted in his feelings
about his mother's pregnancy during the oedipal years, coupled
with her increasing unavailability to him; I also thought that the

need for a hard, toned body, along with his obsessive exercise, was an effort to affirm and strengthen his fuzzy body boundaries. However, by then I was convinced that speaking to those factors—that is, treating his preoccupations as symbolic—was premature and would not be useful.)

I stayed with his concreteness in the sessions, speaking in equally concrete terms about his search for a woman with a perfect body, and his work keeping his own body fit. Gradually, aspects of the sensitive and thoughtful man I had worked with years before reappeared. A new phase of the transference opened. Mr. H. became intensely curious about me, about what I did and read, about what man might have called me on the telephone, and so on. He decided, by way of projection, that I must have been divorced recently and that like himself I was out trying to find another partner. He wondered about the men he assumed I was dating. He cited many ways in which he believed us to be alike: we had similar houses, furnishings, and work schedules. He began to bring with him intellectual and scholarly books that he carefully left in my view. He came to many sessions after or on the way to exercise, in shorts and sleeveless tops. He seemed to be acting on a narcissistic need to have me look at him and admire him, mixed with a wish to seduce me. He wanted to be like me and identify with me. In short, he was becoming more like the person I had originally known, and displaying a much more recognizable transference.

By this time Mr. H.'s language had resumed its original metaphoric style, and since he no longer seemed to need me to limit myself to concrete speech, I reverted to normal. My lack of response to his nonverbal seductive and exhibitionistic acting-in led to more bouts of depression and random homosexual encounters. These were dystonic, for he did not regard himself as homosexual, but he became aware that those impulses emerged when he felt rejected by women. I began to interpret the erotic transference in displacement—in metaphoric, symbolic terms. Mr. H. was now able to engage in this process. He eventually found a loving and caring woman with whom he shared an intense sexual life, but he continued to date others, as he felt that he wanted to wait a while before committing himself. In his final session, joking with me about the women he was dating, he said, "I won't see those who won't sleep with me!"—that is, his analyst!

It can be argued, and I think it is true, that Mr. H.'s concreteness served in part as a defense against the erotic transference, but in itself it was also an issue that had to be worked through. Working through it demanded my participation in the concrete dialogue. I am reminded of Fenichel's (1945) statement that "no sight can actually bring about the reassurance which these patients are seeking" (p. 348). This is a correct appraisal of the insatiable nature of the quest, which ultimately can only be satisfied by repair of the internal narcissistic wound.

Mr. K., like Mr. H., entered psychotherapeutic treatment in a very depressed state. He appeared originally to be a thoughtful neurotic, but subsequently regressed to a shallow and concrete self-presentation in which he manifested hysterical and obsessional character traits. An architect who loved clean, sleek-looking things, he had been very critical of his wife, who was slightly plump and buxom, and who wished (as he felt it) to "spoil" the clean, immaculate look of their apartment by displaying some of her own possessions. Fed up, she had left him, asked for a divorce, and found another man. Mr. K. spent the next few years flooding the analytic couch with tears, dredging up the past in order to understand his inability to get over his loss, get on with his life, and meet someone new. He tortured himself by spying on his ex-wife and her husband, standing outside their apartment until they closed the blinds to make love.

It was obvious that he had been a spoiled child. His mother had favored him over two younger siblings and especially over his father, for whom the whole family had contempt. The primal scene and oedipal implications of the stalking of his former wife were evident both to Mr. K. and to me. After years of crying, he himself likened the endless stream of tears to an endless rope, a symbol that had appeared in his dreams and that represented the umbilical cord—the tie to his mother and to his ex-wife. This metaphor was his last for a long time.

After this realization, Mr. K. began to go out in the evenings in search of another woman, but he couldn't find one who was "right." He fixated on women who were sleek and slim, like the buildings he designed, but none were up to his standards. He seemed a completely different man from the one who had entered treatment mourning his plump wife. Finally he found an aggressive businesswoman who had once been a model. She was tall and slender and he chose her for her appearance, but he admitted that he secretly more enjoyed the company and pleasing sight of her dog, a sleek Dalmatian.

Several more years of analysis ensued. Eventually, the concreteness of our dialogue shifted and the use of symbol and metaphor was resumed, as was a less one-dimensional personality. Mr. K. ended his relationship with his model girlfriend, became involved in a number of philanthropic enterprises, and eventually met a caring and loving woman to marry.

Dr. L., a professor of physics, became severely depressed when his wife told him, "all of a sudden, without any notice," that she was divorcing him and marrying another man. Dr. L. had never suspected that she was unhappy or that she was having an affair. He did not have the energy to go out and try to date and he had never really dated as a young man forty years ago. He was an only child. He had been doted on by his parents, he said, and had only fond memories of his mother and father. He remembered his mother's encouraging him to find a nice girl. He had married his wife for her simplicity, her beauty (she looked like Ava Gardner), and her "goodness." (His conviction of her goodness did not alter, even though she rejected his sexual advances and barely spoke to him during the long years of their marriage.) In his therapy Dr. L. spoke about loss, and his complex relations with his four sons. Gradually the simpleminded idealizations of mother, father, and wife began to break down. Dr. L. was able to come to some real understanding of his marriage, its breakup, and why he had broken down so completely. His splitting defenses altered, and for the first time he realized the depth of the anger he had suppressed for so long.

Dr. L. then began to attend social functions and place personal ads in the newspaper. He received an overwhelming response; hundreds of women sent him letters and photographs. This shy, insecure man turned, within the space of a few weeks, into a connoisseur of women. He rated them by looks on a scale from "dogs" to "lookers," and laughed sadistically at the former. Puffed up with himself and his success, he began to sit for hours in front of the university library watching the women pass by— he reported that only "dogs" seemed to attend his university. His interviews with the women from the personal ads were highly stressful because he became extremely jealous to learn that they had ever been with another man or men.

His jealousy was dystonic. I raised the possibility that it had its genesis in feelings about his father's relationship with his mother. Dr. L. denied this, but my having raised the possible connection to his father proved to be helpful. His jealous feelings began to abate to some level of comfort. He began to feel for the first time jealousy of his wife's boyfriend, now husband, which he had heretofore repressed, but he was still unable to relate this jealousy to any feelings he ever had about his father.

After this period as arbiter of female worth, Dr. L. began to feel better and to flirt with me, trying to find out if I found him to be attractive. Although he maintained that "I don't care what they are about as long as they are good-looking," he seemed also to be searching for a loving woman—more specifically, one who would love him. I worked with him in a concrete manner on his dates. He found a woman who "loved him like his mother did." He reported, "She loves me so much, her whole life has changed because she has met me. She is just happy looking at me. She sits and stares at me for hours." Every day he hoped that he would love her a bit more. He thought she was "hot." In this case, the narcissistic gratification was so great the patient decided to terminate, happy, but not cured.

Dr. L. returned to treatment two years later. His girlfriend had ended their relationship, telling him that he was too selfish for her to bear. This time, in deep pain, he was able to reach into himself and to work more deeply, using symbol and metaphor.

These three vignettes demonstrate the characteristic alternation of the therapeutic work from a mode in which it was possible to work in terms of symbol and metaphor to a more concrete one, and then back again. Each of these men came to therapy feeling unloved and empty. Each had experienced object loss either prior to or during treatment, and while in treatment found someone to replace his former love. Each entered treatment in a state of profound pain. As each began to feel better, each regressed temporarily from using metaphor to a more concrete, shallow experiencing of women. For them to feel better, the narcissistic deficits had to be made good—hence, the regression to body narcissism, and the feeling better, and the concreteness. When the narcissistic deficits began to be repaired, the ego became capable of more advanced object relations and an increased capacity for symbol and metaphor.

There are times when a patient leaves therapy feeling satisfied that he has reached another level of psychic organization and compromise formation, but the therapist does not feel satisfied because the patient is not communicating at the level of symbol and metaphor. I have come to understand that what seems like destructive resistance may in fact be necessary regression, and that it is an error to assume that the treatment has not been effective. As the ego changes stimulated by the therapy become integrated and the full strength of the ego becomes available, the clinical picture can change dramatically.

I will now offer cases of female patients, also previously capable of metaphoric thought and language, who, like their male counterparts, shifted to concrete language at times of preoccupation about their looks. The dynamics of the narcissistic issues may be different, but the connection with concreteness of thought are the same.

Ms. S. was 34 and single when she entered a four-times-weekly analysis. Lovely although somewhat disheveled, she was involved with a man whom her family disliked. They expected that he would jilt her, and they kept warning her of this in no uncertain terms. For the first several months of her analysis Ms. S. was able to use the couch, to free associate, and to bring in dreams and memories. She filled me in about her relationship with her boyfriend T., and she knew that it symbolized aspects of her parents' marriage.

Ms. S. had grown up in Beverly Hills. Her mother, a former actress, was a beauty, but could neither manage her home nor get her children to school on time. She had numerous affairs to which the children were witness. Ms. S.'s father, an attorney for a film production company, was away on business a lot, and had a series of mistresses. Ms. S. described her youthful self as "fuzzy—walking about in a blur" (note that these descriptions indicate the subjective perception of an inadequate visual grasp of the world). She spent her high school years sunbathing and shopping with friends, running up huge bills over which she and her father battled—it was the only way she could reliably get his attention.

Ms. S.'s parents entered her in child and teenage beauty contests, some of which she won. Whenever she gained any weight, her father would take to calling her "Fatso." (He himself weighed close to 250 pounds, but as a man in our culture he felt he was exempt from any criticism.) Ms. S. managed to get through college, majoring in art history. She came to New York and found a job as a researcher for an art gallery.

Before she began her analysis, she had started dating T., a handsome, hard-working, well-educated, rather brilliant man, who, by her reports, both used and abused her. He was interested in the possibility of working for her father. T. criticized Ms. S. whenever she gained a pound, and although his similarity to her father in that respect was not lost upon her, she persisted in trying to please him, and reported that she "loved him to death." (She had some real capacity for self-awareness, but she could not hear the aggression in this metaphor.)

Ms. S.'s analysis progressed well for several months. Then she left her job for a lower-paid one that would leave her with enough energy to see T. at the end of the day. By then they were engaged, and she said that she wanted to have the energy available to plan her wedding. She was not interested in becoming a professional woman or in having a career. All she wanted was to be a wife and mother. She cut back to two sessions a week.

My experience during this period was that Ms. S. went from being a pretty woman to being a silly woman. All she seemed to care about was looking good, staying slim, and buying clothes. T. overtly exploited her, making her wait for him for hours to come home late from work, requiring her to drive late at night to pick him up at the airport, and asking that she entertain his friends and relatives even at times when she did not feel well. She reported feeling tired and run-down and suffered from numerous viruses and allergies. My interpretation that she was somatizing rather than verbalizing her anger at T. and her family fell on deaf ears. She wanted me to serve as witness and container, and she frustrated my efforts to examine what she was doing. This was a "perverse transference" akin to Renik's (1992) notion of the use of the therapist as a fetish, where the therapist is used to serve the thinking function (see Chapter 6).

Ms. S. went home to California to be fitted for her wedding gown. Her father became extremely angry when he saw her in it, and snarled that he didn't like it, that it was ugly. After the wedding and honeymoon, Ms. S. reported anger at her husband for his egregious behavior toward her on their honeymoon (playing tennis all day and leaving her alone at the pool), but she found herself unable to speak up and confront him. Then she began missing sessions, calling me on her cellular phone from the Stair-master at her health club. More than once she said that she would feel too guilty if she did not exercise and since her husband had invited people home for dinner, she had to miss her session. She could not entertain the interpretation that the guilt was really about her anger at her husband and her father.

At this point in the treatment, Ms. S. presented as "empty." She showed little interest in her work or anything other than looking good and holding her husband's attention—especially keeping him away from the topless bars he visited after work with his colleagues. She could not see any parallels between her behavior with him and her desperate childhood behavior with her often absent, philandering father. She reported a dream that she experienced as "gross." "I had a huge zit, but not that apparently large. I squeezed it. There was a huge explosion. A bruise was left." Her associations were to "never be wrinkled" and "a thought of piercing her thigh with a pen to get out the fat."

Kaplan's (1991b) observation came to my mind: "When I came to the various masquerades of feminine gender identity . . . I pointed to the collaboration of the fashion and cosmetic industries with the fetishization of the human body and the trivialization of the female mental and sexual life" (p. 523).

Ms. S. seemed to me to be no longer analyzable or possibly even treatable. At that time I had not yet considered the issues of concrete versus metaphoric language that I am raising here. I continued to attempt to interpret her fears of her aggression toward her father and husband, how she was turning the aggression on herself and trying to work it off through exercise. I had some intuitive feeling that Ms. S. needed to be seen face to face and asked her to sit up during her sessions. Just looking at her, but not commenting concretely about what I saw, proved to be insufficient.

Ms. S. decided to leave treatment, with the excuse that her busy life permitted only time for exercise and trying to look good. I believe now that if I had been able to discuss with her on her own terms the concrete concerns about her body, reflecting back to her what I saw, rather than interpreting her anger or its roots, face-to-face treatment and an ongoing analysis of the countertransference when the "silly woman" material emerged most probably would have led to a better result.

Nevertheless, the patient reported satisfaction with the treatment, for she had after all married T., which had been her stated goal from the start. Over the next ten years, she referred to me a number of acquaintances who remarked on the positive changes they had seen in her as a result of her psychotherapeutic treatment. She had three children and she seemed to them to be content.

Mrs. P., a slender banker, began psychotherapeutic treatment at the age of 36. She was seductive in her body language and dress, but she was soft-spoken and her manner was demure. The miniskirts and tight spandex tops she wore did not look like the usual uniform for the conservative bank at which she worked, but she reported that she liked her work, and that she was well thought of there, and was considered successful. She and her husband led a very sophisticated urban life.

Mrs. P. said that she had come to treatment to deal with her marriage of ten years, since she was feeling uncertain about whether she had married the right man. Soon after, however, the focus of the treatment changed to her feelings about her looks. She was concerned that her husband would find other women attractive, and felt that she lacked "definition" in a crowd of people. (She saw her husband as having that same problem of lacking "definition.") She spent many hours crying about these issues.

She was aware that she was attractive to men, but was obsessed with the idea that as she got older, she would lose this power to attract them. This fear caused her to break down and cry in much the same way she did when thinking about her lack of presence. Her constant need for compliments and attention invaded and diminished her opportunities for conflict-free work and general happiness.

Mrs. P. reported feeling bad from time to time about not being very thin. She felt that very thin women were unattainable and untouchable, and that she "lost power" by not being "rail thin." She said that she wanted to lose ten pounds, but that she liked her pasta dinners. Rather than ask her to associate to the meanings of this, I asked her why, if this was so important to her, she did not diet and lose the weight? I wasn't saying she needed to lose weight, but if she felt she did, there were things she could do about it. My concrete comments were aimed at getting her to engage in a real concrete behavior, as opposed to just endlessly picking on herself. In the next session, the patient, for the first time, spoke of her mother's picking on her and her guilt at being angry at her, which she had suppressed. My concrete suggestion about her concrete issue gave her ego support and strength, which enabled her to tolerate the conscious awareness of her mother's sadism.

My careful tuning to Mrs. P.'s very concrete ideas and my oscillating between concrete idea and metaphor resulted in a successful resolution of this case. I reflected back to her my perception that she wore trendy clothes and noted that she had highlighted her hair. Mrs. P.'s chronically ill mother had stayed too close and undifferentiated for her to be able to internalize her and to develop in a normal way. Mrs. P. was able to attain a more distanced and age-appropriate relationship with her mother and to cease the obsessive jealousy that plagued her with her husband. She became more confident about her looks and not so worried about their meaning for her as she aged.

In a subsequent phase of her treatment, memories came up that clarified the genetic bases of her seductive dressing and its symbolic meaning. She was by then able to understand her seductiveness as a symptom and as a symbol, and with this understanding it abated.

DISCUSSION

Brooks (1993) has most eloquently described the connection among body, language, and thought:

> The body, I think, often presents us with a fall from language, a return to an infantile pre-symbolic space in which primal drives reassert their force. . . . Bodily parts, sensations and perceptions . . . are the first building blocks in the construction of a symbolic order, including speech, play, and the whole system of human language, within which the child finds a libidinally invested place. [p. 7]

Unfortunately, there has not been much attention in the psychotherapeutic literature to such concrete aspects of the experience of the body. Issues of gender and gender difference have been extensively studied, but not such matters as whether the body is experienced as looking good or bad. Sifneos (1975) and McDougall (1989) have addressed the difficulties of those who cannot verbalize their emotions and who express themselves through somatic channels. Sifneos has written about *alexithymia*, a term describing the way some people define emotions solely in terms of somatic sensations or behavioral reactions rather than being able to use meaningful words. The patients I am writing about here have words, albeit concrete ones, for the body and its experiences.

Balsam (1996) has noted the neglect in our thinking about the visual aspects of the external body in the development of the young girl. She believes that we do not listen enough for the surface quality of visual and tactile information and its mental representation:

> The literature has stressed a continued internal focus on the mother, for women, as encompassing a "fixation" on her, implying a state to be hurdled if development is to proceed. This attitude could cause the analyst to try to "help" the patient too rapidly past the inevitable fascinations I dwell upon here. [p. 422]

In her work on daughters' perceptions of their pregnant mothers, Balsam was referring to the patients' fascination with the therapist's clothes, her own clothes, and those of other women—concrete issues. She has addressed some of the same issues I deal with here.

Paniagua (1998), in a paper on the analysis of "acting in," reported that he noticed that his patient, anxious about some job interviews, put her index finger over the bridge of her nose, and he told her what he saw. She was self-conscious about her nose, which she thought was ugly. He then told her that she was hiding her nose from his view. She reported that his view of her nose from his chair was unfavorable. "This clashed with her wish that I found her ravishing (transferential). She fantasized that, perhaps, touching what she considered the imperfection in her nose would make it disappear magically" (p. 507). His intervention is an example of the technique that I have come to use.

During the course of some therapies, the therapist may be speaking one language (metaphor) and the patient another (concrete). The psychotherapeutic literature is replete with the conviction that "listening" is superior to "looking" as the preferred medium of communication between therapist and patient, the use of metaphor being associated with the former mode and concrete language associated with the latter. When patients begin psychoanalysis in the latter mode, they risk being judged as unanalyzable and referred out for psychotherapy, or even considered untreatable. Other patients may begin their treatment using symbol and metaphor, but regress, for a few minutes or for many sessions, to concrete ways of thinking and communicating that confuse and baffle the analyst.

The effect of translating and abstracting, at least in the case of very concrete patients, may be that we miss what is actually being said, and that our patients in return find us difficult to understand. Our patients understand us best when we speak their language, and it is often difficult for them to tell us that they have not understood. As a matter of habit, for example, we should use statements like "You don't like you" in preference to "You have low self-esteem." We should use language that refers to the thing itself rather than an abstract essence when that is what the patient is doing. Furthermore, some people become adept at using symbol and metaphor but do not really connect with what they are saying. As one patient of mine cleverly put it: "I can talk the talk, but I can't walk the walk." I understand my efforts to be in the same direction as Schafer's (1976) elaboration of an "action language," and Gedo's (1996) efforts to communicate with his patients using tropes and affects. They, too, were dealing with the therapist's need to use words that reach the patient. However, they were seeking more affective immediacy, and it has seemed to me that this is not the issue in working with the kinds of patients that I describe here; that resonating with them affectively can in fact be too frightening and/or overstimulating. It is their capacity to perceive their concrete selves that is at issue.

CONCLUSION

I have demonstrated the style of analytic thought and the kinds of technical interventions that can used with such patients, with particular attention to linguistic attunement, the use of concrete language when narcissistic issues about the external body, whether the body of the patient or the bodies of others, emerge in the treatment.

I also have demonstrated the danger of a blind preference for symbol and metaphor, what might be called a rush to metaphor, at times when our patients are not really able to process what we are saying. The therapist must be able to tolerate his own regression and must use concrete language, both for practical and for developmental reasons, when the patient is thinking and speaking concretely. Only then will the patient be able to use the therapist's interventions, grow with their help, and ultimately develop the capacity to use symbol and metaphor genuinely in treatment. When a patient lacks this capacity, symbol and metaphor can be used by both patient and therapist to defend against primitive or uncomfortable material.

6

Working with Women Obsessed with Thinness

Do you want them to write on your tombstone: "She stayed thin"?

My comment to a patient obsessed with thinness

$\mathcal{I}$ have had in psychotherapeutic treatment a number of women patients whose associations began to center mainly and obsessively on their efforts, successful or failed, to achieve the levels of body leanness and muscle tone that this society values so highly. Their obsession with these surface issues, and their complete disregard while preoccupied with them for other concerns (relationships, family, work, children, even their own history and/or its analysis) I thought at first to be a resistance to reaching deeper levels in the analysis. It induced in me profound countertransference feelings of hopelessness and a sense of being caught in a net of shallowness, silliness, trivia, and trivial pursuits. I was reluctant to join these patients in treating their bodies as "things," and unwilling to be coerced into the role of spectator while these women used their bodies in the ways they did. Furthermore, the sense of "thingness" extended to me: at these times, these patients experienced me as a "thing," too, easily disposable or interchangeable, rather than as an individual.

One patient, a 55-year-old woman, extremely intelligent and well-educated, and of normal weight, came for therapy at a time when her son was dying of AIDS, her daughter was on drugs, her husband was having an affair, and she had job issues to resolve. What she talked about in her sessions were the five pounds she wanted to lose, and how hard this was for her. She "dumped" or "evacuated" her problems with her children and her husband into me, requiring me to contain them, so that she could then deal with herself. The hidden agenda of her treatment was her need to ex-

perience herself as intact; I was to focus on her and not on *them*—
to look at her and admire her and so make that experience possible.

The transference–countertransference paradigm that emerged
with this woman felt to me like the phenomenon that a number
of authors in recent years have characterized as "perverse transferences" (Bach 1994, Etchegoyen 1991, Fogel 1991, Reed 1994). In
the perverse transference, as I understand it, the patient's (unconscious) aim is not so much to gain self-understanding through an
analysis of the past as repeated in the present, but rather to use the
therapist in some covert and sadistic way. Whereas in the classical
transferences the patient for the most part experiences the analyst
as a particular internalized figure in a particular internalized fantasy and eventually becomes aware that he or she is doing so, in
the perverse transference, the patient uses the therapist himself or
herself as a fetish (Renik 1992).[1]

The interrelationships between the perverse (in the sense of "that
which is turned away from what is right, reasonable or good" [Fogel
1991, p. 3]), perversions, perverse fantasies, and perverse transferences have yet to be fully elucidated or understood. However, the
perverse transference paradigm I will describe here emerged in the
late twentieth century as a reflection in treatment of a particular
social context. Social reality for many women patients demands
that they be extremely thin, and rewards them for conforming to

---

[1]A fetish can be a nongenital body part (for example, a foot), or an inanimate
object (for example, a shoe), that is essential for sexual discharge to take place
while contact with the anxiety-provoking genital is avoided. In the common
use of the term today, *fetish* or *fetishized* stands for a sexualized and often idealized object, usually a consumer product (for example, a handbag). In the perverse transference, the therapist himself is used rather than his interpretations. In
the perversion, a substitute is used instead of normal intercourse, just as the
perverse transference implies a substitute for the real thing.

a body ideal that requires their depriving themselves of needed food. Lately this demand has expanded to require muscularity and muscle tone, necessitating several hours of working out every day, and sometimes two sessions a day at the gym. When starvation and extensive exercise are not enough, women may turn to such adjuncts as pills (diet pills, diuretics, and laxatives), body wraps, or liposuction and other forms of plastic surgery. All of this perverts and redirects the oral drive, whose purpose under normal circumstances is to satisfy the body's biological need for food (Gamman and Makinen 1994).

This demand is so prevalent in this society that it is difficult to find anyone not aware of it or affected by it. It is not new. At the end of the nineteenth century the tubercular, cadaverous woman was the aesthetic ideal: "'*Sois belle et sois triste*' (be beautiful and sad), as Baudelaire commanded. A woman who was not childlike and innocent was thought to inspire evil desires, with the result that the poets were fond of confusing women with boys" (Jullian 1971, p. 42). The Duchess of Windsor was widely quoted as saying: "You cannot be too rich or too thin." Susan Faludi (1991), Naomi Wolf (1991), and others have hypothesized that as women won new freedoms in the late twentieth century, a backlash arose in response, reinforcing more than ever such crippling ideals. During one single day in my own practice at the time I was writing this book, one patient had to leave in the middle of her session in order to go to the bathroom because she had taken laxatives in order to lose weight; another reported that her husband had told her that he wanted a divorce because, although she was thin enough, she did not have good "muscle tone"; and the fiancé of a third was organizing their elopement so that the hour of their marriage would not prevent her from working out that day.

My observation of these patients leads me to believe that they internalize this demand and treat it as an imperative with moral and ethical authority. From this privileged position it dominates the manifest content of their associations during certain phases of their psychotherapeutic treatment. It also appears to me that such women have in common certain fantasies and childhood experiences. They are not diagnostically anorexic or bulimic, as described by Aronson (1993), Bruch (1978), Sours (1974), and Wilson and colleagues (1984); although they may sometimes starve themselves, binge, or purge, they never get so regressed, or lose so much weight, that they require medical attention or hospitalization. But they envy, admire, and seek to emulate truly anorexic women. Some of these patients have been rail-thin, while others were of normal weight, but all embarked upon psychotherapeutic treatment because of chronic unhappiness and blunted affect.

Ogden (1995) described a patient of his as suffering from "inner deadness":

> She subsisted on a diet of fruits, grains and vegetables and organized her life around a rigorous exercise regime that included marathon jogging and the extensive use of a stationary bicycle. The patient exercised vigorously for at least three hours every day. If the exercise routine were in any way disrupted (for example, by illness or travel), the patient would experience a state of anxiety that on two occasions developed into a full blown panic attack. [pp. 55–56]

Ogden's patient belongs with the group of women I am discussing here. Shortly into treatment, it becomes apparent that they are consumed with thoughts about what they will let themselves eat, and how to avoid eating. They rage at themselves when, in the grip of their bodies' drive for survival, they give in, break their self-imposed diets, and eat something—usually a particularly forbidden or "junk" food—which inevitably they do. These women are generally unaware of the degree to which they idealize men on the one hand and denigrate them on the other. They are unaware of their anger at others. They are chronically tired, yet they exercise several hours daily, and have little time left over for work, friends, or other interests, any of which might help them feel less empty. The media—movies, theater, newspapers, magazines, television—as well as their husbands and boyfriends support what they are doing, and are all too generous in suggesting role models for them to emulate. This year the ones mentioned most are the waif-like model Kate Moss and actresses Gwyneth Paltrow and Calista Flockhart. The social reality sustaining this unhealthy ideal is very powerful, and it presents a considerable problem in psychotherapeutic treatment. Adherence to this ideal is entirely ego-syntonic to these women, and it is up to the therapist to make it dystonic. But work with these patients poses countertransference problems for the therapist, who is called upon to address the surface, since these patients have difficulty connecting to deeper layers of the psyche.

Rapaport (1960) described such a social structure that opposes psychotherapeutic change:

> Often all the therapeutic efforts are to no avail if the patient is continually exposed to situations with which he has no other way of coping but his characteristic defensive behavior, that is, situations in which the very defenses which it is the work of the therapist to weaken and penetrate are continually maintained and strengthened by the environment. [p. 892]

In the cases I am discussing here, the social demand for thinness made it more difficult for me as the therapist to address unconscious issues and to demonstrate to these patients that their obsessive thoughts and low self-esteem were symptoms, and neither necessary nor natural. In my paper on analyzing single women over 30 (Lieberman 1991b), I reported a number of symptoms that characterized this group: "chronic depression, bingeing and starving, obsessing that they must stay thin in order to attract men;

believing that they are physically unattractive and incapable of having relationships with men" (p. 185). In one case, a patient's family harassed her with embarrassing questions: "'How come you haven't found someone yet? Maybe if you take off some weight you'll meet someone right away.' Each successful dieting phase (she was of normal weight) is followed by high expectations and severe disappointment" (p. 186).

In their analysis of asceticism in contemporary culture entitled *The Good Body*, Winkler and Cole (1994) put deliberate fasting and starving into a cultural and historical perspective with moral connotations. They examined the relationship between cultural idealization of control of the self through ascetic practices and rises in eating disorders. In this same volume, Miles described the "pleasure of unpleasure" (p. 60), and Moore addressed the self-denial of abused women who "put lots of energy into trying to figure out what their abusers want, to please them, or to change themselves so their abusers will stop insulting or hating them" (p. 37).

But the women patients I discuss here do not need others to abuse them—they abuse themselves. They suffer from never reaching their unreachable goals of bodily perfection, and they suffer from the eating "crimes" they believe they have committed. I think of them as junkfood Raskolnikovs—their superegos mete out harsh punishment. They come to their sessions declaring profound remorse and guilt over not having attended an exercise class or having eaten a candy bar or cookie. The analytic couch becomes a confessional to the mortal sin of eating sweets, and this sin is not necessarily a repetition connected to such childhood transgressions as stealing cookies from the cookie jar. Yet paradoxically some of these women buy a dress, wear it with the price tags tucked inside, and then return it for a refund, saying, "Everyone does that," and feeling no awareness of guilt over such behavior.

As therapist I am witness not just to this new ego of our times—one in which deficits in body narcissism impair total ego functioning—but to a new superego as well, the contents of which are very different from my old-fashioned model. Continuous countertransference analysis is required to maintain the requisite neutrality. I personally do not find the confessed sin (eating sweets) sinful, but I do experience as sinful the one *not* confessed to (returning the worn dress). Furthermore, until I began to understand what was really happening between my women patients and myself, and found useful ways of addressing it, I experienced the content of the sessions as too trivial for someone with all of my training and expertise to deal with, and I felt guilty about collecting my fee. Later in this chapter, I will elaborate upon the considerable countertransference issues these patients arouse.

I have come to the realization that the women patients who in psychotherapeutic treatment display an obsession with body thinness seem to possess neither adequate intrapsychic internalization, nor adequate cathexis, of their own body surface. I now understand that in treatment they attempt to use me as a trainer who will help them to focus upon and cathect the body surface, to mirror it and reflect it, in order to strengthen its cathexis. When my analytic patients experience pangs of hunger on the couch from excessive dieting, uncomfortable fullness after a binge, cramps from laxative-induced diarrhea, or pain following upon cosmetic surgeries, I now understand that they are not just communicating an experience of masochistic gratification, but a deeper need for *primary narcissistic restoration*. They need to be looked at. They are trying to *feel* something in order to combat inner feelings of deadness and emptiness. Although they report that their efforts are aimed at satisfying the contemporary male's desire for a thin woman, they show, as I have said and will demonstrate below, much contempt for men, and are in general sexually anesthetic and uninterested in sex. They do seek with men the holding, cuddling, and visual attention that shores up the sense of body boundary. Paradoxically, in what can only be regarded as a split in the ego, many of these women simultaneously embrace both feminism and its valuation of independent women, and this restrictive ideal of staying thin so that men will like them.

I cannot say that all of these women belong to the widening scope of psychotherapy, for much of what goes on in their treatment, which I will not report here, falls into the range of the average expectable, and is typical of most treatment. But from time to time in the cases I am writing about there emerges what I think must be described as a "perverse transference," the goal of which is to pull me into certain enactments, in which I in my role as therapist was (countertransferentially) reluctant to engage. My reluctance came in part from the high value that my work as a classical analyst has taught me to place on neutrality, and from my belief that the analyst's task is to bring into consciousness derivatives of inner fantasy and conflict. But I have had to diverge from that stance in order to be effective with the patients described here. In the perverse transferences that emerged in these cases, what was demanded of me was to look at the patient's body surface, and to comment about what I saw. I came to see my role in that context as reluctant spectator.

Truly anorexic patients have been found by Ackerman (personal communication, 1999) to differ substantially from the patients I describe here. She understood anorexics as needing to disappear, to be left alone, *not* to be seen. She cited one patient's pleading in a letter to her:

> "I wanted to disappear—to go away and forget I exist—but—How can I disappear when I'm the center of attention. It makes me want to disappear even more/I am so tired and everyone wants to talk to me, compliment me—STOP IT—leave me alone. . . . Please let me out—out of this world, this body, to that place where I don't feel anything. It's not death—I don't want to die—I want to live in that place where I'm so empty that I'm numb—I live every day to slowly disappear—the goal is peace—"

In this case the conflict over wanting attention (and getting it because of not eating) and not wanting it (because it feels invasive) is quite poignantly clear. My patients, on the other hand, are not looking so much for attention as for a means to see themselves and to be seen more clearly and accurately.

The treatment of women obsessed with thinness is usually accompanied by acting out and by splits in the transference. These patients are adept at mobilizing a host of "helpers," in addition to the therapist, in their task of shoring up the body ego. Visits to trainers, nutritionists, chiropractors, dermatologists, and plastic surgeons are part of their daily routine, and these visits are often coupled with the timing of their therapy hours. Hairdressers, manicurists, and facialists are their confidants, and may well hear their dreams and fantasies before the therapist does.

Psychotherapists have long struggled with the treatment of narcissistic issues within the context of the more standard drive-related transference issues. To the Freudian analyst, the "body" means the biological drives and object-directed wishes that emanate from them. When Freud (1923) wrote that the first ego is the body ego, he was referring to an inner experience of the body, the body imago. Today, when patients refer to their bodies and to their dissatisfaction with them, they usually mean their bodies as seen from the outside by another—size, shape, muscle tone—and from the inside by critical internalizations.

CASE VIGNETTES

Ms. A. embarked upon psychoanalytic psychotherapy when she was 23. She was having difficulty ending her engagement to a young man for whom she experienced considerable contempt. Nevertheless, her mother was urging her to marry him. (The two other patients I will discuss in this chapter also came to treatment after involvements with men they found to be unappealing and "unappetizing"—to use an oral metaphor.) Ms. A. was very bright and beautiful, and she was as thin as a rail: 5'6" and 95 pounds. She reported being a liar, feeling that her lies kept people from knowing who she really was. Eventually a perverse transference emerged in which she lied to me, and by so doing managed virtually to keep me out of her psyche. I have written about this aspect of her pathology elsewhere (Gediman and Lieberman 1996, Lieberman 1991a). I handled her conventionally at that time, and feel that the therapy was only moderately successful.

For Ms. A., her thinness was her only source of quick and immediate positive attention. If Mrs. B. and Ms. C. (whom I will discuss next) had met her socially, they would have envied her! Being thin represented something good she could present to others, who would be duped and not know the real her, who was bad. Wherever she went she was praised for her thinness. As a child she had been a poor eater, and her mother had force-fed her (as her mother was trying again to "force-feed" her the unappetizing fiancé). She would refuse to eat, and could sit before a cold and unappetizing plate of food for hours. When her mother did succeed in forcing her to eat, she would vomit—and her mother would force her to eat the vomitus. As an adult, she starved herself for days and then binged secretly on ice cream, cookies, and potato chips. If her roommate returned home during a binge, she would stuff the food into a large pocketbook, which she kept at her side for that purpose. This eating disorder was multiply determined, but one aspect of it was to ensure that the other person, the object, became the one to take in the "bad food," the lie. By staying so thin, Ms. A. was given praise that allowed her to keep her bad engulfing maternal introject at bay.

As a result of her therapy Ms. A. was able to end her engagement, change her job, and stand up to her mother and her controlling boss. She dated a number of passive, effeminate men who adored her for her thinness. She terminated treatment when she met and became engaged to a plastic surgeon whom she experienced as kind, and who said that he loved her because she had not a bit of fat on her body.

Mrs. B., an attractive entertainment lawyer, divorced after a ten-year marriage. She had one daughter, and began psychoanalysis at 41, when she had been single for nine years and was searching with little success for her next husband. She was chronically unhappy, felt empty, and was puzzled as to why the various men she dated did not wish to marry her. Paradoxically, she did not love or admire any of them, but nevertheless felt rejected by them. Early in her treatment, it became obvious that she suffered from an obsessional personality disorder, the symptoms of which were organized around compulsive closet-cleaning, drawer-arranging, and shopping for clothing seasons ahead of time.

Mrs. B. felt chronically empty and as if she had "no life," despite daily reports of her career as a lawyer, her full and active social life, and her many cultural pursuits. She could experience a bit of excitement when introduced to a new man, but she was sexually indifferent. She assured me that all of her lovers experienced her as a terrific sex partner and that she was adept at deceiving them about her lack of enjoyment of sex and her incapacity to reach orgasm. She could have sex with three different men in one week or be celibate for months on end without complaint. It was all without meaning to her.

The only consistent pleasure in her life was finding and eating new flavors of ice cream. She would report her finds to me as if she had come across some forbidden and perverse pleasure, and she seemed to want to share the pleasure with me, hoping to turn me on. She would say, "Today I am into heathbar crunch," or "Today I am into passion fruit," in a voice that expressed salivation and a sexualized licking of her lips. She found a low-fat cookie with the brand name of "No-No's." In Mrs. B's world, sex was not forbidden; it was quite ordinary. *Ice cream* was forbidden, and ice cream was what counted.

Mrs. B. had had a previous analyst, a man, and it became clear that whatever she had learned from him was experienced by her as superior to anything she might possibly learn from me. Early in the development of the transference I experienced myself as psychically "vomited out," or, as was also evident in displaced transferences to her paralegals and secretaries, "defecated upon." The way she prolonged her profound feelings of emptiness was demonstrated in her unwillingness to take me in, to use me as an object for identification. This began to change only when the negative transference became manifest and could be interpreted. But this took some time, for Mrs. B., in the style of the other patients discussed here, acted quite manifestly grateful for, and involved in, her treatment. She (like Ms. A.) praised my work, and admired the way I looked and dressed and the decor of my office. This flattery covered a deeper layer of basic rejection of what went on between us. Also, if the analysis never ended, she would never lose me.

Mrs. B. came from one of those perfectionistic families described by Bruch (1978), Sours (1974), and Wilson and colleagues (1984). Her parents presented themselves to their children as flawless, encouraged them to repress emotion, and never argued in front of them. Mrs. B. learned early on that she had to stay bone thin in order to be popular and admired. As an adult she was always on a diet. She used laxatives and diuretics, embarked on all kinds of exercise programs, and went regularly for liposuction to remove the evidence of the ice cream binges that collected around her abdomen and thighs. Mrs. B. regularly visited plastic surgeons for consultation, both here and abroad, and had had her facial features remodeled a number of times. She received much social approval from friends who concurred with her opinion that she was being good to herself when she undertook these surgeries. Although she felt emotionally flat most of the time, she became ecstatic when she could turn one of her friends on to going to one of her plastic surgeons. Further adding to the ego-syntonicity of her symptoms was the fact that in her social and professional world, there were no role models imparting different values. The task in her treatment was to demonstrate to her that her obsessions, which she considered to be normal, were not in fact normal, and that they were related to fantasies and events in her childhood and her neurotic way of seeking love. As a further complication, Mrs. B. routinely visited a number of physicians in her stated goal of self-maintenance—periodontists, dermatologists, gynecologists, proctologists, chiropractors—and these figures all served to split the transference and to keep the narcissistic problem intact. Her relationship with one plastic surgeon seemed to be a perverse and sexualized one, as she supplied him with new customers whom she had "turned on."

Constraints of space permit me to present only a small portion of the reconstruction of Mrs. B.'s childhood. Through the analysis of dreams, memories, and the transference, it emerged that Mrs. B. had been expected to be a perfect, beautiful, and clean child who was to make no noise and to know nothing of family problems or illnesses. Important issues were never discussed. It became apparent, despite her protestations to the contrary, that she suffered from a lack of motherliness. Her basic needs were cared for, but in a sterile way. Nothing was soft and warm. I had the sense that there had been "food without food," "mother without mothering." For months on end, in what I eventually came to understand as a perverse transference, her associations were full of empty chatter about clothes, diets, and face-lifts, all presented to me in a way that made it impossible to deepen the material. In the countertransference, I began to feel hopeless, and resentful of having to listen to such a barrage of shallow talk, but I searched within myself to find a way to get through to this patient.

During one particularly cold winter, Mrs. B.'s dieting regimen seemed to be breaking down. Frustrated with the treatment and realizing that my neutral classical stance was getting us nowhere, I tried something new. I confronted the patient with the way her snacking, bingeing, diuretics, and laxatives were jeopardizing her health. I wondered why she did not stop at her local market, and I named it specifically, buy some dishes of low-fat foods, and provide herself with some nourishing dietetic meals. When she had a cold, I mentioned the possibility of her purchasing for herself a soup or a stew, a "comfort food." In other words, I became very concrete. She brightened up—she had never thought of food as "comfort." In this discussion with my patient I had unwittingly but instinctively filled in some gap in the mothering imago—Lacan (1977) would have called this a "suture."

This might seem like a standard supportive intervention, and supportive it was. The concreteness of my suggestions provided something the patient needed at that moment, thus stimulating ego development. It demonstrated the mutative function of what I call *mundane interventions*, the kind that most probably take place in many analyses but that do not find their way into the literature.

A few months later progress led to regression. Mrs. B. had her eyes done, an unnecessary procedure that no amount of interpretation could prevent (in this context see an old but still relevant study of polycosmetic surgeries by Menninger [1934]). For the next few months as she entered my office she would raise her face so that I could look her squarely in the face before she lay down on the couch. Her associations in those sessions made it apparent that the underlying activated dynamic was not competitive, exhibitionistic, or homoerotic (although it had aspects of all of these), but was connected to a need for my gaze, a need for me to look at her and to confirm that she was intact. Once I realized that need, I began to make occasional concrete references to the new appearance of her face and to the surgery. She was able to experience me as "seeing" her.

Interventions such as these, stimulated initially perhaps by the countertransference affects of impatience, frustration, and boredom, were surprisingly helpful in breaking through the treatment impasse. Mrs. B. became increasingly able to talk of matters of relationship, of caring, of loss, and of meaning. For the first time she began to acknowledge thoughts, feelings, and fantasies about me. Prior to that I had been "just anyone," an "anyone" not to be thought about or missed.

I saw Ms. C. four times weekly in psychoanalysis for over ten years. As in the other cases, a dynamic of "purging of the analyst" occurred, making the work seem interminable. She entered treatment when she was 26, describing herself as "a basket case." She was working as a saleswoman, living in a tacky studio apartment, and feeling bad about her looks and her body, especially about what she perceived to be her large derriere. She also felt deeply ashamed that her breasts were overly large. Ms. C. was of normal weight, but she experienced herself as heavy and was always on a diet. Aside from her sulky expression, she was actually quite pretty. She had been rejected by her boyfriend, who had ended a virtually sexless relationship of two years. She felt profoundly rejected by him, even though she had experienced him as physically repellent.

She was the fourth of five children from a socially prominent family. All of her siblings were boys. She, like Mrs. B., had been raised to be good, beautiful, thin, and socially adaptive, the end goal being to find a rich husband. Instead, Ms. C. was sulky and

belligerent, acted like a tomboy, and was much punished for her
rebelliousness and her futile efforts to separate from her controlling mother. Her mother forced her to exercise as a preteen
in order to reduce the size of her derriere, which was the target
of family jokes. Her father referred to her as "Porky" upon a
number of occasions. As an adult, Ms. C.'s primary concerns were
her body and her clothes. Her mother taught her to sleep only
in certain positions in order to maintain the tone of her facial
skin. She avoided eating good food, and when she cooked she
made food that was tasteless in order to avoid temptations that
might lead her into putting on weight.

I can't discuss all the details of the complex analysis of this
severely narcissistic and masochistic woman, whose manifest treatment issues centered around castration anxiety, penis envy, and
sibling rivalry, and defended against the less conscious ones of
oral frustration and thwarting of affection and dependency needs.
She was envious of, and competitive with, most of the women
she encountered. Her parents encouraged a morbid dependency
on them, rewarding her for being sick. Over the years, as with
Mrs. B., the transference was split, as Ms. C. regularly visited
chiropractors, orthopedic surgeons, gynecologists, and dermatologists. Despite these interferences with treatment, some
changes occurred. She became able to find work in a field she
liked and to attain a high level of competence in it. And after a
number of years, she became able to experience sexual pleasure
and to become conscious of her sexual fantasies, which excited
and aroused her.

Prior to the awakening of her sexuality, a period occurred in
which Ms. C. took cooking classes, invited friends to dinner, and
cooked with her new boyfriend. This brief period of progression then led to regression. She began to report a fear that she
would not be loved because she was not thin. Ms. C. had, during the course of her analysis, a series of woman friends from

whom she would take advice. I remarked to her that although in her sessions with me she might come to a conclusion about something, she then needed her friends' advice before she would act on it. Her response, a profound belittling of me, was the verbalization of her chronic refusal to take me in, just as she had tried to refuse her mother's influence on her. How could I know anything about sex or relationships, she wanted to know, for I was "a nobody" just like her. The analysis of her sadistic attack on me facilitated real psychic change, along with some transient identifications, heretofore warded off, that furthered psychic growth.

Additional changes occurred when I began, in an enactment reactive to Ms. C.'s provocations and ongoing belittlement of me, to alter my technique in certain ways. I had come to doubt that she was analyzable, and therefore began to let go of my analytic stance. Ms. C. brought in some photographs of an island off the coast of Maine that she had visited. Until that time, she had never traveled or shown any interest in anything outside her immediate existence. I commented on the beauty of one photograph of the sea. The following week she reported having framed that particular photo, neglecting, in her usual fashion, to acknowledge that we had spoken of it. It seemed to me that after many years, a process of internalization had begun, due to the relaxation of my interpretive stance and a positive, concrete comment about something she must have experienced as a part of herself.

I then began to make, over time, a series of uncharacteristic (for me) interventions. When she spoke of her body, her exercises, her weight gain or loss, her frustrating clothes-shopping expeditions, all areas that seemed so unanalytic, I began to acknowledge what I actually saw. I began to express what I concretely, rather than symbolically, understood, and I did not address the issue in terms of its deeper meanings or possible genetic links. I would say, for example, by means of clarification or con-frontation: "You feel disgusting and sweaty, yet you are wearing a wool sweater on a hot day"; "You say that you cannot find clothes that are elegant because of your wide rear end, yet you ignore the fact that overblouses are the fashion this season"; or "You say that you have no new clothes. Isn't the outfit you're wearing now new? I haven't seen it before."

It was difficult for me to make such statements. I felt the way I imagine an Orthodox Jew who eats bacon must feel. I asked myself, What is an analyst doing in this territory? I have since come to understand that interventions such as these are exactly what such patients need. They need to know concretely that the analyst sees what they are doing, that the analyst knows and notices, in a way that their parents did not. After a session in which I made a comment that referred to my gaze and to some-thing I saw about her, Ms. C. brought in the following dream: "We were in adjoining beds. You cut the cord to my white noise-maker." My interpretation was: "Now you are going to let me be heard."

DISCUSSION

The obsession with thinness has been addressed in the literature from various points of view. Orbach (1978) regarded it as "a flight from femininity." Gamman and Makinen (1994) argued that "some women 'pervert' the oral drive for sustenance to assuage narcissis-tic feelings of inadequacy in relation to their self-identity" (p. 139). Louise Kaplan (1991b) viewed it as an enactment of a perverse strategy; she saw the bingeing and vomiting to be fetishistic.

In my treatment of these patients, I have come to believe that they make use of the therapist as a spectator, by which I do not mean a voyeur. The therapist's focus on their bodies helps them to supplement an insufficient cathexis. In the perverse transference that develops, the patient tries to get the therapist to look at him or her in order to repair the feeling of deficit, to "suture" a tear, in the Lacanian sense. In this endeavor the therapist herself is used, rather than her interpretations. This often takes much time in the therapy, since the internalization of a mirroring, approving object is insufficient and must be both met and worked through before the patient can really work analytically. Statements that indicate concretely to the patient one's awareness of small body changes, or changes in clothing—that is, of what is on the surface, rather than within the psyche—are the raw materials of this work.

The classically trained analyst usually feels uncomfortable during this phase of the treatment and such feelings must be monitored. This is not a "corrective emotional experience" in the sense that Alexander meant that term. This confirmation of what is on the surface, and the use of concrete language appropriate to the developmental period from which the narcissistic problem arose, eventually permits the treatment to progress to issues that pertain to inner fantasy and conflict, the areas the therapist was trained to work with and the discussion of which make her feel that she is doing her job. It is my contention that the analyst will be doing her job, when this perverse transference is mobilized, by reflecting back to her patient some of her concrete observations about the patient's appearance (or of displaced related issues, such as Ms. C.'s photos).

In an article on a different topic altogether, Caper (1994) described a session with a female patient who dreamed about silk blouses, and who spoke of her preference for wearing skirts that were shorter than the one she had worn to her session on the previous day. Caper wrote: "I said that she seemed to feel that it was too dowdy for her, that she would prefer something sexier" (p. 908). This was experienced by the patient as a "beautiful interpretation." The therapist felt that it freed her to wear sexy clothing, and that he was no longer experienced by her as some archaic superego figure trying to desexualize her. Caper went on to say: "The mind needs reliable information about itself—truth, if you will—just as much as the body needs food" (p. 909). I agree with Caper on this latter point. I believe that what worked was his acknowledgment to the patient of what he actually, concretely saw—the visual truth of the dowdy skirt of the day before.

In the course of the therapy of patients obsessed with thinness, I have found it necessary at appropriate moments to confront them with my perception that they embrace this societal ideal at least in part because it relates to their own issues. I point out that most women do not pursue thinness to such a degree, or give it the priority that they do. It holds special importance for them because of their need to take in and then to eliminate what is taken in. They need to feel left out, like second-class citizens. Eventually the link between what they say about their obsessions and the genetic roots that give rise to them becomes clear, and they become more able to examine their inner conflicts and fantasies.

These periods of confronting of my patients with my perception that their own issues are part of the problem have proved to be a particular challenge to me. Confrontation arouses anger and defensiveness. For example, one day Mrs. B. presented me with a book on face-lifts, a thinly veiled recommendation. In the countertransference, I am forced daily to confront my own struggle with aging as bodily perfection continues to elude me.

As I work with these patients, I am daily pulled into the terrain of reality, for, as Inderbitzen and Levy (1994) have written:

> Reality is especially well-suited for purposes of defense against unconscious instinctual and moral pressures because of its compelling visibility, its often engaging both analyst and analysand experientially (as in interaction), its here-and-now quality, its "socializing" nature, and many other attributes that contrast with the

confusing, slippery, and often fantastic quality of what can be inferred about unconscious drive and superego forces during analysis. [p. 785]

Confronting these patients about their goals can take place at various points. For example, when they complain of fatigue, the therapist can make statements such as: "You are starving your body and that is why you have no energy." Or when they break their diets and enjoy a meal, "Do you see how you feel? Why do you deprive yourself of such feelings?"

It is impossible to analyze these patients more deeply until some of the acting out abates. Acting out may occur in the use of diuretics and laxatives, or in visits to the surgeons and diet doctors who cut them, touch them, look at them, and enable them to split, even splinter, the transference. Unable, on a deep level, to trust the therapist or the therapy, they often rely on an ever-changing panel of advisors in whom they can confide and from whom they receive concrete advice. After this phase, the therapy can really progress as they begin to see how their behavior is connected to the wish to be rid of specific inner tensions.

Therapists should think about the use of the couch at the times when this kind of perverse transference is mobilized. According to Goldberger (1995b), there are times when the couch serves as a distancing device, enabling the patient to avoid speaking of shameful topics. At times it may have more to do with the therapist's need than that of the patient. Patients who manifest ego deficits and for whom the "as if" quality of the transference is tenuous are more likely to become engaged in a face-to-face encounter with the therapist. The therapist must evaluate whether words alone are sufficient, or whether the patient must be seen face-to-face. I will consider this further in Chapter 7.

The women patients discussed here shared certain dynamics: They all felt rejected and unloved, and they all received attention from their parents mainly for their looks. They were quite willing to accept the masochistic gratifications of chronic pain in the form of hunger, body aches, and postsurgery pain. Some had progressed somewhat to the oedipal phase, but were severely let down by their fathers, who made no pretense about their lack of interest in them as little girls, and their preference for their mothers' company. This led to a profound oral envy of their mothers, a refusal to internalize them or what they could realistically provide, and a profound envy as well of other women whom they saw as having what they did not. Fantasies of magic, such as, "Some women have that magic touch and can get any man they want," were prevalent. This was associated with the goal of thinness as potentially providing the missing something that eluded them. They managed, on an anal level, to turn to feces, to eliminate and evacuate, whatever they did take in, and their chronic inner experience was one of emptiness.

Etchegoyen's (1991) view of the perverse transference is that the therapist is seduced into scopophilia, or the therapy is subverted so that interpretations become surface pseudo-interpretations. It is my observation, however, that in the cases discussed here, the patients experienced the therapy and its insights internally as food that must be nibbled on or eaten sparely and then evacuated. Sometimes these patients flattered me; sometimes they belittled me; but eventually all of them evacuated many of my efforts. The slowness of the process of internalization under such circumstances prolongs treatment. What gains are made are attributed to the advice of others or to the passing of time; each of these women has said to me: "It would have happened anyway." The slow progress fuels the patient's need to perceive the therapy as useless and to try yet another diet or another surgery. As I have said, metaphoric language develops at the time that body image is being consolidated; my concrete interventions addressed the patients at the point where development had stopped, both narcissistically and linguistically. I will discuss this further in the next chapter.

Etchegoyen (1991) summed up the countertransference reactions produced by patients in the perverse transference with the comment that "these people really make you want to quit doing analysis." The countertransference must be constantly monitored. The therapist is daily immersed in a world of superficial values personally eschewed. The patient's self-hatred often turns on the therapist's body as a target of sadistic attack. The patient is envious, competitive, and contemptuous of the therapist. The therapist must connect with the patient's pain and suffering. While being personally attacked and belittled, the therapist must lead the patient on a journey inside herself so that she can challenge a compelling social reality.

7

To See or Not to See

I cannot put up with being stared at by other people for eight hours a day (or more).

Freud (1913, p. 134)

$\mathcal{W}$ith the above admission, Freud gave future therapists permission to structure the psychotherapeutic situation so that they would be personally comfortable enough to conduct their work on a daily basis. Whether having patients on the couch serves the patient and the therapy as well as it does the therapist is a question that has been debated for decades. Is the use of the couch, and the fact that the therapist is heard but not seen by the patient, facilitative and ultimately curative, or not? And if it *is* facilitative, then what exactly does it facilitate? As Jay (1993) has observed, "The couch thwart[s] the scopophilic-exhibitionistic potential . . . abet[s] the blankness of the analyst as crucial to the transference process" (p. 335). The potential advantages of this thwarting are well known, but what of the disadvantages? What happens to communication when one of its most important pathways is removed? If the couch is not of equal benefit to all patients, then how can we tell who is likely to benefit from its use, and who is not?

One of the prime justifications for the use of the couch is to break through defense. The therapeutic situation places limits on the patient, who "is compelled to reject certain instinctual demands and certain allurements on the visual plane" (Major 1980, p. 466). According to Goldberger (1995a), however, there are times when the couch itself can be used for defensive purposes, for example serving as an isolating and distancing device that enables the patient to avoid speaking about shameful topics such as masturbation. In a case she cited, the patient told her therapist, "Sitting face-to-face is a confrontation: you'll see something I don't want you to see. You don't know my face, my eyes. It's kind of private" (p. 28).

Goldberger goes on to say that the couch can also protect the personal space of the patient. Although it may be used for defensive purposes, or at times have more to do with the therapist's need than that of the patient, some patients may require the perception of a private, less vulnerable space before therapy can take place at all.

Therapists are often unaware of the significance some patients attach to looking or not looking at them. Traub-Werner's (1998) detailed report of a male patient with a voyeuristic perversion (see Chapter 2) contains no discussion of the patient, who was overstimulated visually as a child, trying to look at, or be looked at by, his therapist. Instead there was a discussion of the therapist's "voyeurism" being stimulated in the "listening mode," of the therapist's looking forward to "looking through ears" at the stimulating tales his patient told, and a fascination with his role as spectator to these tales. Riess (1988), on the other hand, reported looking away from one woman patient upon hearing a car crash outside her office. Her patient experienced a strong reaction: "She spoke about her great need for my looking at her and my talking to her as confirmation of the reality around her, both of which she constantly doubted" (p. 400). This patient had been accustomed to reading cues from her mother's face all through her life.

Plotkin (1997), interpreting an older male patient's formidable resistance to working on the couch, found that the patient's visual involvement with her served as a resistance to memory. "The transition to the couch was discerned by the patient as a punishment since it meant loss of visual contact. . . . As soon as he took his eyes off her, he remembered pain and remarked: 'I can't stand not seeing you'" (p. 11). The couch was associated with pain, death, and loss. He felt too alone on the couch.

In his sensitive article about the role of "face to face" in therapy and its relation to the smiling response, Weissman (1977) concluded, "We learn to use our eyes to read emotions in others, to express emotions of our own, and to communicate with others" (p. 447). He realized well into the analysis of an adult patient that she suffered greatly on the couch and that this suffering gratified her masochistic wishes. Her need for visual contact came from an early separation from her mother, and her facial searching reproduced an effort to coax depressed parents out of their bad moods. To keep her on the couch would have reinforced a repetition of her masochistic misery, "permitting the gratification of constantly reliving her childhood neurosis without having to undergo personal change. By remaining faceless, I would have continued to be the absent mother" (pp. 446–447).

On the other side of the coin, there is the matter of the therapist's own working style, and the conditions and input that best suit his own therapeutic equipment. Moriatus (1995) empathically considered the situation of the working analyst in an issue that he edited for *Psychoanalytic Inquiry* entitled *The Relevance of the Couch in Contemporary Psychoanalysis*. Most of the contributors to that collection took the position that listening was superior to looking. Like Goldberger, Moriatus made the observation that having the patient on the couch guards the analyst's personal space; it serves as a "protective shield" for the analyst, enabling the analyst to listen and to apply certain personalized rituals in the process: "These rituals are minute but highly sensitive behavioral patterns that reflect the analyst's idiosyncratic ways of regulating tension. Familiar examples are doodling, writing, smoking, closing one's eyes, changing posture, sipping coffee, and even daydreaming and dozing" (p. 407). Moriatus supported these tension-regulating and -reducing behaviors, which enable the analyst to stay engaged in a neutral way in the work, but any of which, if viewed directly by most patients, would stimulate thoughts of being boring or being rejected by the analyst.

The bodily actions of the therapist reveal to the patient how the therapist is receiving, or blocking, his or her communications. Freedman and Lavendar's (1997) study of the (videotaped) nonverbal behaviors of therapists also spelled out in detail a wide range of adaptive bodily adjustments made by therapists while engaged in face-to-face treatment. Bodily actions of the therapist during the listening process were filmed and coded for rhythmicity (motor actions in phase with the ebb and flow of speech) and arrhythmicity (shielding behaviors unresponsive to the patient's speech). Rhythmic actions include head nods, foot kicks, lateral hand to body rhythms, and posture shifts. Arrhythmic actions include repetitive bilateral self-stimulation with one hand or finger rubbing the other, and self-regulating head nods.

For those of us who conduct traditional analysis using the couch as well as face-to-face therapy, the possibility of changing one's chair, one's field of vision, one's posture, of being able to move or cross one's legs, to stretch if necessary, is vital to a sense of physical and psychological well-being. It is not that analysts are completely immobile while sitting face to face with their patients, but they are under scrutiny, and because of this their movements are not as fluid. A woman analyst wearing a knee-length skirt, for example, will generally be more aware of herself in crossing her legs when her patient is looking at her.

The following case vignette illustrates some of the pitfalls of face-to-face treatment.

Dr. Y., a self-observing, sophisticated analysand, entered analysis in order to understand a number of self-destructive political moves and actions he had made at the university where he taught. From time to time he did not want to lie on the couch. I noted that these need-to-sit-up sessions usually preceded or followed my vacations, or occurred when Dr. Y. was in an agitated emotional state. His agitated states were usually precipitated by some-

thing happening in the transference, but Dr. Y., despite his so-
phistication, generally attributed them to something in his life
outside the treatment. One day he came into his session in an
angry mood and sat on the couch looking at me. I was experiencing the beginning symptoms of a viral infection, had taken
an antihistamine, had not slept well the night before, and was
trying to suppress a tendency to cough. I was also aware of a
slight twitch in my eyelid. All in all I was not physically comfortable, to say the least. After several minutes Dr. Y. reported
that he had noticed that I played with my hands, and he wondered whether I had problems too. (The hand movements he
noticed were of the arrhythmic shielding variety of behaviors
noted by Freedman and Lavendar [1997]. These movements, as
contrasted with rhythmic body movements that are in phase with
the ebb and flow of the patient's speech, are "unresponsive to
variations in the patient's phonemic system" [p. 84].)

I saw Dr. Y.'s statement as most likely stemming from a fantasy
about masturbation, but because of the likelihood that I *had* been
holding onto my hands in some unaccustomed way in adjusting
to my own physical discomfort, I did not follow up on this theory
with my patient. In addition, I thought that Dr. Y. would have
felt assaulted, as do many patients in psychoanalytic treatment
when they address a visible reality and are made to feel that their
reality testing is being questioned, and their realistic perception
being twisted and turned by the analyst into a fantasy. Both
realistic perception and fantasy are always operative in different
degrees, but at that moment both the patient and I were pulled
toward the reality end of the spectrum. I made a note of Dr. Y.'s
comments and was able to use them later in the analysis when
the timing was better. What was real in the face-to-face situation was an obstacle at that time to on-the-spot analysis.

Dr. Y. usually wore contact lenses, and on the occasions that
he wore eyeglasses in his sessions, I often experienced him as

wearing a mask. One day he remarked from the couch that when he wore his glasses he could search for flaws in the way the books on the bookcase in front of him were lined up, like the "flaw" he had discerned in my hand movements (and the flaws he always commented upon in others' actions). In this instance I had no difficulty inquiring about his search for a flaw in the book arrangement; it was not my body, but a rather (to me) neutral extension of it, that was under scrutiny. The analysis of Dr. Y.'s looking behaviors led to his recollection of watching his aunt, who lived with his family, get undressed and parade before him in her underwear when he was a boy, and then to the fantasies he had at times of being a woman.

Dr. Y.'s case raises the issue of patients who usually use the couch but who from time to time need or want to sit up, either on the couch itself or in the chair they sat in when beginning treatment. There was a time when one did not permit such "acting in," but only analyzed the resistance and why the patient wanted to sit up. My clinical experience has convinced me that many patients cannot really say why they want to sit up at the moment they experience that wish. But when they are permitted to sit up, the meaning of the wanting to look at the analyst can emerge.

Other patients are able to "get around the couch contract . . . getting the most out of the eye-movements before and after the 'hour' as defined by the couch position" (Jacobson 1995, p. 309). Goldberger's (1995b) patient told her after three years in treatment that she glanced at her face each day as she entered the office in order to "see what the weather is." Therapists are aware of patients who scan their faces before and after the hour with searching eyes, and of those who avoid looking them, sliding past as they come through the door with their eyes cast down. Fleming (1975) noted the separation anxiety of a patient who had suffered early object loss and who obtained some relief in looking at her before and after being on the couch, in "lingering moments." In my experience, the questioning of either extreme of behavior can sometimes lead to self consciousness and suppression of the natural response, yet at others may yield fruitful information about whatever transference fantasy is operating at the moment.

A striking clinical vignette illustrates further the link between the visual image (of the therapist) and separation. Hopkins (1999) was caught off guard once by a patient who brought a camera into a session and snapped her picture. The patient returned with the photo and its negative the next day. This was understood to be a kind of photographic "rape," and a measure of how much the patient needed to hold onto an image of her for fear that her internal image of the therapist would disappear. (The patient's mother believed that photographs captured one's soul, and she herself refused to be photographed; if she found a photo of herself, she would scratch out the eyes.)

Patients regulate what they see and do not see even when face to face. Years ago Riess (1978) predicted the recent studies of the mutual gaze of mother and child, and presciently grasped also the importance both of the early phases of eye contact between mother and child as an indicator of their emotional involvement and the importance of visual communication in the forging of preverbal affective ties. She described an adult patient who could not telephone strangers without anxiety: "He became aware that he always needed to scrutinize the faces of people with whom he was talking to 'read' their expressions and assure themselves of their approval of his statements.... He had to take his cues for his own views from the other persons' faces" (p. 391). He had learned to scan his mother's face for clues to her quick emotional eruptions and abandonments. This patient averted his glance during treatment, thus sparing himself the task of scanning for the analyst's approval or disapproval.

I have patients who in the middle of a session will suddenly look back to see my face, and I recall one man who would roll around onto his stomach, look at me, and then roll back. In each case, something has been generated that leads to the need to check me out and make sure that I had not left the room, that I was awake, still liked them, was not making fun of them—whatever the fantasy was that produced the need for the visual search. Some people are afraid to look, out of fantasies related to fear, envy, or something else, and get on and off the couch without looking at me and do not ask to sit up. It is important that such aversions of the gaze also be analyzed and understood. These phenomena are at risk of being missed if the analyst insists too rigidly on the couch.

The therapist's office and office building, the lobby and elevators, the therapist's car—all of these are visible extensions of the therapist's body that from time to time come under attack. Some patients verbally attack the body of the therapist in order to defend against their own shame at having problems, at being patients. For some, lying on the couch enables them to avoid feeling the shame they feel about being patients (Broucek 1991), which should not, of course, go unanalyzed. They have a sense of hiding when on the couch rather than being "really" seen by the analyst face to face. Jacobson (1995) and Wolf (1995) noted that patients who are told they are not well suited to the use of the couch (that is, not analyzable) often feel mortified. As one who has written about deception and deceptive patients (Gediman and Lieberman 1996, Lieberman 1991a), I would hope to make some definitive statements about the role looking at the therapist in the eye or the therapist looking at the patient in the eye plays in encouraging truth-telling, rather than the couch more easily facilitating deception. I cannot. In fact there seemed to be no difference—deceptive patients were on the couch and also face to face. Competent liars are able to look at a person straight in the eye and seem sincere!

Patients are usually not very aware of being in the therapist's line of vision when they are on the couch, and therapists vary in the way they position their chairs and the actual view this affords them. When my patients are on the couch, I am particularly aware of the back of their heads, of their hands and hand movements, and of their feet. Meissner (1998) describes aspects of on- and off-the-couch observations and how the physical body characteristics of both patient and therapist influence the situation:

> We can observe the patient's posture on the couch—relaxed, tense, motionless and rigid, or moving spontaneously and freely. Are arms crossed or not, are hands open or mobile, or clenched and restrained; does he twiddle his thumbs, scratch? Where does he put his hands, on his chest, behind his head? What does he do with his right or left hand? [pp. 281–282]

"Our patients speak; we listen. But sometimes our patients act and we watch." In her paper on the written dream, Stimmel (1995) was able to learn the meaning of a patient's dream and "dirty secret" by looking from her chair at the scrap of paper in her patient's hand, on which was written the dream she was telling. This was a bit of stationery from a hotel the patient had gone to with her lover, a married man. Stimmel concluded that "sometimes the concrete visual representation of the thing, which is the closest an analysand can come to showing the analyst the 'raw' dream, enlightens us in a way that language simply cannot" (p. 666).

A patient and therapist sitting face to face usually have reciprocal frontal views, but the physical distance between the therapist's and the patient's chairs varies according to the therapist's preference, which is true also when the couch is used. In the case of chairs, those that are lighter weight can be moved by both patient and therapist to suit themselves. There are cross-cultural differences as well in the distance between chair and couch or between chair and chair. In Israel, patient and therapist sit closer to one another than they do here, regardless of the size of the office they are in (Kushnir-Barash, personal communication, 1999). All these variations and others affect how much each can see of the another, and how it feels.

The therapist who gives up the protection of the couch gives up something real. When a patient stares at the therapist for many hours from his chair and then comments upon the therapist's looks or clothing, critical or negative commentary can be experienced as more hurtful and difficult to deflect than when such commentary comes from a patient on the couch. Real physical characteristics of the therapist serve as lynchpins for the attachment of transference derivatives (Meissner 1998). One of the occupational hazards of psychotherapy as a profession is being verbally assaulted in that personal way from time to time. When the patient is on the couch, one can more easily defend oneself in one's mind by "moving" the criticism into the realm of fantasy and transference and saying to oneself, "It's transference—this person doesn't even really know what I look like, for he hardly has a chance to look at me." Personal criticism is difficult to deal with, especially when it approaches sensitive aspects of one's body image, and some degree of defense used by the therapist may be both necessary and adaptive. If this is not sufficient, countertransference reactions such as depression, withdrawal, anger, or even sadistic counterattack may ensue.

Many (but not all) psychotherapists look and dress like academics. Many male therapists wear glasses and have beards. Many women in the profession eschew the fashionable and the trendy and resist the kinds of cosmetic alterations that many in the broader culture value and espouse. They often take pride in so doing. In Malcolm's *Psychoanalysis: An Impossible Profession* (1981), the pseudonymous central figure Dr. Aaron Green disdainfully referred to the Columbia Psychoanalytic group as "sharp dressers," and by implication "lesser" analysts. Malcolm asked him:

"What's the matter with them now?"

Aaron frowned, and said in a low, dark voice, "They're sharp dressers."

I laughed. "Is that all?"

"Isn't that enough?" Aaron said. He laughed too.

"Do they tell you how to dress at New York Psychoanalytic?"

"No. But let me tell you a story." [p. 53]

Aaron went on to describe the soft-shouldered Abercrombie & Fitch black-and-white herringbone tweed jacket that was the jacket of choice of his colleagues; it made him feel that he really belonged to that group. Exactly that choice, however, might make him vulnerable to ridicule and attack by patients from other parts of the community at large.

When therapists are personally attacked on the basis of what patients see, rather than on what they hear, much intrapsychic work must be done to restore neutrality and the capacity to work in a benign way. Many years ago I heard a tale about an elder-statesman analyst who, viciously attacked by a patient for his large, bulbous nose, replied: "It is not so in my internal representation!" Burka (1996) wrote about how she and her patients dealt with her being overweight. There is a considerable literature about pregnant and impaired therapists that addresses questions about what patients can see but may not speak of, or, on the other hand, may make use of in sadistic attacks.

It can be very hurtful to be attacked and criticized by a patient who has noticed something unflattering about one's person. Although there are many reasons that patients attack their therapists in such ways, in most cases envy is an important underlying factor, and envy is often exacerbated by and focused upon visible elements.

Ms. A., a single woman in her thirties, entered a reduced-fee psychotherapy with the conscious goal of understanding why she had no husband and no career to speak of. She lived an impoverished life in a small, seedy apartment. It was apparent from her remarks about others that a displaced mother transference had been activated, with strong feelings of hatred and envy of me (who, in her fantasy, had "everything": father, looks, clothing, furs, jewelry, and a successful career). At an appropriate moment, I asked her if she were aware of being envious of me. Ms. A. remarked that the only thing I had that she might want was a sweater she saw me wear from time to time. The sweater, in my own estimation, was one of my least attractive and least valuable possessions. In addition, my more intangible personal qualities, the fact of my professional identity, the possibility of my having a family (which the patient did not "know" but could easily surmise) were all passed over and never referred to in Ms. A.'s associations.

It is at times difficult to work neutrally with people whose envy leads them to devalue you—to mock who you are and reject your efforts to facilitate change and psychic growth. Stony withdrawal or counterattack are not uncommon countertransference behaviors that can be destructive to the treatment, as in the following example.

Ms. C., whom I have described in Chapter 6, for years would not admit to having any feelings or thoughts about me, a resistance that I interpreted as a considerable obstacle to the progress of her treatment. She came into the office one day and said sarcastically: "I suppose I'm supposed to comment on that [a new framed photo of Freud's couch]." I asked her to say more. She replied, "Nothing. I'm just doing what I'm supposed to do." I had been belittled and devalued for years by Ms. C. and now I felt attacked again and needed to re-establish my narcissistic equilibrium. Rather than be silent (a form of withdrawal I sometimes resort to after being attacked), I replied that it was a photo of Freud's couch (a comment within the realm of a technically "acceptable" departure from classical technique) and that I had just purchased it in London (a comment that was in this case not acceptable, since Ms. C. could not travel anywhere as a result of her many phobias). This competitive remark exacerbated Ms. C.'s envy even more, and the topic was dropped by both of us. I felt internally mortified by my lapse, and could go no further in an analysis of my provocative patient's envy in that session.

Whether patients lie down or sit up for their sessions, for some it is a shock to see their therapists outside the office. The shock value, especially when the therapist is with other people, is not unlike the shock experienced by a child suddenly confronting the primal scene. In the office situation, the visual stimuli are to some degree constant and predictable, and patients soon adjust themselves to them in a way that defends against affect. Such defenses are usually not in place when patients suddenly see their therapists outside the office, another indication of the psychotherapeutic vitality of sight.

Dr. D., a mental health professional, was aware of my vacation trips and of the existence of my family. Nevertheless, she could only picture me spending the weekend break sitting in the waiting room reading the magazines left for patients. At a weekend professional meeting, she encountered me being greeted and embraced by several colleagues right in front of her; in her session the next day she could not remember ever having seen me at the meeting at all.

It is instructive to consider the possibility of no visual input at all. Increasingly, the practice of allowing only rare telephone sessions as parameters, when a patient is ill or out of town, is being replaced by more frequent telephone sessions, or even entire treatments conducted on the phone. Writing about the advent of telephones with video, Kaplan (1997) has coined the term "telepsycho-therapy" for "psychotherapy conducted by a therapist at a location different from the patient's through bidirectional communication technology supporting real-time interactivity in the audio, audio-visual or text modalities" (p. 227). He reported cases in which a videophone was used, and no differences from standard treatment was found, once the patient and therapist had become accustomed to the use of the instrument. Kaplan, however, believed that he himself needed the visual cues some others did not seem to need.

Aronson (1990) described working with a dangerously ill anorexic woman who began therapy and then refused to come in and see her. (This is an example of the "disappearing" phenom-enon described by Ackerman, which I refer to in Chapter 6.) Tele-phone sessions and the therapist's answering machine were used as a transitional space that eventually was outgrown and no longer needed. The severely underweight patient began her treatment by averting her eyes, and proceeded to complete avoidance of the overstimulation of face-to-face contact with her therapist for sev-eral years. She had been cross-eyed as a baby and her mother had been unavailable to her. Aronson reconstructed that she had expe-rienced little "dyadic, face-to-face gazing and vocalization—the interactional sensory-motor experiences that are the precursors of psychic structure . . . [and] little mutual gazing, mutual smiling and sharing of excitement" (p. 168).

Lindon (1988) detailed several cases of psychoanalysis by tele-phone conducted with patients who were away on business or on vacation, or who could not come in for their sessions because of paranoid fears. Except in those cases where the patient felt threat-ened by physical nearness of the analyst, no significant differences between office and telephone sessions were found. The telephone was not automatically used as a distancing device.

Despite these reports, I believe that there must be something special in the psychological makeup of those who choose telephone analysis. Zalusky (1998) considered it to be a "therapeutic compromise" that is "inherently conflictual" but may be the "best treatment available for a particular patient." She reported on the case of her patient Annie:

> With only my auditory sense available, I was able to hear her differently. Annie's basic good nature, her enthusiasm and her delight to be in the room with me could no longer mask the depth of her passion, her loneliness and her depressed affect. The telephone tended to facilitate unconscious-to-unconscious communication. [p. 1229]

Using the telephone, Zalusky could walk freely around her office, alleviating her chronic back pain. She wondered about her own need to see her patient, even if her patient did not need to see her. Annie was afraid to see her, afraid that if she saw her she would not be as perfect as she was in her fantasy; she was afraid of her greed, that if she saw her she would want her all of the time; she was afraid of sexual arousal. In addition, the phone sessions enabled Annie to repeat the intimacy she had experienced, as a child of divorce, with her father, with whom she often communicated by phone. Zalusky concluded that telephone analysis can at times intensify, rather than dilute, the transference:

> Without the visual presence, the fantasy of the analyst may be untethered, lost in inner space. In a regular analysis, if an analysand should fantasize that his analyst is as sexy as Marilyn Monroe, he may not, as he arrives at or leaves the session, be able to escape the fact that she looks more like Hillary Clinton. [p. 1236]

The telephone patient will not know that the therapist has survived his attack by seeing her smile at the door the next day, and the therapist will not know that the patient has taken drugs, is naked, and so on. The telephone patient has to work harder to visualize the therapist and this facilitates the ability to form a mental representation of a caring other.

Mrs. H., an advertising executive, presented with considerable discrepancies between her well-organized and fashionable physical appearance, her well-respected position in her profession, and the primitive issues that prevailed in her marriage to an adulterous clothing manufacturer. She never used her time to address the latter problem, which mortified her, and she focused instead on the areas from which she took pride. I recommended four sessions per week, but Mrs. H.'s busy schedule would permit only two. From the very beginning of her treatment, she could not get to her sessions on time. She began to call me from her car phone while I was waiting for her, to inform me of her progress in getting to my office. One evening she asked me if she could begin her session on the car phone—that traffic was so bad that she despaired of ever getting there on time. I, by now almost ready to resign the treatment, decided to break with standard technique and agreed.

Mrs. H. spoke in a way that seemed no different from the way she spoke in her sessions. Midway through her car phone sessions, she would announce that she was outside the office, terminate the call, park the car, ring my doorbell five minutes later, come in and finish her forty-five minutes face to face. I permitted this practice when the patient needed it. After about six months, the delays became shorter and Mrs. H. began to come to her sessions on time, no longer needing to distance herself from me. I understood this as having been this patient's way of allowing herself to develop a sense of control and trust. She had used distancing devices to regulate how much she "took in" of me as the activation of an overpowering, critical, and toxic maternal introject threatened quickly to emerge in the transference—a situation that might have led to the patient's premature termination. The car phone enabled her to keep her composure and equilibrium and to titrate my influence. It is also possible that her intense envy of me, whom she saw as calm and unruffled in the face of her own inevitable storms, was too much for her to manage when treatment began. Eventually she was able to internalize that calm.

Clearly there are enough pros and cons on all sides of the who-can-see-what issue to keep arguments flying for years. Ultimately, what really matters is not the use of the couch per se, but the facilitation of the patient's freedom of verbal expression (Goldberger 1995b) and the therapist's capacity to work comfortably. Two issues seem to me to be essential in the couch versus chair debate, and in the ongoing discussion of the use and usefulness of the couch in facilitating an analysis: (1) the position one takes about the importance of the visual observation of *affect* in analysis, and (2) the position one takes about the *level of communication* facilitated by looking as opposed to listening.

In the *Psychoanalytic Inquiry* issue devoted to the relevance of the couch, Lichtenberg (1995) referred to Stern's (1985) work on the importance of scanning the mother's face for the development of security feelings in the infant. He strongly stated the position that "analysts who choose to deprive themselves of the opportunity to view their patients' affective expression, relying only on verbal exchanges, either do not appreciate the significance of affects or are willing to work with one hand tied behind their back" (p. 284). Patients do not put everything into words, and when they are on the couch, the analyst may not be aware of the tears, winces, or smiles that memories and associations evoke.

In Sadow's (1995) view, the couch suppresses the "generative mode" of thinking, and looking disrupts the flow of the analytic process:

> The disciplines of the couch, talking and listening, tend to protect and promote the analytic process; although looking—to objectify and to make real—is ultimately an important aspect of the analytic process, it may disrupt the process when it is introduced prior to the acquisition of an adequate database derived through the generative mode. [p. 387]

He feels that Freud preferred the couch, among other reasons, as a way of avoiding the stress of maintaining the generative (or more creative, intuitive, introspective) mode of thought while looking and being looked at. Sadow implied that the generative mode is more intuitive and more empathic than, and thus in opposition to, the more logical (organized, analytic) mode the analyst can sustain when the patient is on the couch. For the analyst, looking is stressful, and according to Sadow detracts from what he has to do as analyst. By this I think he means that looking evokes empathy and thereby draws the analyst into the patient's story, making the analyst (he feels) less of an analyst.

Ogden (1996b) and Ross (1999) have argued from a different perspective. From his reading of Freud's technique papers Ogden inferred that for Freud looking involved secondary process thinking, whereas the couch arrangement "helps provide conditions of privacy in which the analyst might enter a state of reverie in which he gives himself 'over to the current of [his] unconscious thoughts' (Freud 1913, p. 134) and renders his own unconscious receptive to the unconscious of the analysand" (p. 885).

Ross (1999) explored the hypnagogic state of the supine patient and how it resonates with the empathic reverie of the unseen therapist. For Ross, to be free from looking and being looked at while he works means that he can look inside himself. As one who thinks in visual images, he believes that he can do this more effectively with the patient on the couch, creating a kind of "movie in his mind."

Tremendous demands are placed on the therapist's ego when he has to oscillate between these two modes. Looking and being looked at add to the psychological demand, and at the same time increase the burden of processing the additional, and sometimes contradictory, information gleaned through visible facial and bodily communications.

Implicit in the above arguments is a basic disagreement as to what successful therapy requires: A therapist who daydreams or a therapist who uses secondary process? A subjective therapist or an objective therapist? There is also disagreement as to what matters: Are verbal expressions worth more than nonverbal ones? These questions all refer back to the larger debate about what is actually curative in therapy: verbal interpretation of dreams, memories and associations; empathy with the patient's affective state; attunement with a broader subjective state, including bodily movements and rhythms, which require a visual channel of communication. But these are to some degree artificial distinctions, and should not be considered mutually exclusive.

Different theoretical models of intrapsychic development and enabling of intrapsychic change influence the interpretation of clinical experience. Feldman (1997), a Kleinian, quoted Bion (1958) as describing

> the beginning of a session with a psychotic patient, who gave the analyst a quick glance, paused, stared at the floor near the corner of the room, and then gave a slight shudder. He lay down on the couch, keeping his eye on the same corner of the floor. When he spoke, he said that he felt quite empty, and wouldn't be able to make further use of the session. Bion spells out the steps in the process by which

the patient first used his eyes for introjection, and then for expulsion, creating a hallucinatory figure that had a threatening quality, accompanied by a sense of internal emptiness. [p. 229]

Grotstein (1995) takes the position that "bonding and attachment in the infant–parent situation is facilitated by the mutual eye-gaze act. Perhaps analysis, unlike the birth situation, is a unique event in which the very forfeiture of the gaze option allows for an opening of the channels into the interior of each participant" (p. 400). Grotstein believed analysis could succeed only if its form *differed* from the initial bond with the parent. Others have argued that the framework of analysis must *replicate* aspects of the original dyad in order to succeed. This is the more common view.

Mitrani (1998), another Kleinian analyst, described the case of Carla, a patient who had suffered early object loss. Carla feared being "spilled and gone." After weekend breaks she scanned the analyst's face while passing through the doorway on the way to the consulting room. She left the analyst feeling self-conscious, as if her lipstick was crooked, or powder left off. Yet when the analyst asked the patient about it, she said that the analyst always "looked the same." Her mother had been in an accident as a child, and as a result her expression was fixed as if in disdain. Carla could never tell if she loved her. The analyst interpreted that "she seemed to need to feel like a flowing-over and joyous baby—she could be seen and held in my facial expression, so that she could not spill away and be lost again" (p. 113). The analyst's self-consciousness informed her that she had become a receptacle for the frozen maternal imago.

Gedo (1996) has been quite vocal (and radical) in his position that the analyst himself must provide visual feedback to the patient—"it may be necessary to reinforce one's intended meanings by adding the language of gestures and facial expressions to our repertory" (p. 11)—and has wondered whether the use of the couch might be contraindicated. He recommended that the analyst "should always sit in a place an analysand can survey visually—if the choice of looking at the analyst is clearly left to the patients, those who need visual cues to grasp the analyst's meaning will almost always avail themselves of the opportunity to gather them" (p. 11). (I disagree with Gedo's belief that the patient will choose whatever will help him. This was not so in the case of the woman who masochistically prolonged her childhood misery in Weissman's case, and in the cases of the envious women I mentioned above.) Gedo noted that patients' monitoring of the analyst's facial expressions can be problematic, but he considers that preferable to not being able to see their expressions himself, because of the importance of cues obtained therefrom:

> To facilitate these observations I have always positioned my chair so that I might look at the analysand's face more or less from the side, rather than having a view of the top of the patient's head or glimpsing a face upside down. I have always insisted on supplementing the analysand's associations with information I could collect through direct visual observation. [p. 73]

As an outcome of her survey of developmental work on mirroring, Haglund (1996) recommended mirroring techniques for the stimulation of psychic growth and concluded that:

> dyadic matching appears essential to the development of self-esteem, cohesion, and efficacy in infants. Therefore, increased attuned interaction by the therapist with patients experiencing difficulty in these areas could promote growth and structural change. Specifically face-to-face seating to maximize eye contact, vocal matching, and affective attunement on the part of the therapist seem critical to increased self-regulatory capacity and the positive capacities that depend on it. [p. 242]

Bucci (1997) in "Discourse in Good and Troubled Hours," distinguished between verbal and nonverbal processes, and then made additional distinctions within the nonverbal mode. She found that

> the analyst perceives and responds to his patients on multiple and continuous dimensions, including some that are not explicitly identified. The analyst is able to make fine distinctions among a patient's states . . . including distinctions in sensory bodily levels sometimes using his own feelings as indicators without being able to express these feelings in words. [p. 158]

This kind of processing, which Bucci calls *subsymbolic processing,* or emotional information processing, is often body related and expressed first in gesture or facial expression and only later eventually moves into reflection and verbal elaboration. This is the kind of "computation" the infant uses to position himself at his mother's breast, or the child uses to climb from a table, or the dancer or the athlete uses in his or her work. It uses all the senses.

Beebe and Lachmann (1998) explored the relevance of studies of mother–infant gaze to adult therapy, and cited Bucci's work. They see psychoanalysis as

> currently seeking an expanded theory of interaction. This theory must ultimately address the nonverbal and procedural as well as the verbal dimensions of the interaction. . . . The nonverbal, procedural dimension is usually out of awareness but it provides a continuous background of moment-by-moment mutual influence. Parallel to the exchanges occurring on a verbal level, patient and analyst are continuously altering each others' timing, spatial organization, affect and arousal on a moment-to-moment basis. [p. 509]

Stern and colleagues (1998) took a "relational" position with regard to analytic treatment. They noted that interpretation has historically been tied to intrapsychic dynamics rather than to the implicit rules governing transactions with others, and they believe that this emphasis is currently shifting: "Procedural knowledge of relationships is implicit, operating outside both focal attention and conscious verbal experience. This knowledge is represented non-symbolically in the form of what we call implicit relational knowing" (p. 905). For them change is generated in a "moment of meeting"—the intersubjective context is altered when one achieves this implicit relational knowing.

They described a patient who entered analysis because of poor self-esteem with regard to her body and her inability to lose weight. When she was a child, her parents had her dance for them, and would watch her with admiration. She associated this to her experience of being watched by her analyst from some superior position. Then she spoke of bodily fears: "After a prolonged silence Molly said, 'Now I wonder if you're looking at me.' (*The now moment began here*)" (p. 913). The analyst, put on the spot, replied: " 'It kind of feels as if you're pulling my eyes to you . . .' 'Yes,' Molly agreed. (*These two sentences made up the moment of meeting*)" (p. 913). According to these authors' conceptualization, there was a minimum of transference-countertransference involved.

The relational position is that the therapist participates with the patient in an interaction. A traditional transference interpretation would address the exhibitionistic wishes of the patient that the therapist repeat what her parents had done. I might label this as an example of the therapist as reluctant spectator being pulled into a perverse transference, as I have described in Chapter 6. (These authors also presented a failed "now moment" when a patient tried to show the therapist a scar from a burn, something the therapist would not permit.)

Whatever one's theoretical position, such research findings must be incorporated into contemporary psychoanalytic theory and practice. In most psychoanalyses conducted these days, there is a preliminary phase in which analyst and patient sit face to face, whether for the initial consultation in which analyzability is assessed or, more often, for a period of psychotherapy that prepares the patient for analysis. This sometimes lasts several years. During this phase, whatever its length, visual communication takes place and visual assessments of each another by the members of the dyad are made. Each takes note of what the other looks like, characteristic bodily movements and gestures, and effective ways of making or avoiding eye contact. This information affects and informs the subsequent on-the-couch phase for both. We need data on these matters: how to determine the optimal length of the face-to-face period, whether one or both modalities should be used, the experiences both patient and analyst have of one another in these two modes, and how they are similar and how different.

These various arguments for the use of the couch versus the chair in psychoanalysis raise the consciousness of analysts about these issues and challenge some of the rigid formulas that govern psychoanalytic technique, particularly when they do not take visual issues sufficiently into account. It is too simple to say that face-to-face treatment uncovers preoedipal and preverbal issues and that on-the-couch treatment is best suited for oedipal and symbolizing issues. Use of the couch or chair should take into account the degree to which patient and/or analyst are *visuel* (Jay 1993), the way each processes auditory and visual cues, and the way each uses facial cues to know another person. It has to do with what any particular analyst needs to know a particular patient's affects (when the patient can't speak about them, for instance), or, on the other hand, whether the analyst prefers and needs to concentrate on the patient's words. But these dichotomies do not really exist. It is the mixture of all these factors that should determine the choice of couch versus chair.

Therapists have idiosyncratic reactions, too, and, these reactions warrant consideration when making the decision with any given patient to use couch or chair. Some patients are overstimulating, others so understimulating that the therapist needs to move around for fear of becoming sleepy. The therapist should be able to feel comfortable and alert when working with a patient. The patient's wishes should also be considered.

Some flexibility should also be allowed about whether patients sit up or lie down at different points in therapy, provided that the therapist is tracking the transference and resistance meanings of such shifts. We usually think of sitting up as a resistance, but as Goldberger (1995a) has cautioned: "Analysts need to be alert to the possibility that their strong preference that the patient use the couch may interfere with perceiving the subtle ways the couch abets their own avoidance of and defense against strong affects in the transference" (p. 39). Similar issues will undoubtedly come up as new technologies become available and are used by therapists and patients, for instance, the videotelephone and the Internet.

Psychotherapeutic treatment should be tailor-made to the individual patient in the context of that person's individual therapist. It may not be until the patient is well ensconced in treatment that enough is known about his or her need to look or be looked at for the couch/chair decision to be an informed choice.

8

One Therapist's
Countertransference

A narcissist is anyone better looking than you are.

Gore Vidal

Mr. P. was an exceptionally handsome advertising executive who entered psychoanalytic therapy at age 35 because of an obsessive love for a married woman. He didn't understand why she seemed so much more valuable to him than the various single women who made themselves available. Only after several weeks did he mention that she frequently complimented his looks, telling him that he was cute or good-looking, which his mother had never done. These compliments were precious to him. (A split image of his mother had been emerging, as a good companion, but neglectful. His father was remembered in a very shadowy manner. It seemed that as the child of divorced parents he had been left on his own, with insufficient parenting and attention.)

After several months Mr. P. appeared to be letting go of his obsession with Mrs. L. He commented that she seemed unable to leave her husband, and he made critical comments to the effect that he believed that she was doing no real work in her own analysis, and that it was "crazy" that her analyst had her lying down on the couch. He himself, he said, needed to look and be looked at. In fact, his caring for Mrs. L. had begun to diminish after a chance encounter at the theater one night. In their brief conversation she admitted to having gained five pounds and he believed that it seemed more like ten. This made her far less desirable to him.

Mr. P. loved athletics and worked out every morning, and then again in the evening, in a small gym he had built in his apartment. He came to one session reporting that he was looking forward to meeting a new woman. He had heard from the person who arranged the date that she had a body "filled with muscles" and that she worked out all day long. Mr. P., who had considerable difficulty spending even one evening alone, was at the time already conducting two simultaneous affairs in addition to the one with Mrs. L. He spent most of his time with one of the three women who, he reported, massaged him for hours and was totally in love with him although he just liked her.

As his sessions progressed, Mr. P. became more and more attached to me and to seeing me. It was clear to me that he was flirting with me as he flirted with every woman he met, boasting of his sexual prowess and of the number of orgasms he gave his women. His wardrobe was expensive and carefully put together. His grooming was immaculate at all times. When the temperature reached 100 degrees, Mr. P. arrived for his sessions in his shirt sleeves, but with no visible sign of perspiration or physical discomfort.

I found that I was wearing suits rather than my customary skirts and blouses on the days that Mr. P. came, transparently rationalizing this behavior, and that I was straightening my hair prior to his sessions. To my surprise, I did not want to incur his negative opinion of my clothing or grooming. I was not aware of any sexual feelings toward Mr. P., a man considerably younger than myself, and whom I experienced as too "plastic," a "Ken" needing a "Barbie" to complete him. But his grooming stimulated in me a most unaccustomed self-consciousness.

I began to monitor carefully my considerable countertransference reaction to Mr. P., which was quite different from the clearly negative reactions I had from time to time toward the men I wrote about in Chapter 5. At the beginning of our work he was unable to express his concerns in words, certainly not words that expressed his profound inner sadness and sense of worthlessness. Yet despite his presentation, I did not experience him as a man who denigrated women. Only intellectually did I find the shallowness of his dealings with them repellent. I saw him instead as sadly and masochistically longing for a woman to love him and affirm him—and at times as wishing to be a woman himself, and I found that my uncharacteristic self-consciousness and concern about my clothing and grooming told me things about Mr. P. Messy emotions and a messy love life were covered over by well-cut clothing and perfect grooming. My lack of sexual response to him reflected the undeveloped sexuality that he tried to disguise with the Lothario mask that he wore. His obsessive exercise, his quest for a hard-muscled woman, and his need for compliments all pointed to the kind of narcissistic deficit so typical of many of the patients described in this book and of so many men and women in our culture today.

When patients cannot verbalize what is bothering them, the therapist's countertransference can be an important tool informing the work. Ogden (1996a) reported finding himself straining to look at the designer labels on the jackets of his patient, which had seemingly been left on a chair for his scrutiny. In the process he became aware of how his own voyeurism had been stimulated by his patient's subtle behavior, and from this was able to recognize her exhibitionist wishes.

Bonaminio (1999) vividly reports the case of an adolescent boy with gender identity confusion whom he became able to understand through the use of visual cues, such as the effeminate way in which the patient touched his hair and the patient's unfashionable hairdo. In the treatment the therapist's facial expression became the focus of the patient's near-delusional attention. Bonaminio quotes the patient:

"What's wrong? What happened? Why do you look at me like that?" At that point, his brilliant and mobile eyes, still keeping eye contact, start looking carefully at my whole body, at times looking around it, until his gaze rests near my right hip, at just outside my body. In this way [he] seems to try to block the origin of my emotional expression, which he felt as very persecutory.

The first time this happened I ended up looking at the table on my right hand side, as if I had left something embarrassing lying on it. . . . The discharge now moves inside myself, making me experience transient and fleeting sensations of alteration in my body scheme. As if depersonalized, I feel some kind of growth or a hole, a pit, in my right hip. [p. 3]

Bonaminio was able to understand that he was feeling what his patient feared feeling—examined, scrutinized, and controlled. Visual issues kept emerging as the treatment deepened. The patient fantasized that he was transparent, able to be entered with a penetrating gaze by anyone who wished. The therapist interpreted: "In order to hide what you don't want to be seen, you are forced to show it through a caricature of yourself" (p. 6). In this case, as in my work with Mr. P., countertransference helped clarify what lay under the patient's more visible mask. In both cases, the countertransference informed interpretations made to the patient, but no self-disclosure was made in either case. I did not say to Mr. P., for example, "I find myself fixing my hair prior to your sessions and wonder if we could explore what that's about." Some therapists might find such an intervention useful. But I make this point to indicate that countertransference can be used without self-disclosure by those whose theoretical inclinations steer them away from it.

Furthermore, I think there are reasons to be cautious about self-disclosure in work with these patients. It is not always a simple matter to handle, particularly when it is *my* body and *my* looks are the subject of my patient's preoccupations, or when it seems that such issues are just beneath the surface or are being raised as thinly veiled displacements.

It appears to me that at the beginning of treatment, and sometimes for many years after that, narcissistic patients tend to experience the therapist as a blur, both visually and auditorily. Their self-object differentiation is poor enough that self and object are ill-demarcated. Many narcissistic patients experience any personal comments by the therapist as alien. They either say directly or imply indirectly, "Who invited you to talk? This is my session, my time." They are needy and hungry for exclusive attention, and they do not focus on the attributes of the therapist. They exclude him (as they themselves have been excluded). I believe that this has to do with envy, which destroys the capacity to experience others in benign ways that feed the self. Paradoxically, much of what the therapist has to say or offer beyond becoming an object with whom to identify cannot be internalized. They are surrounded by interpersonal possibilities but unable to make use of them. The therapist's countertransference is more likely to be related to feeling ignored and excluded than to the use being made of him in the patient's thoughts. It is this kind of situation that gives rise to the common but unfortunate type of self-disclosure in which the therapist tries to bring interpersonal life to the session by telling the patient about himself.

Jacobs (1999) has thoughtfully classified three types of self-disclosure: (1) slips and errors, (2) deliberate acts of sharing phenomena arising in the therapist's mind during the session, and (3) answering questions about one's self. Jacobs notes that some patients may hear disclosures differently from the way that the therapist intended them, causing considerable pain and blocking progress. On the other hand, withholding can repeat the experience of nonresponsive parenting and thus shut down fantasy. Clinical decisions must be made, therefore, depending on the patient, where he is in the therapy, and the state of the transference. Jacobs reported a case in which looks and looking were manifest. A woman patient, who had been critical of his appearance, suddenly began to change and describe him sympathetically. He realized that he had left within her view a copy of the alumni magazine of his college, which was also the one her first and greatest love had attended. He reports, "I had a need to alter the patient's perception of me, to impress her, and to deflect her criticism" (p. 167). Jacobs feels that for some people with narcissistic deficits insight and the working through of conflict are not enough; that they may need "a kind of neodevelopmental process in which their internalization of the analyst's view of them, as selectively disclosed in the course of analytic work, aids in the development of a more realistic self-representation" (p. 181).

My experience of Jacobs's three categories is that slips and errors (such as the kind of effort to enliven a session that I described above) usually are problematic, but can sometimes be turned into something useful, grist for the mill. An example of this is the incident I described in Chapter 7, when I told Ms. C. about my trip to London. The patients I am dealing with here do not usually ask questions. They do not want to know about me; in fact questions would be proof of great advances in development. So the third category isn't relevant here, and I will limit myself to the second category—those cases in which I might voluntarily disclose to the patient something about myself or my reactions to the issues at hand.

My own theoretical belief is that psychotherapeutic treatment is about the patient, and about understanding the patient's projections. The patient will seek to enhance me or detract from me, make me visible or invisible, as he or she needs to do. As Mrs. B., whom I described in Chapter 6, began to become more aware of herself, she became more aware of me as a separate person. At one point, speaking of her perception that it was socially desirable in her group to be extremely thin, "a social x-ray" as Tom Wolfe (1987) put it in *The Bonfire of the Vanities*, she gently said to me, "I guess it's no secret that you are bigger than me," her way of speaking about my own visible lack of adherence to such an ideal. I told her that although I was aware of the cultural ideal, I did not agree with it— that I could not do my work if I were constantly hungry and physically uncomfortable, that my own social and professional groups shared my belief that one should eat and exercise to be healthy, and that starving and overexercising were neither healthy nor valuable. With that admission, I believe I gave Mrs. B. permission (1) to allow herself to be aware that other group ideals existed; (2) to follow the dictates of her own social group, if she so wished, and to be different from me, if she so wished; (3) but also if she wished, to think things out and be different from those in her group.

The therapist's body can be a mirror, reflecting back to the patient who the patient is, by being different from or similar to the patient, different from or similar to the societal ideal. The therapist's physical imperfections can serve as a relief from the demands of harsh ego-ideals and/or from characterological competitiveness.

The kinds of self-disclosure I believe are suitable in psychotherapy are those that model a vision of psychologically healthy ways in which to live. I have had in my practice physicians who want to play music, or attorneys who want to write, and who wonder if this means that they are conflicted and troubled about their choice of profession. I am willing to say, in such cases, that I think one's work goes better when one uses other brain cells from time to time, and that I myself have a passion for art and in my free time give lectures in a museum.

Patients reflect back to me their perceptions of my body in dreams, or less directly in their allusions to other women. I, like all therapists, appear in my patients' dreams with different kinds of bodies, at various ages, and so forth. It is quite a challenge to maintain a strong sense of one's self at the end of each day! I have been dreamed of as a go-go dancer, a biker chick, and an elderly nurse with deep gashes in my cheeks and breasts so long that I can throw them over my back. One patient told me that she was convinced for years that because I was blond and she brunette, there was no way I could possibly understand her. One very pretty woman patient told me that she was glad that I was pretty, because I would not plague her with gratuitous attacks the way unpretty, envious women did. Another patient, on the other hand, told me that she would not hire a music coach who was so pretty that she could not bear to be in the same room with her, the intimation being, of course, that there was no such problem with me! Listening for references to the transference in dreams, memories, and associations, I often find my physical characteristics present, as they are, or in distortion. I was ill with the flu one winter and gained some weight. A physician patient told me that he was afraid I would die, just as he worried that his overweight father, who had had a heart problem, would die. Considerable oedipal material including erotic wishes for me as the oedipal mother were emerging at the same time. My patient was a parentified child who took care of his parents. He was also an adult physician. So his concern for me was in part a defense against wishes that his father would die; a defense against recognizing the emerging erotic wishes for me, representing his mother; a characterological (and defensive) taking care of others; and a professional opinion—all at the same time. In this case, I interpreted the transference, rather than acknowledge the reality that I had gained weight. I would be less than candid however, if I did not admit that on the very day my physician patient spoke about my weight I started a diet!

The transference picture can be confusing when read in displaced form. For example, one male patient reported feeling more sexually attracted to one of his woman lovers than to the others and was puzzled as to why. He described three characteristics descriptive of her. Only one applied to me. To what extent does one understand it as transference?

Most of my patients do not really see me, and they do not seem to notice physical changes in me such as new clothing or a haircut. They often do not notice changes in my office furniture or layout. It may be that the need to see me as constant blocks perceptions of change. Envy may do the same. After a month's vacation one year, I returned with a dark suntan, quite a drastic change from my normally pale skin. One patient came in and challenged me: "Where's your tan?" In such cases I do not bring myself into the picture. I am there for their projections.

On the other hand, I do frequently address a specific kind of comment.

Ms. R., a 25-year-old woman, said to me: "I do not know why I am agreeing to work all weekend at the office. I would like to meet a man. This is the best time of my life. I look my best, my body is at my best, before I begin to sag . . . [silence] not to be rude."

I asked: "Be rude, what are you speaking about?"

"Well, you are my mother's age and her body is not what it used to be and when I speak I hope that you are not feeling hurt."

The patient in this instance was denying her very strong wishes to hurt me, which became quite manifest in the next few sessions.

Reality factors do trigger transferences and resistances. I enjoy shopping for and wearing fashionable clothes. Since I sit all day and must be comfortable, I wear looser-fitting and longer clothing than I wear when I'm not working. I try not to wear clothing that is visually distracting. I am aware of the visual impact of my clothing, jewelry, and possessions upon my patients, especially those who do not have much money and/or are envious; at times I may re-frain from wearing a new suit or pair of shoes in order to be sen-sitive to a particular patient's feelings, just as I might not raise the fee of someone who has just lost a job, or notify a patient about an upcoming vacation the day that he has broken up with his girl-friend.

I work in an office in my apartment in which the decor is quite colorful, filled with art and small objects, visual stimuli that often come up in my patient's associations and dreams. I personally feel comforted and soothed by the libidinal pleasures offered by this decor and I would feel very deprived if I had to work in a more traditional and visually blander office setting.

My experience working at home is what has convinced me of the preponderance of transference factors over reality factors in psychotherapeutic treatment. My patients could be privy, if they wished to be, to all kinds of personal information about me, but they don't try to find out about my life. They are just not inter-ested until the point comes much later in treatment when reality factors begin to converge with transference wishes and fears. Over the past twenty-five years, my patients have met, in chance en-counters, my children, my significant others, my friendly neigh-bors, and my colleagues. This has done little to disabuse some of them of their transference fantasies of me as celibate, friendless, and isolated.

In this book I have emphasized the importance of listening to the concrete patient's associations, and of participating in concrete dialogue. I've also acknowledged how difficult this can be. I am no different in that respect. My struggle to become a professional woman meant disengaging myself from timeless, slow-paced con-versations and often enjoyable gossip with women my age who do not work and do not have the time management concerns that I have. To speak concretely about such issues as thinness, diets, plas-tic surgery, and cooking for me represents going back to the place that I originally came from, and worked very hard to leave. It is pleasurable, for it represents my bond with other women, especially my mother, but I also experience it as regressive and dangerous, an unproductive space. I must remind myself when I am working with patients who have long been deprived of the formative aspects of such concrete language, that this space is very productive for them, and it requires my being in it with them.

Like many of my patients, I grew up in a family that considered appearance important and judged people by what they looked like. Fortunately for me, my formative years saw icons like the curvaceous and voluptuous Marilyn Monroe, Brigitte Bardot, and Elizabeth Taylor (just an earlier form of sexism, of course) rather than the waiflike Kate Moss and Gwyneth Paltrow. My developing feelings about my rounded body were organized around different ideals from those prevalent today. I was fortunate to have received a lot of nurturance and attention for my intellectual pursuits and achievements. Nevertheless, I live in the same world as my patients do, have dieted when I thought it necessary, have involved myself more and less willingly in various beauty interventions, and have had to cope with the bodily changes that accompany middle age and menopause. There are times when I have to sort out on a daily basis where my issues end and theirs begin. I wonder sometimes how much of my day should go into the pursuit of beauty instead of my work or interests or friends or family. I do not feel a burning need to be looked at constantly, and my work and other interests are extremely gratifying, but a certain amount of social approval does comes from looking good. When I go to my health club, I am greeted by age-mates who resemble Ogden's patient, or Mrs. B. from Chapter 6. These women do not work, but they work out several hours daily, going to the club twice a day. They are deeply involved with their trainers around the development of their muscles. I would be less than honest if I pretended that I am impervious to these social demands.

Issues of body narcissism surround me constantly. I overhear bits of conversations on the train: a 30-year-old man says to his friend, "You should see her—all muscles. She works out three times a day." His counterpart thirty years ago might have said, "You should see her—she's stacked." It is impossible not to notice that women are still being treated as objects, despite all the advances they have seemingly made. Once bartered by the pound in the Middle East, and foot-bound to be desirable in China, women now read fashion magazines that describe models with perfect bodies: hard like a bamboo pole. I mentioned this to a very well-known educator I met at a party recently and his response was, "Well, I suppose that it is just women's fate that they are supposed to look like sticks." Women, too, accept this fate and do not question it. There is little sense of outrage on their part.

I find it frightening that this ideal—see also Faludi (1991), Gilman (1998), Greer (1999), and Wolf (1991)—tends to obliterate the characteristics that make a woman a woman. I work with women who cannot become pregnant because of excessive dieting or who fear becoming pregnant because they will gain weight. Young women in their twenties are developing osteoporosis. Many are so thin that they do not have breasts. They then incur much risk having implants and the health threats—as evidenced in a host of law-suits—attendant upon them. Teenage girls who develop large breasts have them reduced and sacrifice forever sexual sensitivity as well as the possibility of ever being able to breast-feed. The latest development, I hear, is having several ribs removed in order to look thin. Women are praised for working out all day rather than working at something productive—a number of young married women I know left their jobs after they gave birth mainly in order to have time to work out, rather than to tend to their babies. They find that they feel more successful, and that they get more social approval, for being thin and toned than for working. I have spoken to numbers of successful single career women, divorced or widowed, who complain that they have difficulty competing in the social arena with women who do not work and who spend all their time in the search of beauty.

I regard this as yet another war against women, one that women themselves permit, participate in, and often embrace. Women have been freed from their kitchens only to be chained to their treadmills. Almost every week, the Sunday Styles section of *The New York Times* contains another story about role-model women who jockey for the best table in the best restaurants and then order lettuce and bottled water for lunch. At least Betty Crocker produced some biscuits, some cakes. The statement "She works out all day" may be the contemporary ritual purification of our culture's vision of the evil woman, replacing the former "She cooked and cleaned all day long" and "You could eat off her floor."

Just as men may gratify masochistic wishes through overwork or being battered in contact sports, women punish themselves by depriving themselves of food and hurting their bodies in strenuous exercise. Some will not leave their homes if they gain a pound, for their clothes, purchased in small sizes, do not fit. It is unthinkable for them to purchase larger sizes. I know of a couple who returned early from their honeymoon after the new bride panicked in a foreign land because "all the food there was fattening."

Bordo (1999) has documented the fact that in a curious form of parity, men today find themselves to be in similar positions as women. (I would consider this "equal-opportunity victimization.") Men are increasingly getting into body-building, bulimia, and cosmetic surgery.

These issues cannot simply be dismissed as artifacts of sexism or superficiality. I met at a party a number of years ago an elegant woman who spent two years of her adolescence at Auschwitz. I asked her how she had been able to survive this experience. She told me that she and a friend, dressed in rags and forced to spend the day sweeping and cleaning, planned each day the trip to Paris they would make when they were released, with particular focus on the clothes they would buy and how they would have their hair styled. Such is the importance of appearance and its libidinal function in the psyche.

In a related twist on this issue, I have also seen patients whose life goals are being sabotaged by insufficient attention to their appearance. It is hard enough to address these issues tactfully when the patients themselves bring them up, but it is even harder when they avoid them altogether, or actively refuse the therapist an opening. I saw a talented young lawyer who was applying for jobs in conservative Wall Street firms. He refused to compromise his principles by cutting his long hair and shaving his beard, and so was not offered a job. My addressing his refusal to make these changes resulted in barrages of insults about my bourgeois clothing and possessions. In the case of a female lawyer, it was apparent to me that her seductive clothing and long sexy hairdo were compromising her career development. Here, too, I met with abuse rather than a collaborative effort on the part of the patient.

Analyzing issues about a patient's appearance is one of the most difficult and painful tasks of a therapist. It opens up all kinds of fantasies and memories that are usually related to shame and humiliation, and sometimes to sexual abuse. The therapist's wish to avoid hurting the patient is coupled, after a little experience, with the wish to protect herself, for inevitably such attention to the patient's appearance, to his body or clothing, will elicit a severe attack on the therapist's person. What ensues may not in fact be "grist for the mill," that time-honored rationalization for therapeutic bloodbaths. It may result in termination, or if not that then in so much disruption of the positive transference that previous treatment gains may be reversed. It is vital to deal with these issues, but equally vital to deal with them with extreme tact, especially when it is not the patient who brings them up.

Psychotherapists are supposed to be neutral, and yet at the same time manage to impart to their patients a vision of what makes for a psychologically healthy and meaningful life. In discussing here the unhealthy end of the spectrum of body narcissism, I don't want to give short shrift to the importance of the healthy end, feeling that one looks good and feels good, and doing one's best to remain healthy. I regard our culture's obsession with thinness to be wasteful and unhealthy. I said to one woman patient who complained that her life had no meaning, yet spent a good part of each day at the gym on a treadmill: "Do you want them to write on your tombstone:'She stayed thin'?" I believe that there is too much important work to be done in this world to allow our patients to remain unquestioningly trapped in values that are so counterproductive and even destructive to our culture.

I have stated my position on these matters in a self-revealing manner most unlike my usual stance, because although I feel that therapists, despite being experts on human behavior and human foibles, should be neutral with respect to most values, I feel that they must not be neutral with respect to values that undermine mental or physical health. The therapist who is critical of some aspect of the broader society may be perceived as a noble rebel (or alternatively as an abject failure) by his patients and society alike. The therapist must lead the patient on a new journey, for as Schafer (1970) so eloquently put it, "The patient is simultaneously an ardent defender of the existing society that is to be reordered or replaced as well the potential center of a new society he is about to bring about. There is an inner hell to be traversed and an inner society to be transformed" (p. 283).

IV

APPLIED
PSYCHOANALYSIS

9

The Artist as Spectator
and Spectacle

Art is the mirror of life.

Heinrich Wolfflin (1932, p. 226)

$\mathcal{I}$n this chapter and in the one that follows I venture into applied psychoanalysis. I use some of the additional lenses that other fields provide to explore even more of the twists and turns of looking and being looked at, of seeing and being seen. I share Kuspit's (1998) conviction that "applied psychoanalysis is only nominally and conveniently about the artist; it is about the psychological workings of a certain culture as reflected in its so-called works of art" (p. 10).

CONTEMPORARY ART REFLECTS CONTEMPORARY CULTURE

In this exploration I discuss artworks with an eye to issues of spectatorship and spectacle rather than beauty. Late-twentieth-century art has an edge to it that reflects the culture around it, and this is a culture in which spectatorship reigns. Despite the great emphasis placed on beauty and on physical perfection, it is paradoxically true that human beauty is seldom depicted in contemporary art. Instead, many contemporary artists concern themselves with issues of human conflict and human paradox in works in which they themselves are either spectacle or spectator. Their art can be characterized as "desublimated" and often contains mundane content, in striking parallel to the concreteness and often mundane content presented by many contemporary psychotherapy patients.

The works that I discuss here have led some viewers to believe that the artists themselves are disturbed. In general, this does not seem to be the case. These works are of a genre in which madness is *simulated*. The artists discussed here are not part of a "lunatic fringe" but are known and respected by the art community. Therefore, when I characterize a particular artist as an exhibitionist or as a voyeur I am not making a diagnosis. I am commenting only on the art that he makes, an art that reflects something inside him that in turn reflects the culture.

The history of art is intrinsically tied to theories about vision and about what the eye can do and can process. From the anamorphosists of the sixteenth century, who made paintings, drawings, and prints that seemed distorted when viewed frontally, but looked normal from the side or in a mirror, to the surrealists of the twentieth century, whose distorted images, transcending the real, were supposedly drawn from the unconscious and based on dreams, artists have played with and challenged the optical experience. Much surrealist art had to do with fragmented bodies with eyes and windows so that people could be looked at inside and out (Jay 1993). Magritte, for example, addressed the "betrayal of images," and showed how words introduced into a painting could challenge its visual meaning, such as in *Ceci n'est pas un pipe* (1928) in which the words (in English translation "this is not . . . ") make the viewer doubt what he clearly sees (a pipe).

As in the great art historian Heinrich Wolfflin's epigram cited above, some of the art made in recent years can be experienced as a mirror of life in the therapist's consulting room. I will demonstrate this by juxtaposing clinical vignettes with the artworks they reflect.

CONTEMPORARY ART REFLECTS CONTEMPORARY PSYCHE

The writings of Freud, Klein, Winnicott, Lacan, and others have greatly influenced the artists of the last thirty-five years. Psychoanalytic writings are now included in the curricula of our major art schools and psychotherapeutic treatment is now a part of many artists' lives. Freud's insistence that his patients speak about the unspeakable broke long-standing cultural taboos. As a result of his work and the openness it encouraged, contemporary artists now feel free to express visually ideas that were once forbidden, and to show what never before could be seen, at least in public.

This development affords psychotherapists an alternative pathway for considering and working through residual discomforts and anxieties about the body and its functions: becoming familiar with a branch of contemporary art that has to do with body and gender. In my experience responses to visual representations can be at times more visceral and immediate, more emotional and more compelling, than they are to auditory communications. Visual sensations tend to be experienced more directly, and thus can short-circuit the kinds of intellectualizations and denial to which words lend themselves.

My focus here is on the related psychological issues of exhibitionism and voyeurism as they are represented in art, specifically in a selection of artworks that challenge and activate therapists' affects at least as much as do our exhibitionistic and voyeuristic patients. In the first part of this chapter, I discuss the works of women artists in which these issues are manifest, particularly in the context of power and control. I then proceed to a discussion of analogous work done by male artists, in which the artist appears first in a masochist way as spectacle and finally as spectator of the taboo (looking at death itself). I consider art of this type to be desublimated. The very word *sublimation* connotes the *sublime*. This art is anything but sublime. Following a tradition set by Duchamp (who early in the second decade of the twentieth century presented mundane, everyday objects—"ready-mades" such as brooms, bicycle wheels, urinals—as art), contemporary art differs from the art of previous centuries in its closeness to everyday life, to the mundane, and to the abject and the debased.

Take for example the work of performance artist Mona Hatoum, who constructed a video installation in which a doctor produced interior and exterior views of her body using endoscopy, colonoscopy, and echography. Displayed on the floor inside a cylinder large enough for a person to go into, and accompanied by a soundtrack of the artist's heartbeat, the circular-shaped images of Hatoum's orifices, tissues, blood vessels, and internal organs created the effect that one was standing on the rim of a volcano looking down into its crater, evoking in the viewer a sense of imminent sense of danger and dislocation. This artist exhibited herself on the inside.

In a similar vein, there are patients who enact in the clinical situation a wish to be looked at by, or to look at, the therapist. Often therapists do not analyze these exchanges or really understand them. Art can help us to better understand these exchanges. The performance artists I discuss here evoke in their viewers affects that are similar in many ways to those evoked within the patient–therapist dyad. They compel their viewers to look at sights that, given the choice, they might well have chosen not to look at. They make the viewer into a reluctant spectator (see Chapter 6). The viewer, like the therapist, is there to look, but has generally not bargained for what is displayed for him to see. In addition, these artists treat their own bodies, and the bodies of others, as objects, just as we find some of our patients do.

In *Three Contributions to the Theory of Sex* Freud (1905b) commented on the pleasures of looking and observing, and noted that vision is implicated in a system of control. Voyeurism gives pleasure by enabling one to position oneself against another, by enabling one to submit the other to a distanced and controlling gaze. (This power aspect of the gaze is the predominant one I will deal with in this chapter, as opposed to the less aggressive bonding aspect covered in Chapter 3.) To be both subject and object of the gaze is the essence of exhibitionism. Since the body is covered, sexual curiosity is continuously aroused. This is normal.

Freud noted that inhibitions around voyeurism and exhibitionism are related to conflicts around sadism, and that they develop in an interconnected way with shame issues around voiding and excretion, since the excretory organs and the genitals are in such close proximity. (See Chapters 2 and 3, to review Freud's theory.)

My view of exhibitionism, voyeurism, and perversion is that they are culturally defined concepts; what is permitted and what is forbidden varies from culture to culture and in gender-specific ways (see Chapter 2). Issues of time and repetition are quite relevant, for the perversions are based on needs and fantasies that are insatiable. A mere peek will not suffice for the voyeur, nor will a mere flash suffice for the exhibitionist. Therefore, one cannot label as a pervert one who has had a one-time perverse experience. The inner drive of the pervert will lead him to endless repetition of the perverse act, which even so ultimately brings him no satisfaction.

The theme of the power of the beholder and the powerlessness of the subject of the gaze as Freud conceptualized it has permeated the writings of feminist theorists and art and film critics in recent years. It is impossible in this context to do justice to the richness of the ideas that exist in that literature. As one example, Irigaray (1978), one of the French *antivisuels* influenced by Sartre, noted:

Investment in the look is not as privileged in women as in men. More than other senses, the eye objectifies and masters. It sets at a distance and maintains a distance. In our culture the predominance of the look over smell, taste, touch and hearing has brought about an impoverishment of body relations. The moment the look dominates, the body loses its materiality. [p. 50]

John Berger (1972) is widely noted for this statement:

Men act and women appear. Women watch themselves being looked at. This determines not only most relations between men and women, but also the relation of women to themselves. The surveyor of woman in herself is male, the surveyed female. Thus she turns herself into an object and most particularly an object of vision—a sight. [p. 47]

Griselda Pollack (1988) commented on the "sexual politics of looking" of the late nineteenth-century "flâneur," the impassive male stroller:

> The flâneur symbolizes the privilege or freedom to move about the public arenas of the city observing but never interacting, consuming the sights through a controlling but rarely acknowledged gaze, directed as much at other people as at the goods for sale. The flâneur embodies the gaze of modernity which is both covetous and erotic. . . . But the flâneur is an exclusively masculine type. [p. 67]

She continues: "One of the major means by which modernity is thus reworked is by the rearticulation of traditional space so that it ceases to function primarily as the space of sight for a mastery of gaze, but becomes the locus of relationships" (p. 87).

In Laura Mulvey's (1975) classic Freudian and Lacanian tract, "Visual Pleasure and Narrative Cinema" (see Chapter 10), she noted that films give us pleasure rooted in voyeurism, fetishism, narcissism, and identifications with the ego ideal of the male gaze. Mulvey is famous for this assertion: "Women are passive icons of the male gaze and the camera's gaze is male. Women connote 'to-be-looked-at-ness'" (p. 366). Doane (1988–1989) and Gamman and Marshment (1989) have addressed some of these same issues. Contemporary women artists, who like the rest of us have been exposed to these writings and have thought and spoken about these issues, are now engaged in actively photographing themselves, other women, and men as well; they (and we) are much more aware of the power structures tied up in their representations of gender.

A recent exhibition at the MIT List Center entitled "Mirror Images: Women, Surrealism, and Self-Representation" (Chadwick 1998) showed a number of women artists' self-portraits, influenced by surrealism, in which the female body is explored in a wide, nontraditional variety of ways, asserting a feminine identity and notion of femaleness that extended beyond traditional stereotypes. Knafo (in press) has done some noteworthy research on this subject.

Self-portraits were typically done by artists seated between mirror and canvas, and today the art photograph often replaces or supplements the mirror. In the case of the self-portrait, the artist requires the viewer to look at the artist, and to give the artist narcissistically gratifying time and attention. Chuck Close, when asked why he made his paintings of himself and his friends so large, quite blatantly acknowledged his exhibitionistic agenda when he replied that it would then take the viewer so much longer to pass on by!

In his discussion of the late Francis Bacon's portraits, Winnicott wrote about Bacon's narcissistic strivings: "In looking at faces, he seems to me to be painfully striving towards being seen" (1971, p. 114). He reported that Bacon said "he likes to have glass over his pictures, because when people look at the picture, what they see is not just a picture; they might, in fact, see themselves" (p. 117).

This theme of the mirror, and particularly of women admiring themselves in mirrors, is a prevalent one all through art history, a topic thoroughly addressed by Schneider (1985) and Chadwick (1998). Elizabeth Sussman (1996), discussing a show of Nan Goldin's photographs called "I'll Be Your Mirror," wrote that the traditional doubling of the view of the woman by placing her before a mirror increases the "visual fiction of possession" by the male artist and the male spectator. In Goldin's photographs, on the other hand, the sense of male possession traditionally suggested by the mirror image is reversed. Here the doubling acts as self-confirmation and self-possession, since the artist is a woman herself.

THE WOMAN ARTIST

I will now examine the works of six contemporary women artists for their voyeuristic, exhibitionistic, and perverse meanings. In some of these works the artist herself is a performer, her face, body, and actions the subject matter of the piece. My understanding of these works is that the viewer is drawn into a "perverse" relationship with the artist, feeling coerced to gaze at her and coerced to see what the viewer might have chosen (if given the choice) not to see. The artist in such works is functioning in an exhibitionist mode, and the works themselves seem to be derivatives of issues around exhibitionism. In other works, the artist herself seems to be functioning as a voyeur. The subject of her piece seems to be imprisoned by her in an analogously perverse relationship; that is, if given the choice, one feels, she would have chosen not to be viewed by others, especially strangers, in that particular way. The viewer in this case becomes in a way the "voyeur of a voyeur." In both of these cases the viewer is drawn into a perverse relationship with the subject of the art work. The sadomasochism of the artist crosses the boundary from the art object to the viewer, who must then absorb and master it. The viewer is in a sense psychologically bound, and a "rape of the eye" occurs. It is most probably for this reason that this kind of art makes many people angry and defensive enough to reject both the works and the artists. It activates conflicts around scoptophilia, exhibitionism, voyeurism, and sadomasochism—in short, it evokes a lot of anxiety.

I believe that patients involved with us in perverse transferences, who induce us to look at them in ways that make us uncomfortable, or in which we feel trapped, activate similar responses in us. Therefore, I will intersperse my exploration of these themes in art with some clinical vignettes that seem to me to be analogues that speak for themselves. In each clinical case, it becomes apparent that the underlying perverse structure in the patient's psyche was interfering with the patient's work and/or love life.

The Woman Artist as Exhibitionist and the Viewer as Voyeur

Carolee Schneeman, Janine Antoni, and Orlan are representative of the many women artists who use their own bodies as the subject of the gaze; Cindy Sherman, Hannah Wilke, and Ana Mendieta were their antecedents.

Sherman is a talented and well-known contemporary photographer. Her work has evolved from a series of photographs of herself in various film roles (her 1978 "Film Still" series) through her assumptions of different identities from history, art history, and contemporary culture (1983). She attempted in these works to control the objectification of women by making herself the object of her own gaze as well as of the gaze of others.

Hannah Wilke died of lymphoma in 1993. In her early performance work, she posed nude in ways that both extolled and ridiculed the female nude in art, for example, urinating standing up like a man, or holding a gun (1978). In the late 1970s her work became more serious as her mother had cancer and she photographed the ravages of the disease upon her mother's body. In the 1980s her own tragic turn came. She photographed herself between 1991 and 1992, and gave her husband instructions as to how to photograph her in the various stages of her illness up until her death.

Ana Mendieta lost her homeland, Cuba, as a young woman. Comparing this trauma with being ripped from the womb, she imprinted herself on the earth and photographed her imprint, pressing it into sand, etching it with dirt, drawing it in blood, and torching it in flames (1973–1977, 1976). Her silhouette splayed on the earth was an uncanny premonition of her death in a fall from a window.

Works related to these have been done by male artists, some of whom will be discussed later in this chapter: Vito Acconci, Bruce Nauman, Chris Burden, Yasumasa Morimura, Yves Klein, Bob

Flanagan, Lucas Samaras, and Arno Minkinnen. But their concern is not the issue of being the object of the other sex's gaze and the power that is lost in being so.

Carolee Schneeman

Carolee Schneeman has been a pioneer since the 1960s in the development of the genres that eventually came to be defined as body art, performance art, and installation. She believed that the body is in the eye, that sensations received visually take hold in the total organism. Her work was controversial and marginalized because of the directness of the sexuality it expressed. Although it would seem that a woman artist's dictation of the terms on which she would allow her body to be viewed would be a liberating step, her work was not embraced by feminists because it was not explicitly anti-patriarchal.

In *Eye-body* (1963), a happening (happenings were art events of the 1960s and 1970s that combined planned and spontaneous performance with artistic creation and found materials, often including audience participation), the original action consisted of a number of self-transformations undertaken by Schneeman, who interacted with various materials in her studio in a nude, trance-like state. These were captured on film over the course of a couple of hours. Her performance combined sensuality, myth, and humor. In *Meat Joy* (1964), slabs of raw chicken, sausage, and fish were thrown onto a wet paint-splattered floor by eight barely dressed performers who then interacted with the pieces of meat and with each other. In *Bloodwork* (1972), Schneeman hung the actual record of her daily menstrual blood dripped onto paper on a wall. In two of her best known performance/installation works, *Up to and Including Her Limits* (1973–1975) and *Interior Scroll* (1975), the artist expressed her belief that archetypal gestures are pulled from the collective unconscious into the present. In the first work, a video featured Schneeman, long crayons attached to her hands, suspended for long periods of time in a harness, her entire body used as a tool, as she created drawings across massive paper surfaces that the sweep of the rope allowed her to reach. In *Interior Scroll*, one of her most notorious performances, Schneeman stood naked, slowly unwinding a scroll on which was printed a text on "vaginality" from inside her vagina while reading it to her audience. Her body was presented as the source of knowledge. In the 1980s her amalgamation of performance, eroticism, and photography, and a search for the historical antecedents of her repertoire of archetypal forms, led to *Infinity Kisses* (1982–1986), a filmed documentation of the daily kissing ritual with one of her cats, each separate image representing a single day in which she was awakened by the sensation of the cat pushing its tongue into her mouth.

Strong visceral reactions to Schneeman's work echo in more muted form in the following clinical vignette. (In this vignette and those that follow it I have underscored the patient's exhibitionism and voyeurism, and set aside the very complex accompanying psychodynamic picture.)

Lucy

Lucy, a tall, dark-haired 28-year-old cable TV news commentator, much accustomed to being in the public eye, found herself unable to leave her 4-month-old baby at home to return to work, as she had planned. She would not even leave her to return to therapy, and so Dr. Z. invited her to come for her sessions with the baby, to understand what was happening.

She arrived at Dr. Z.'s office in a mink-lined coat carrying her baby daughter, who was dressed in a snowsuit made of the same fabric and similarly mink-lined. She and her daughter had been posing together for publicity shots; articles about her as a new mother had been published in a variety of newspapers and magazines. She fantasized bringing her daughter to work and appearing with her on television.

In the session, the beautiful mother could not take her eyes from her beautiful baby. She stared at her throughout the session. She told Dr. Z. about her adoration of the baby, her surprise at how totally she had embraced being a mother, and her lack of interest in pursuing her career without the baby. When the baby cried, she found her pacifier, licked it clean, and put it in the baby's mouth. She reported a dream in which she was in a theater and it was unclear as to whether she was in the audience or onstage. She found herself to be intensely jealous of her nanny's attachment to the baby, and was afraid that the baby would love the nanny more than herself; when they were in a room together she thought that the baby looked at the nanny more than at her. At that point in the session, the baby cried again, and the mother opened her blouse and nursed her, the two locked together in bliss.

Dr. Z. felt herself to be a reluctant spectator to this scene, which bordered on the perverse. The issue was not so much the breast-feeding of the baby, but the entire context in which it occurred. The potential for this mother's exhibitionistic use of her baby emerged in the therapist's mind as a serious and daunting possibility, especially since at the time the therapist was being reminded daily of the murder of the child beauty queen Jon-Benet Ramsey. Over the course of the next few months, Dr. Z. focused her interventions on Lucy's conflicts around exhibitionism. This work enabled her to separate from the baby sufficiently to resume her work.

Janine Antoni

Janine Antoni's works, which were influenced by artists of the 1960s and 1970s such as Schneeman, combined sculpture and performance, and carried messages about female gender roles. The viewer had to look at Antoni herself for the length of her performance, and to think about the artist herself during the process of creation, empathizing, perhaps, with her pain and suffering while contemplating the finished piece. Antoni has said that she does not begin with an idea, but rather with the experience, the process. The meaning of the piece becomes apparent only later.

In *Chocolate Gnaw* and *Lard Gnaw* (1992), 600-pound pieces of chocolate and lard were cast as cubes and then chewed on by her; she then spat out the chewed chocolate and lard. Her mouth was the tool. The chewing took one and a half months. At first the viewer, who does not see the actual performance, which was private, examines the finished Donald Judd-like cubes, which are aesthetically pleasing objects. When the viewer learns, however, of the process, that is, of how the art was made, pleasure is turned into pain as the viewer contemplates the artist's hunger, her struggle with intake of fattening foods, which are forbidden to women in our society, the biting and spitting impulses activated in the artist as a result of oral frustration. The viewer imagines the sores in the artist's mouth, the pain in her teeth, concrete symbols of the masochistic female role. The viewer who seeks a pleasant experience of objective aesthetic contemplation finds himself or herself instead experiencing what it is like to be inside the artist's aching mouth.

Similarly, *Lick and Lather* (1994) presents the viewer with fourteen classical busts of Antoni's face and throat, seven made of chocolate and seven of soap. By licking and washing, Antoni changed the appearance of each. She "interacted" with them either by lathering her hands on her own face or by licking her sculpted image as a way of changing its physical look. The viewer is here, too, drawn into the artist's bodily experience, feeling the blisters and pain in her tongue and mouth. Antoni's work has been characterized both as narcissistic and as a manifestation of narcissistic disavowal, for at first she presents her own image but then she effaces it.

In *Loving Care* (1992–96), a performance piece done live and available on video, Antoni puts the Loving Care brand of hair dye on her long mane and does a floor-level dance, mopping the floor with her hair, a commentary that condenses the notion of woman as servant with the notion of woman as servant to beauty. Painting and mopping the floor are given parity. Observers must gradually back out of the room as she at first invites and then rejects their view, and in her own way with her dye-covered mane of hair controls it. She thus reverses the notion that the one who looks is in control. In the beginning she is on the floor and vulnerable, but she gains power as she makes the spectators leave. The artist Yves Klein in Paris in the 1960s had used women's bodies as paintbrushes in his works. But the women artist who uses her own body is now the one supposedly in control.

In *Slumber* (1996), an installation piece that occupied a large space at the Guggenheim Museum in Soho and in other places, Antoni slept in the gallery connected to an electroencephalograph (EEG) machine that recorded her rapid eye movement (REM) sleep patterns. The REM printout became a drawing of her unconscious. During the day, she wove a blanket at a huge loom using her EEG patterns as a design and chatted with visitors. Each day in each city in which *Slumber* was showing, she went to a department store and purchased a nightgown to be worn when she slept in the museum that night. Ribbons torn from the cloth of her nightgown were sewn into the woven blanket that contained the record of her dreams. Antoni sat at the loom or on the bed graciously speaking to admiring visitors about her work. When asked about the pain that seems to accompany all of her work (sleeping in the cold museum being one example), she replied that it is about being disciplined, about taking her body to its limits, about seeing how far it can go. For her it is not, at least consciously, about being in pain, but about transcending pain. Here, too, viewers are at first invited in and then are asked to leave when the museum closes and Antoni goes to sleep, once more controlling the gaze.

In *3 Legged Race* (1996), a site-specific piece, she renovated the kitchen of a slum apartment. She hoisted herself into the room by pulley, painted the walls white, picked up linoleum layered with newspapers going back seventy-five years, and laid down a new floor. Playing voyeur herself, she read the love letters of the long-departed woman tenant who had lived there. Visitors viewed her work through a window. They could not enter the room. Once again, the viewer-voyeur is kept at a controlled distance.

Works such as these have been characterized as fetishistic, denying the viewer any clear representation of the artist's body, but presenting materials that have come in direct contact with it: the paint, the floor, and the rope. In other words, the materials include the blanket, the nightgown, the chocolate, the lard, the hair dye. In this case, as in the others presented here, the viewer becomes more involved with the artist and her body than with the artistic work itself.

Orlan

Whereas Antoni's work curiously evokes sympathy in the spectator (perhaps due to her youth and beauty), the work of the French performance artist Orlan, who works with similar themes, generally evokes viewers' antipathy for her art dealer, her doctors, her nurses, and most of all for the artist herself. Her material is her own body and skin. She has given her body itself to art. She produced two series of videotapes of plastic surgeries entitled *The Reincarnation of St. Orlan* and *Omnipresence*, which she transmitted internationally. In these procedures (which in our society are usually done privately and secretly) she had her face sculpted into the "quintessential female form"—part Venus, part Diana, and part Mona Lisa—all designed by computer while audiences all over the world watched.

The doctors who performed the surgery and the nurses who assisted them dressed in medieval garb while Orlan read from a French psychoanalytic text and electronic music provided the background for this Orwellian operation. Daily photographs were made of her recovery and displayed in art galleries. Pieces of her hair, her skin, and her bandage, and petri dishes of her fat, were sold as if they were relics, along with the surgeon's bloody gowns. In Antoni's art, materials that have come in contact with her body are presented as art. Here there are no fetishistic stand-ins. The viewer here must watch the surgery, watch Orlan's skin pried away from its moorings, witness the pain and bruises incurred in this artist's quest for beauty, figuratively be inside her narcissistic problem. Orlan recognizes the aggressive component in her work: "I wanted to do a performance that would be like a bomb in intellectual society. . . . Most people cannot look at things like the opening of a body, like death, like suffering, but these things are very normal. Everyone wants to see flowers."

The following clinical vignette resonates uncannily with the work of both Antoni and Orlan.

Susan

Susan, an attractive, slim 41-year-old attorney and married mother, came for analytic treatment with Dr. Y. to deal with her bulimia, which was out of control. She experienced powerful wishes, to which she daily submitted, to eat large amounts of chocolate. She had had her eyes done in her twenties and thirties, and parts of her face and knees lifted.

Susan's public persona was that of an extremely beautiful and elegant woman. She spent hours every day on machines in her health club, working out with a trainer. The compliments of the women around her reinforced her perverse preoccupation with physical perfection, in whose pursuit she daily sought out and paid for the careful attention and ministrations of physicians and their surrogates.

In her analytic treatment, however, Susan quite visibly manifested and spoke of the misery and emptiness plaguing her. She found endless ways of enticing Dr. Y. to look at her. She strutted around the office to get him to look at her before getting on the couch. She held her face right in front of his as she entered and left her sessions. He felt that a perverse transference was activated in which Susan was inducing him to treat her body as an object in the very way that she herself experienced it. Susan forced him to look at her to see if she was indeed heavier or thinner or altered in some way, the looking serving to shore up a fragmented sense of self.

The Woman Artist as Voyeur and the Viewer as "Voyeur of a Voyeur"

The works of the next group of women artists cast the viewer as witness to the artist's own voyeurism, as "voyeur of a voyeur." These artists are photographers. This type of work is also not exclusively the domain of women artists. Male photographers have also had voyeuristic agendas, from Brassaï's forays into Parisian brothels, to Mapplethorpe's homosexual explorations, to Josh Sturges's shots of prepubescent females. But in the case of contemporary women artists, here again the hidden agenda is that they are being empowered through the gaze, which belonged previously exclusively to the male artist's domain.

Nan Goldin

Nan Goldin's works serve a "bridge function" for the first two sections of this Chapter. Some of her work is diaristic; it deals with herself, her body, and her diverse sexual object choices and proclivities, and records the most painful and private moments of her life for the whole world to see. She shows herself in the act of breaking up with her lover, the camera in the room recording the painful scene. One month after having been battered by her boyfriend, she stares again into the viewing lens, her face disfigured, her eye smashed and bloodshot, making a permanent record of an event that her forgiving psyche could not deny.

The rest of her work similarly chronicles her friends' most private moments in life and in death: Nan kissing her woman lover; two male friends bathing together; two transsexual friends kissing; her friend Fiona after breast surgery; her friend Cookie at her husband's funeral. Goldin is renowned for her sensitive photographs of her friends as they were sick and then dying of AIDS, here and in Europe, in hospitals and at their graves. Her friends offered themselves, warts and all, as subjects of her gaze. They gave her, by posing for her, their private issues to be made public and shown in art galleries, museums, and slide shows (the most notable of these called *The Ballad of Sexual Dependency*), as well as in a number of widely distributed books.

Goldin's personal recording of the events of her life and of those of her friends enabled her to hold onto relationships, which are tenuous, and to give them permanence. Her images also give a reality to events that one might tend to deny. For her, seeing is believing. She has said, "I photograph when I am afraid of something. It gives me a sense of not being so powerless." Goldin denies that her work has to do with voyeurism, since the subject of a voyeur's gaze does not know he is being watched, whereas her subjects know they are being photographed. Since the viewer is unknown to the subjects of these photographs, the viewer experiences both the pleasures and the discomforts of voyeurism when looking at these photos, and the awareness that friends who at age 20 consented to the wide distribution of these photos might feel differently twenty years later.

In photography, according to Goldin, female sexual excitement has been legitimate subject matter, but male sexual excitement as viewed by a female has not. The women she depicts looking at themselves in the mirror are self-possessed, rather then possessed by the male gaze. She hopes to depict a kind of self-contained eroticism.

Sally Mann

Sally Mann's photographs of her three children generally evoke shock and dismay in viewers from the mental health field. When I (Lieberman 1994) presented Mann's work to an audience of psychoanalysts, it seemed that everyone there experienced her work as abusive to her children. In the art world these photographs are generally regarded as works of a not unusual type, and are considered to be normal manifestations of a nonhypocritical mother's love. Her works, artistically of the highest quality, are published in widely disseminated books, as well as displayed in museums and galleries. In her curious synthesis of motherhood and work, she has photographed her children nude (they ran around that way on her property during the summer months); in private scenes, for example looking battered (with a black eye; in a bed soaked in urine); with the camera's focus on their genitals; or nude with adults in various stages of dress, which seemed to render the adults much more powerful than the children. What psychoanalysts believe should be kept private is made public. The viewer becomes a voyeur of the artist's voyeurism. Sally Mann's children had no choice, no power, no control over being her subjects and these photographs will be in the public domain throughout their lives.

The following case vignette elicits similar affects.

Mary

Mary, a 32-year-old single clothing designer, entered psychoanalytic therapy when her father brought his current mistress, who was 26, to live with him, and Mary found herself unable to show her designs to clothing manufacturers.

When she was a child, her father had traveled most of the year for his work and was usually away with whatever mistress he had at the moment. When he was gone, her mother was barely functional and chronically depressed. Like her mother, Mary adored her father and was unable get angry with him. During the times when her father was at home, she and her brothers were often asked to sing and dance for her parents' many guests. The entire family swam in the nude in the pool behind their home. When she became an adult she would leave her job and whatever boyfriend she had at the moment in order to join her parents in Florida. When her father called, she would drop everything in order to join him. Nudity prevailed on these vacations. Her father would often quip, "Incest is best." In her psychotherapeutic treatment secrets and omissions, disappearances long and short, reflected her attempts to defend herself against memories of overstimulation and chronic invasion of her privacy.

Zoe Leonard

Zoe Leonard deals with issues of power as a lesbian artist and as an admitted voyeur. During one phase of her career, she photographed women in such sexually evocative poses as modeling on a raised runway. She focused on their legs as their skirts billowed upward. She then went through a phase that she herself labeled as "creepy" in which she traveled to Europe and photographed male and female anatomical models (now in medical museums but once used to teach anatomy in medical schools) with exposed viscera. For her exhibition at Documenta II in 1992, she photographed her women friends' genitals and hung the photos in a very conservative German museum where they were surrounded by paintings of dukes and duchesses and the like. She was able to inject funny, sexy images into a claustrophobic atmosphere.

In her work Leonard attempts to reverse Mulvey's (1975) assertion that we identify with the male gaze by making the active gaze a female one. Her work can be regarded both as a demonstration of artistic exhibitionism, and of her voyeurism in looking while taking the photographs. It is sadistic, a trick played on the viewer (particularly the male viewer, in whom castration anxiety in sometimes aroused by the sudden unexpected sight of the female genital).

Ruth

Ruth, a successful 30-year-old actress and self-proclaimed femme fatale, reminiscent of Joan Riviere's (1929) "women masquerading as women," usually sat facing Dr. P. with her legs crossed, wearing five-inch-high sling-back heels, swinging them back and forth in a seductive manner. Her skirts were quite short and it was impossible to miss an occasional glimpse of underwear. One day early in treatment, she came into her session in a hysterical state, complaining that her husband was "useless." She reported that in bed he refused to look at her genitals while they were making love. "I don't understand it, they are quite pretty. I am just lovely down there." She was quite unaware of her seductive wishes toward Dr. P., who felt pulled sadistically into a voyeuristic-exhibitionistic enactment. She tended to experience silence as a rejection, and empathy as a seduction, and interpretation of her sexual wishes with regard to her therapist at that early phase of the treatment seemed to pose a real danger of early termination.

THE MALE ARTIST AS SPECTACLE

I now turn to the voyeurism and exhibitionism in the works of male artists. Ever since Freud wrote his important paper on masochism (1924), it has been assumed that women are more masochistic than men, whether for biological reasons or because of their inferior roles in society. Nevertheless, in my survey of the works of some noted male artists—counterparts of the females discussed above—I discovered that the male performance artists far exceeded their female colleagues in their penchant for exposing self-torture and pain to public gaze. They make themselves into pitiful or heroic spectacles before their spectators, inciting both sadism and voyeurism in those whom they successfully invite in to see the taboo and forbidden.

The visual image of male suffering has been prevalent in the history of Western art. We are all familiar with images of Christ suffering on and off the Cross and St. Sebastian pierced by arrows. Only in recent years, however, with the development of performance art in Europe and then (in the 1970s) in the United States has the suffering of the artists themselves been the subject matter of art. Before that artists *depicted* suffering. I have come to the conclusion that the more extreme forms of suffering inflicted upon themselves by male artists emanate from their attempts to portray cultural conflicts about voyeurism, exhibitionism, sadomasochism, homosexuality, and anal eroticism. O'Dell (1998) has thoroughly discussed this genre.

Early performance art incorporating self-flagellation and other kinds of self-abuse was characteristic of the Austrian Actionist school (for example Nitsch, Muehl, Brus, and Rainer). Schwarzkögler (1940–1969) killed himself jumping from a window after having amputated body parts, he alleged, in the service of art. In trying to break through taboos connected with the body, he mutilated his penis in numerous performances.

These Austrians influenced the noted German artist Joseph Beuys, who in one performance had a young man punch him in the face. With blood running down his face he lifted a crucifix and remained absolutely still. In his performance *I Like America and America Likes Me* (1974) he arrived at a New York art gallery by ambulance from the airport and spent three weeks in a room-sized cage with a coyote, dressed as a mad shepherd covered by a felt cloak. He then returned to the airport in the ambulance.

Beuys in turn influenced Dieter Appelt, who in a one-hour event entitled *Symmetry of the Skull* (1977), stood nude on a podium holding animal skulls. He then hoisted himself up to a pipe suspended from the ceiling and hung by his ankles. In *Black Box* (1979) he lay immobile for two hours on shallow water with his eyes closed.

These artists had lived through the violence and tragedy of World War II in Europe, and had all experienced personal trauma. The American artists I present next did not experience the war, yet chose to express themselves in similar ways.

Paul McCarthy in the 1970s presented himself as an extreme of abjection and self-humiliation, inducing considerable pain in the viewer. In *Painting, Wall Whip* (1974), a video, he swatted the walls of a loft with a tarpaulin dipped in paint, whose weight often lifted him off the ground. He used his hands and face as a paintbrush, smearing his body with paint, then ketchup, then mayonnaise, and finally with raw meat or feces. In *Class Fool* (1976), he held a doll between his legs hopping on a ketchup-slicked floor with his feet slipping out from under him. This viewer, at least, experienced acute anxiety defending against the sadism aroused by these anal-sadistic acts.

Chris Burden flirted with his own death in *Shoot* (1971) when he had someone actually shoot him from a distance. The shot went into his arm, but might have been fatal. In *Transfixed* (1974), he had someone nail him to a Volkswagen, which was then backed out of a garage and into a busy street in Venice, California. In another performance in 1975, he lay motionless for hours enclosed under a sheet of glass without water or food. Finally someone put a glass of water within his reach. He then went home, leaving the audience to deal with the possibility that they might have let him die. His work induced painful guilt in the viewer.

Tehching Hsieh lived entirely outdoors for a year. He spent another year in a cell in his studio without talking or reading, and yet another tied to another performance artist.

The much-acclaimed artist Matthew Barney appeared in a video as an accomplished athlete/drag queen testing the limits of his physical endurance and recording his adventures. In *MILEHIGH Threshold: FLIGHT WITH THE ANAL SADISTIC WARRIOR*, homoerotic satyrs demonstrated their physical endurance. In the *Jim Otto Suite* (1991), the artist received blows to the stomach and performed bizarre rites of healing through many applications of Vaseline and the manipulation of a hydraulic jack around his abdomen. The relation between the macho athlete and the seeking of anal-erotic stimulation is clear. It appeared to me that viewers of both sexes become considerably aroused and anxious during these performances.

Those works of Bruce Nauman that belong to this category are painfully obsessive, repetitive, unpleasant, and violent. In one video he plays a violin tunelessly tuned to the notes D E A D. Lights flash on and off. It is a fun house pushed far beyond fun. In another work he shrieks over and over: "Get out of my mind, get out of my room." In *Poke in the Eye/Nose/Ear* (1994) the video records him brutally poking himself. Nauman's narcissistic pain was expressed in a poignant print that said, "PLEASE/PAY/ATTEN-TION/PLEASE."

Bob Flanagan, who has since died, was one of the most extreme cases of public spectacle in his masochistic self-abuse. In his battle with cystic fibrosis, he sought to control the pain from his illness with self-inflicted and self-controlled pain, piercing his body, his nipples, and his penis, hanging himself by a harness, and so on. In *Visiting Hours* (1992) at the New Museum of Contemporary Art, he moved into and lived in the museum. Visitors spoke to him and to his woman friend (who assisted in his torture), viewing photos and videos of his painful sexuality. This attempt to fight sickness with sickness seemed quite blatantly related to castration fears and to homoeroticism.

This trend is still going strong, as is evidenced in the work of still another artist whose works were prominently displayed, along with others of this genre, at the 1999 Venice Biennale. Zhang Huan, a member of a Beijing group of artists who are devoted to social issues, sat nude in one performance for three hours in a public toilet, his body smeared with honey in order to attract flies (1994). In another performance (1998), he lay on a mattress of ice without his pants for 10 minutes while dogs tied to the end of the bed barked.

In this art, these so-called masculine feats of heroism seem to represent a masculine masquerade that defends against anal sadism and feminine wishes. What extremes these artists go to in order to be looked at! The curious interaction one finds in the clinical situation between masochism and narcissism becomes manifest. One wonders too about the psychological makeup of the frequent spectator of such events.

VOYEURS AT THE MORGUE

In our culture, we look at the dead only briefly, if at all. We are often told, "Don't look," when someone has been killed in an accident or a dead person is carried out of an apartment house. Only the nearest of kin are allowed into morgues. Most coffins are closed, and when they are left open many who come to the service or wake choose not to look at the dead person.

Artists for some reason have at times been, or felt themselves to be, exempt from this taboo. They have been commissioned to create mummies and death masks and for centuries they were permitted to depict Christ dead, both on and off the Cross. Leonardo da Vinci and Michelangelo studied cadavers to learn how to draw. Caravaggio used a dead prostitute as a model for the Virgin Mary, but evoked outrage in so doing. One of Rembrandt's most notable works is *The Anatomy Lesson* (1632), in which doctors in training view a cadaver. And Freud himself had in his collection quite a number of paintings that depicted death.

Recently the British artist Anthony Noel-Kelly, despite a connection with the Royal Family, became notorious and was eventually jailed for the possession of corpses, from which he made plaster casts for his sculpture. As cited above, the performance artist Chris Burden flirted with his own death in his work by having himself shot, or by risking electrocution or death by fire. Nan Goldin photographed friends dying of AIDS, in hospitals, and in coffins. The Starn brothers did a series on the dead in which they framed and boxed photographs of Champaigne's painting of the dead Christ, putting their collage before the public as if it were a relic of adoration. Cindy Sherman evokes images of the dead and mutilated in some of her recent photographs. Gerhard Richter did a series of grisaille paintings from police photos of the dead. Joel-Peter Witkin's creepy images and the fetishistic assemblages done by Bruce Connor, so very evocative of death, belong to this category.

Our personal reactions to such art seem to be connected with the nature and extent of our defenses against voyeurism, exhibitionism, necrophilia, and universal unconscious wishes to sleep with and look at the dead. Necrophilia as a perversion usually involves sadomasochistic and oral practices with the dead, and the dead person usually represents the mother, for death itself is frequently depicted in fantasy as a devouring Mother Earth. The act represents on one level an attempt to incorporate the object and thus to restore it. On another level, the object, being dead, cannot retaliate against the aggressive impulses expressed. As in voyeurism, there is a sexualization of looking. Sadistic impulses are involved, since looking takes the place of destroying (one could say to oneself: "I did not destroy it, I merely looked at it"). Here, too, the dread of talion punishment prevails and creates anxiety, because the dead person cannot return in order punish his aggressor (the one who looks) and the guilt is never assuaged.

As I have said, there are instances in which the artist is both a exhibitionist and voyeur who perversely pulls the viewer into looking at something he or she would not willingly have looked at, making the viewer "voyeur of a voyeur." The artist who displays his voyeuristic product to the viewer acts as an exhibitionist as well. These dynamics seem to be particularly operative in the photographic works of Andres Serrano.

Serrano worked with the taboo against looking at the dead and its various implications in his *Morgue Series* (1992). I want to make clear that the following discussion is not about Serrano or what "makes him tick." It is about ourselves—our own reactions to his subject matter and to looking at the dead.

Andres Serrano, an artist whom Senator Jesse Helms took on in combat, became notorious for his work entitled *Piss Christ*, a photograph of a crucifix submerged in a glass tank of his own collected urine. His technique uses glorious light and color that contrasts with his subject matter: body fluids—blood, milk, semen, urine, menstrual pads. In the works I will discuss here he treats death as an aesthetic matter through the use of subdued lighting and black backdrops for 4 x 5 prints, which he bonds to Plexiglas. Viewers are drawn in, attracted to the prettiness of his Cibachrome photographs, and then are shocked by the subject matter. These visceral responses are sought by the artist, who perversely and sadistically seduces the viewer and then shocks him. Today's artist no longer just relates to his subject matter, in this case a cadaver, but has an agenda with the viewer as well.

Serrano spent two weeks in Europe working on his *Morgue Series*. He photographed fifty or sixty bodies (they could not give permission; nor were their relatives asked for permission). His subjects died by homicide, by suicide, by illness. The titles of the photographs reveal the causes of death: *Hacked to Death, Rat Poison Suicide, Burn Victim, Broken Bottle Murder*. These words are needed to give the images identity. The viewer is seduced into wondering about the dead person and the story. Is it gross or engrossing? Is this a boundary violation that the coroner should not have permitted? Is Serrano a voyeur, an exhibitionist, or both, and are we voyeurs of a voyeur?

(Noel-Kelly has described his own difficulty in obtaining body parts: "To get them was a sweat, under cover of darkness. . . . I had the police on me once because someone had tipped them off. I still had some dead body parts which I hadn't used, and I had to destroy them" [1997]. It is apparent that such artists are motivated and tantalized by the forbidden as well as by the threat of punishment lurking around the corner.)

Serrano is an artist who has been in therapy, but he admits that he has not analyzed his fascination with the dead or where inside himself this work comes from. He feels that doing this work makes him less afraid of his own death, and he works spontaneously and analyzes after: "I've found that my work is pretty instinctual and much like dreams. When you have a dream, you may not choose a lot that's happening or why. Then after the dream is over, you sit on the couch and you think about it."

It is apparent that this artist had to touch his subjects in order to arrange his shots. In *Totem and Taboo* Freud (1912b) wrote about the explicit taboos in many primitive cultures about touching the dead. The viewer finds himself looking and thinking: "How could he do it? Could I do it? It is difficult enough to look at the photos let alone be in the cold morgue with the dead bodies." When we look at Serrano's work we are thinking about the artist himself. He is in the work. He is thus an exhibitionist as well as a voyeur.

The following are some examples from *The Morgue Series*:

Fatal Meningitis II: A photograph of a 2-year-old who nearly drowned, survived, but then developed meningitis. Looking at this sweet innocent baby evokes tears. He is like an angel. The viewer is compelled to think: "What if he were my baby, how would I feel?"

John Doe Baby II: This photo is of disembodied hands that do not seem to belong to a baby or child and can only be identified as such from the label. The name and the hands evoke a profound sense of lack of identity and dislocation in the viewer.

Infectious Pneumonia: This is the face of a woman the artist calls "the woman in red." She died of AIDS. Initially, with her shrunken body and face, seeing her as a whole, Serrano found her to be repulsive. By covering the top of her head, he found a way to repair her and to make her beautiful. Note the reparative aspect here. With the cloth over her head, she could be anyone. Here identity is not so much dislocated as disguised (Lehmann 1994). [1]

Death by Fire: The skin of a man who died in a fire seems like a lava pit. It looks more like a piece of sculpture than a limb.

Hacked to Death: This photo was made as Serrano zoomed in toward the bloody groin and underwear of a man hacked to death by his wife who had stabbed him fifteen times with a large kitchen knife. Serrano found the image to be "painterly," objectifying it, rather than subjectively experiencing it or identifying with the man or his wife (Lehmann 1994).

Hacked to Death II: Here the artist zoomed in on a dull unseeing eye planted in the blood-smeared face. The eye does not look out but seems to convey a feeling of inner contemplation, wondering perhaps why his wife did what she did.

Death by Drowning: The viewer experiences this as an art object removed from its subject matter, a man who died. Instead the viewer is seduced by the artist to look at the gleaming moist quality of the gray, and the many tones of color embedded in the gray. One forgets that this is flesh and human hair. One can deny the fact that the skin belongs to a person, and has turned color as a result of that person's having drowned.

AIDS Related Death: The immaculate manicured hands of a female AIDS casualty present an image of repose and call to mind the hands in Michelangelo's *Pietà* inspiring feelings of awe and reverence.

Many reactions occur to works like these. Some viewers are drawn to the images, others are horrified. Some find that they catalyze thoughts about illness and death, or they wonder about the characters and why they wound up in the morgue. Were they family-less? Was there no person who had power to keep them out of the morgue? There is the possibility of disidentification in the thought "They're dead, I'm not." Some find these works to be empty and a bore. The art critic Peter Schjeldahl (1993) wrote about Serrano that "his relentless aestheticizing defuses the psychic mechanism of identification (*that could be me or my loved one*) which can make pictures of the dead particularly unbearable" (p. 91). For Schjeldahl, most compelling was the image of Serrano himself, "doggedly coaxing beauty from shambles hour after hour amid the morgue stinks" (p. 91).

Serrano himself is reported as having said, "I photographed these people after the moment of death. I never knew them as human beings. I never knew what language they spoke, what their religious or political beliefs were, how much money they had, or who they loved. All I know about them is the cause of death. . . . It seems to me that death is a strange equalization—we all eventually meet in a mutual space" (Blume 1993, p. 37).

Serrano's work is similar to pornography in its focus on body parts. The fragmentation is in itself seductive. But Serrano does not see his work as pornographic. In pornography, bodies are also photographed in fragments and decontextualized. But pornography is crude and artless, and is intended to stimulate sexual feelings, which is not Serrano's intent. (In his *History of Sex* series in which explicit perverse sex acts were photographed in brightly lit, aesthetically beautiful contexts, the effect on most viewers was paradoxically sexually flat, even boring, not what the artist intended.)

The dead in our culture are whisked away out of sight by officious professionals who cremate them or embalm them or put them in coffins or mausolea where sight and touch is limited and contained by these professionals' rules. Walter Benjamin (1983) observed that we have managed to avoid the sight of the dying and death as living "dry dwellers of eternity" living in rooms that have never been touched by death. Serrano reminds us that in Victorian times, people would take photographs with their deceased ones in their arms as a "momento mori." In India the religious travel to the River Ganges with their dead relatives, wash the bodies in the holy river, and then burn them. It is a very different way of mourning that allows such physical contact with the dead.

These days, perhaps as a result of a change in attitude in our culture about what may be looked at, fathers are invited in to view the births of their babies and many videotape the entire event. This would have been thought "creepy" twenty-five years ago. More and more women nurse their babies in public, challenging others to look at them without embarrassment, or without inappropriately eroticizing a normal sight. Therefore, we must ask whether there might come a time when we can freely look at our dead relatives if we wish, photograph them if we want to, without being labeled as perverted.

In this speculation I am not sanctioning the efforts of photographers to market death photographs of Princess Diana (pictures of her *alive* sold for $100,000; pictures of her *dead*, for $1,000,000), the dead Nicole Brown Simpson, or the dead Jon-Benet Ramsey. Salman Rushdie (1997) experienced the death of Diana as pornographic, referring to the camera with its unavoidably "phallic long-nosed snout, giving pursuit . . . while the object of desire, in the moment of her death, sees the phallic lens advancing upon her, snapping, snapping" (p. 68).

However, Serrano's works make death visible and aesthetic. Through the use of subdued lighting, careful focus, and black backdrops, the viewer is drawn in rather than repulsed. The tension between the beautiful photos and the gruesome subject matter is confusing, however. One might wonder whether his transformation of the gruesome images into something beautiful (and vice versa, too) is really more respectful of the dead than the apparent boundary violation of going into a morgue, photographing dead people, and publishing the photographs without the relatives' permission. His work is upsetting because it arouses fears and conflicts about necrophilia, voyeurism, and exhibitionism. It arouses castration anxiety, our fears of our own death, and the murderous wishes we harbor toward others. His photographs are of something "real," whereas paintings of the dead invite the possibility of denial that a real person died. Serrano has said that he does not view the dead bodies as corpses: "To me, they are not dead, inanimate objects. They still have a life, a humanity, and a spirituality" (quoted in Garbarino 1993, p. 81).

These works fall under the definition of "art" because they transform. They are reparative, in the sense that death signifies loss, and these works in a sense restore the loss. Segal (1991) sees the act of creation as

> having to do with an unconscious memory of a harmonious internal world and the experience of its destruction; that is, the depressive position. The impulse is to recover and recreate this lost world. The means to do it has to do with the balance of "ugly" elements with beautiful elements in such a way as to evoke an identification with this process in the recipient. Aesthetic experience in the re-

cipient involves psychic work. This is what distinguishes it from pure entertainment or sensuous pleasure. [p. 94]

Similar ideas appear in the writings of George Pollack (1989), who postulated a "mourning-liberation process" in the creative act.

We look and are looked at all through our lives. It is sometimes helpful for those of us who work with patients' issues around voyeurism, exhibitionism, and body narcissism to examine our own reactions to these issues in a modality different from that of the written or spoken word. Segal (1991) states, "Art is not an internal communication; it is a communication with others, and much of the work consists of creating new means of communication" (p. 109). When I wrote at the beginning of this chapter that I see art as "a mirror of life in my consulting room," I might have spoken of the mirror of art as a magnifying mirror, enlarging and exaggerating what is seen, so that it can be really seen.

10

Visual Themes in Film
and Literature

I see only from one point, but am looked at from all sides.

Lacan

The narrative arts—literature and film—are often said to reflect our lives. I am not so sure that this is true. To the extent that they *do* reflect our lives and ourselves, they do it in a Lacanian mirror: that is, they reflect us back to ourselves in a form greater and more heroic than we really are. Characters in literature and film are more beautiful than we are, more competent, more gifted, and much braver. They are at times much crazier than we can ever let ourselves be. The world of literature is a world of risks and challenges that most of us are afraid to live in. We go to movies and we read novels to encounter people who are "realer" than we are, who can show us ourselves more clearly than any amount of self-scrutiny will allow. Stories show us in magnified forms qualities, behaviors, feelings, and situations whose reality we can tolerate only in very small quantity. That is their attraction, it seems to me, and that also gives them their great power to expand our grasp of the intricacies of human nature. The imagination and skill of the narrative artist allow a perspective on human psychology and experience that can never be achieved by real life alone.

The visual issues that permeate our culture—voyeurism and exhibitionism, the power of the gaze, and the lure of image—are as present in the narrative arts as they are in the graphic arts. As in the visual arts, countertransference reactions to these issues as they are exaggerated in storytelling can expand awareness and understanding of related but less obvious manifestations in the clinical situation. And much can be learned from film and literature critics, who are themselves often psychoanalytically informed, but with a perspective different from and enriching of our own. Unlike clinical psychoanalysts, however, they tend to pay great attention to these issues in their reading of literature and viewing of film.

This chapter takes an impressionistic tour of the world of literature and film, in hopes of increasing awareness of how the issues elaborated in this book can manifest themselves in these arts, and I provide some relevant critical commentary on the nature of beauty and *the gaze*. The works I cite enhance our awareness of the universality of these issues and of the importance they play in clinical presentations.

Death in Venice: *Vision, Love, and Death*

There is no greater distillation of the narcissistic psychology of vision in literature than Thomas Mann's (1911) *Death in Venice*. Voyeurism, exhibitionism, homoeroticism, fear of aging, and the desire for embodied beauty all pervade this novel, which is no less visually evocative than the film it gave rise to, and which explores the worship of youth and beauty by an aging man. It is a poignant and tragic evocation of the lures and limitations of spectacle and spectatorship. The protagonist Aschenbach is a quintessential voyeur, who comes alive only as he becomes obsessed and possessed by the sight and charm of the androgynous youth Tadzio: "The observer thought he had never seen, either in nature or art, anything so happy and consummate" (pp. 25–26). He watches him, and the boy knows that he is being watched. They come a step closer as Aschenbach, a solitary hotel guest, wistfully observes the lively play of handsome adolescents on the beach of the Lido of Venice and then the social encounters of the charming families who come to dine at the Grand Hotel des Bains.

> At that moment Tadzio came through the glass doors into the room. To reach his own table he crossed the traveller's path, and modestly

cast down his eyes before the grey-haired man of the lofty brows—
only to lift them again in that sweet way he had and direct his full
soft gaze upon Aschenbach. [p. 37]

The erotic visual dance between the two intensifies and continues:

> Daily Aschenbach would wait for Tadzio. Then sometimes, on his
> approach, he would pretend to be preoccupied and let the charmer
> pass unregarded by. But sometimes he looked up, and their glances
> met; . . . but in Tadzio's eyes a question lay—he faltered in his step,
> gazed on the ground, then up again with that ineffably sweet look
> he had. [p. 50]

The aging Aschenbach stares at himself in the mirror, aware that
he has lost his attractiveness. Nevertheless, the perverse Tadzio (a
male Lolita) visually seduces the older man, who became weak in
the knees from the mere sight of him. They play a game of visual
cat and mouse, torturing one another through the withholding of
glances: "The lad would cast a glance, that might be slow and cautious, or might be sudden and swift, as though to take him by
surprise, to the place where his lover sat. Aschenbach did not meet
the glance" (p. 59).

Aschenbach's need to gaze at Tadzio is so compelling that he
cannot bring himself to leave Venice even under the threat of a
spreading cholera epidemic; in fact, he barely notices when he
himself falls ill. At the end of the tale, the dying Aschenbach des-
perately tries to make himself young again, to transform himself
back into what he was. He dyes his hair and mustache and puts on
makeup. He sits, ill and perspiring, with hair dye dripping down
his face, on the beach watching Tadzio.

> Once more he [Tadzio] paused to look; with a sudden recollec-
> tion, or by an impulse, he turned from the waist up, in an exquisite

movement, one hand resting on his hip, and looked over his shoulder at the shore. The watcher sat just as he had sat this time in the lobby of the hotel when first the twilit grey eyes had met his own. [p. 74]

After this final act of mutual gaze, Aschenbach collapses and dies.

Mann captures in this mesmerizing story both the deathly enchantment of narcissistic preoccupation and its solitude; he captures the pathos of lovers who try to connect but cannot, suffering profound experiences of rejection when the loving look is not returned. Aschenbach and Tadzio play a grown-up version of the "chase and dodge" game of Beebe and Lachmann, which I described in Chapter 3. Aschenbach's desperate attempt to recapture his youthful looks echoes the desperate efforts of the patients I have described in these pages, who imagine that they will attract others by the way they look. But Aschenbach loved and looked and suffered impotently, as do many of our patients. The loving gaze goes unheeded, recapitulating, I think, the infant's search for an unresponsive mother.

THE BODY IN NARRATIVE ART

Aschenbach's despair over his aging brings to mind Brooks's (1993) comments on the use of the body in literature and art since the eighteenth century: "Modern narratives appear to produce a semiotization of the body which is matched by a somatization of story: a claim that the body must be a source and a locus of meanings, and that stories cannot be told without making the body a prime vehicle of narrative significations" (p. xii). Citing such works as Shelley's *Frankenstein*, Zola's *Nana*, and Milton's *Paradise Lost*, he describes at first a tension between body, symbol, and language. This tension moves back and forth, finally allowing a hesitant unveiling of the body in literature in the works of Balzac, Flaubert, Proust, the more repressed Dickens, the Brontës, James, and Hardy, followed by a breakthrough in Joyce's *Ulysses*. He states:

> Literature continues to display a greater reticence about the representation of the body than painting. . . . Literature may be less interested in contemplation of the naked body per se than in the body as the locus for the inscription of meanings. . . . We live at a certain distance of spirit from materiality, while recognizing that it is a false distance—that spirit, whatever it is, depends on matter. [p. 20]

The Pillow Book

A literal depiction of "the body as the locus for the inscription of meanings" appears in Peter Greenaway's 1997 film *The Pillow Book*, a tale of voyeurism, exhibitionism, and perversion. This is the story of a Japanese-Chinese girl whose calligrapher father wrote on her skin on every birthday, when she would also witness him submitting sexually to his homosexual publisher. She develops a perversion about having to have her skin written upon, based upon her need to be looked at. She then woos the male lover of the publisher and turns the perversion into writing upon *his* skin, with herself as voyeur. She thus turns passive into active, at the same time seducing, in displacement, her father.

According to Tylim (1998), the skin-writing is a way to hold on to her father, to give an illusion of permanence, of immortality. At the end of the film, her mother writes on her pregnant stomach, and she does the same with her newborn child. What Lacan calls *nom du père*, "the Word of the Father," is written upon her skin. (According to Lacan, it is the Father, or man, not the Mother, or woman, who brings language to the child. Only when things are symbolized, when words can be used, can the self emerge.) I find this to be especially ironic, for just as Lacan's writings can be almost impossible to understand, this girl cannot see the words on her skin. As verbal symbols they have no meaning. Even seen in a mirror they would be reversed and incomprehensible. Ultimately in this film words have no meaning; there is no symbolization and wishes are acted out in perverse form. The writing is the father's and the daughter's perverse way of looking for love, of trying to make it permanent.

THE VICISSITUDES OF THE GAZE

Brooks also addresses the topic of the male gaze in literature. He uses Freudian theory to explain the male need to stare at the female body and to differentiate himself from it:

> Sight, knowledge, truth and woman's body: such a nexus intertwines central and highly charged attitudes and gestures of our culture. Man as knowing subject postulates woman's body as the object to be known by way of an act of visual inspection which claims to reveal the truth—or else makes that object into the ultimate enigma. Seeing woman as other is necessary to think about the self. [p. 97]

Brooks's is a fairly recent formulation, however. Much critical discussion came out of the film and art worlds in the 1970s of the power of the gaze, particularly as it affects and reflects male–female relationships. Berger's (1972) much-quoted statement that "Men look at women. Women watch themselves being looked at," to which I have referred before, catalyzed a debate that has lasted more than twenty-five years. The film critic Laura Mulvey wrote an ironic and widely cited paper, "Visual Pleasure and the Narrative Cinema" (1975), in which she claimed that the camera's gaze is male, that women in films are passive icons, and that the aim of films is to give men scopophilic pleasure. Men need to turn women into

perfect fetishized objects, Mulvey thought, in order to avoid castration anxiety: "The paradox of phallocentricism . . . is that it
depends on the image of the castrated woman to give order and
meaning to its world" (p. 361).

Mulvey took as her point of departure "the way film reflects,
reveals, and even plays on the straight, socially established interpretation of sexual difference that controls images, erotic ways of looking and spectacle" (p. 361). She used psychoanalytic theory as a
weapon to demonstrate how patriarchal society has influenced film.
She stated: "Woman . . . stands in patriarchal culture as signifier for
the male other, bound by a symbolic order in which man can live
out his fantasies and obsessions through linguistic command by
imposing them on the silent image of woman still tied to her place
as bearer of meaning, not maker of meaning" (p. 362).

What Hollywood offered, in her opinion, was "skilled and satisfying manipulations of visual pleasure"(p. 362). She cited Lacanian
theory about the mirror (see Chapter 4) as it relates to film: "It is
the birth of the long love affair/despair between image and self-
image that has found such intensity of expression in film and such
gorgeous recognition in the cinema audience" (p. 365).

In support of her thesis Mulvey cites as evidence the films of
such actresses as Lana Turner, Marilyn Monroe, Jane Russell, and
Audrey Hepburn: "The presence of a woman is an indispensable
element of spectacle in normal narrative film, yet her visual pleasure tends to work against the development of a story line, to freeze
the flow of action in moments of erotic contemplation" (p. 366).

In films at least, says Mulvey, men are not the object of the gaze.
They make things happen: "A male movie star's glamorous characteristics are thus not those of the erotic object of the gaze, but
those of the more perfect, more complete, more powerful ideal
ego conceived in the original moment of recognition in front of
the mirror" (p. 367). The male enjoys the woman in the film and
is fascinated by his own image on the screen as one who gains
control of and possession of the woman.

Mulvey believes that filmmakers have taken two approaches in dealing with the castration anxiety aroused by the sight of woman: (1) voyeurism, associated with sadism, in which "pleasure lies in ascertaining guilt (immediately associated with castration), asserting control, and subjecting the guilty person through punishment or forgiveness" (p. 368); and (2) fetishistic scoptophilia, which "builds up the physical beauty of the object, transforming it into something satisfying in itself" (p. 368). She describes three kinds of looking, all going on simultaneously: (1) the camera recording, (2) the audience watching the product, and (3) the characters looking at one another. All are organized around castration fear as evoked by woman. The audience is fixated and therefore cannot distance from the film. She concluded, "Women, whose image has continually been stolen and used for this end, cannot view the decline of the traditional film form with anything much more than sentimental regret" (p. 373).

Mulvey notwithstanding, I noticed many years ago that William Holden held his own as the recipient of the gaze when he appeared with Kim Novak in *Picnic*. It is true that this male object of the gaze was a scorned man, and not regarded as a good catch for the heroine. Lately, however, there really has been some change in these matters, as in the roles played by Harvey Keitel in *The Piano* and Leonardo di Caprio, a latter-day pinup if ever there was one, in *Titanic*. Since the "outing" of one of the most masculine of movie stars, Rock Hudson, the viewing public seems to have become skeptical of hypermasculinity, and the men on the screen are no longer as one-dimensional as they once were.

American Beauty, The Governess, *and* Artemisia

In *American Beauty* (1999), for instance, the 42-year-old husband and father of an adolescent girl spends hours building muscles in order to win the approving gaze of his daughter's blonde model/

cheerleader friend. The daughter is herself watched (as she well knows) by the adolescent boy next door, a voyeur who spies with his video camera on her, as well as her father, in various states of undress. He looks at them not directly, but through the camera. But the gaze becomes reversed when the boy and girl make love, for he lets her use the camera to look at him.

Films that are set in earlier periods imply that the woman who returns the gaze will be punished. In *The Governess* (1998) Minnie Driver plays a nineteenth-century Jewish governess who is photographed in the nude by the children's father. He ends their love affair after discovering that *she* had photographed *him* sleeping after they had made love. In *Artemisia* (1998), a true story set in the seventeenth century, the artist-daughter of the famous artist Gentileschi at first secretly sketched her own nude body. Then she began to draw male bodies. Her teacher, her father's friend and colleague Tassi, deflowered her, then claimed that her sketches of men proved that she was not a virgin. Despite her love for him and the depth of their visually based communications, she was brutally treated by him and by others. In these cases, the woman's gaze, expressed in photographs and drawings, is used to get love or to hold onto love, but it results in the loss of the love of men who believe that the gaze is a male prerogative.

The Blue Room

There is a difference between theater and film. Members of the audience at a play can choose whom they wish to look at among the characters in the scene. In a movie, the director chooses where the camera's focus lies and how the total scene is cropped. That is why, according to Mulvey, cinema differs from theater in its voyeuristic potential. It can shift emphasis: "Going far beyond highlighting a woman's to-be-looked-at-ness, cinema builds the way she is to be looked at into the spectacle itself" (p. 372).

When I attended the Broadway production of *The Blue Room* (1998), a modern version of Schnitzler's *La Ronde*, I watched the audience unabashedly gaze and gape at the mostly nude body of Nicole Kidman, the female star, her genital only flimsily covered. Many people had brought binoculars for the occasion, a public spectacle for which some scalpers were charging $1,000 a ticket. All of the publicity referred to *her* body. The male star, Iain Glen, who is to my mind at least as attractive as Kidman and certainly as talented an actor, displayed full, impressive, frontal nudity for several minutes. Nevertheless, he was largely ignored by the audience, and seldom mentioned in the press, by either male or female journalists. Perhaps envy was the explanation for this, on the part of both sexes!

THE GAZE, CONTINUED

Two decades after Mulvey produced her seminal tract, Gamman and Makinen (1994) disagreed with her, contending that she exaggeratedly universalized male experience, and that all kinds of various identifications can be made. They objected to the wholesale application of her model:

> At times it has seemed to us that every representation of a "strong" woman is analyzed in relationship to the phallus, rather than on its own merits. Clearly it is reductive to argue that all images of powerful women constitute phallic replacement. The omnipotent mother surely needs a space in her own right, within film theory, and perhaps can be looked at through female eyes. [p. 181]

They observed that men in film also wear phallic props, and concluded that "to acknowledge the male body as a site of erotic spectacle is absolutely necessary" (p. 182).

S. Moore (1994) also observed that times have changed in her analysis of the films *Mean Streets, American Gigolo,* and *Saturday Night Fever.* Each film emphasized an active female gaze. She observed, "The striking thing about contemporary images of men is that at least some of them seem to acknowledge and even embrace a passivity that was once symbolically outlawed. The feel is softer, their gaze unthreatening" (p. 54). She continued:

> The fear experienced by men of women's Medusa-like stare, which petrifies everything in sight, is in reality a fear that the female gaze will soften everything in its path. Yet this softening has *already* been achieved in many of these new representations of men and such a mythology may actively obscure what is different or disturbing about the female gaze. [p. 59]

Film critic Molly Haskell (1987) likewise addressed the female need to gaze: "Are men the only ones who 'gaze' and even appropriate and convert the object-woman into their own fantasy worlds?" (p. 383). She noted that in the 1980s:

> [A]s stars, women would disengage themselves from the 'gaze': the male perspective that . . . had frozen women in postures that catered to male needs and anxieties rather than allowing them to express their own desires. Instead, women virtually disappeared from the screen, as sex objects or as anything else, for a decade. [p. 375]

And Young (1989) made note of an odd twist on the question of knowing who exactly is in power, as exemplified by Madonna's videos, which:

> at first might have seemed to confirm a feminist's worse fears about sexualized images of women. When, for example, Madonna confidentially returns the fetishist's gaze while wearing his favorite sexual accessories, she reveals herself to be in the possession of knowl-

edge; she knows because she is looked at and now is *looking back.*
[p. 184]

Basic Instinct

Today's women can be active in their exhibitionism, knowing that
men are looking at them. They may actively court this look and
return it. A quintessential example of this was the film *Basic Instinct,* which A. K. Richards (1998b) analyzed. The key character,
played by Sharon Stone, is interviewed by suspicious police about
the murder of her lover. Sitting in a chair facing her accusers, she
turns to the hero:

> "Ever fucked on cocaine, Nick?" As she says this, she crosses and
> re-crosses her legs in such a way as to display her vulva while act-
> ing as if she does not notice what she is doing. . . . The sight of the
> female genital stresses the whole roomful of men. She flashes her
> genital at them with the same aggressive intent and effort as a male
> flasher has toward his female victims. [p. 8]

Richards points out that shortly after this an image of the Medusa
appears on a television screen: "The Medusa is an image of the
vulva, hairy all around; a face, but not a face; a mouth, but not a
mouth; and life-giving when young, but horrific to see and death-
dealing to the young heroes who encounter her" (p. 14).

THE GAZE ACCORDING TO LACAN

Lacan has had a major impact on contemporary film theory in his
distinctions among the Imaginary, the Symbolic, and the Real. His
concepts of the mirror stage and the gaze (*le regard*) are universally

cited, although not necessarily well understood. Walls of translation, from French to English Lacanese and then from Lacanese to English (and possibly first from French Lacanese to French!), make true comprehension difficult. *A Triumph of the Eye Over the Gaze: Everything You Always Wanted to Know About Lacan But Were Afraid to Ask Hitchcock*, edited by Zizek (1992), presented a cornucopia of Lacanian ideas as they relate to mass culture. The "eye," Lacan said, differs from "the gaze." In reviewing the Zizek book, Elsaesser (1995) wrote:

> For Lacan, as for Zizek, eye and gaze are placed a-symmetrically to one another, in the sense that the gaze is always on the side of the object, making the point in the picture from which the subject viewing it is already being gazed at. Far from assuring the self-presence of the subject (i.e., the gaze as instrument of mastery and control), the gaze introduces an irreducible split: I can never see the picture at the point at which it is gazing at me. The eye is thus already observed: *essi est percipi*, but with the added dimension into which the first look and the second look are folded, an en-folding of looks that induces a kind of ontological vertigo, making us doubt not what we see, but the very possibility of there being a place from which to look. [p. 633]

In Hitchcock's films, for instance, the gaze is invisible, the eye of the characters looking and being looked at being more powerful, until at the turning point the gaze overwhelms the eye.

Story of the Eye

The eye has been both denigrated and exalted in film and in literature. Jay (1993) traced *antivisuel* influences in France during the nineteenth century, and in so doing explored themes of voyeurism, exhibitionism, and taboo as they relate to the gaze. He reported that the surrealist Georges Bataille finished his pornographic *Story of the Eye* (1927) with a description of an enucleated eye of a garroted priest inserted in the anus, and then the vagina of the heroine, as the narrator realizes that he finds himself "facing something I imagine I had been waiting for in the same way a guillotine waits for the neck to slice. I even felt as if my eyes were bulging from my head erectile with horror" (quoted in Jay 1993, p. 220).

The eye was rendered ignoble in this fantasy. Bataille's father was blind and he himself was traumatized in World War I, having been exposed to blinding light. Jay analyzed as well films made by Buñuel and Dali that present little pleasure in the visual and in which eyes are actually mutilated. (To my mind there has been no more frightening image in film history than that of eyes coming out of a head in the French film *Diabolique*.)

Proof

On the other hand, the *importance* of eyes emerged poignantly in the Australian film *Proof* (1992), about a blind photographer whose mother had given him a camera when he was a boy in order to help him "see." In his childhood she described the world to him. She taught him to listen and to smell and took him to drive-in movies and described the scenes. The plot is organized around the theme of lies. The boy tried to catch his mother in a lie. Since she was angry at him for being blind, she lied to him as a punishment. He learned to use photographs to check up on things that happened outside of his presence, and used the photos as proof when he felt betrayed and lied to. His issues of loss emerge in the context of his fantasy that his mother had died to get away from him, because she was ashamed of him.

LACAN'S MIRROR AND THE SEARCH
FOR BEAUTY

Witham-Levinstein (1996) provided a comprehensible summary of Lacan's relation to film theory by way of Lacan's (1954–1955) work on the mirror:

> According to Lacan, the mirror stage is not simply a moment in development but a process in which the subject's relation to her image is revealed. The subject becomes aware of the body then in a correlative manner. Lacan asserts that the whole form of the human body gives the subject an imaginary mastery over her body (one which is premature in relation to real mastery). The subject thus anticipates the achievement of psychological mastery and this anticipation will leave its mark on every subsequent experience of effective motor mastery. Since this is the original experience through which a woman sees herself, reflects on herself and conceives of herself as other than she is, it entirely strikes her fantasy life. This means that the ego is founded on the basis of that imaginary relation. [p. 5]

I interpret this to mean that in contemporary film theory the spectator in front of the screen occupies the position of Lacan's child in front of the mirror. Primary identifications are made. The cinema screen is another mirror. The cinema involves the spectator in the Imaginary. But in this case it is not the spectator's own body that is reflected on the screen. The voyeurism of the spectator has to do with the primordial experience of the mirror in the primal scene, of voyeurism without exhibitionism.

It is impossible to do justice to the voluminous study of beauty in literature. But Jenijoy LaBelle's *Herself Beheld: The Literature of the Looking Glass* (1988), explores specifically in the literature of the past two hundred years the theme of women looking at themselves in the mirror, confronting themselves, and finding out who they are:

> Through the mirror, we can gain insight into the reciprocal inter-changes between interiority and exteriority as these create what a woman is to herself and to her culture. The reflection in the glass is at once both the self and a radical otherness an image privileged with a truth beyond the subjective and at the same time taken to be the very essence of that subjectivity. [p. 9]

La Belle believes that women find themselves in the mirror, whereas "men look at their faces and their bodies but what they are is another matter entirely" (p. 9).

In *The Face of Love: Feminism and the Beauty Question* (1995), Ellen Zetzel Lambert presented the perspective on beauty that she has acquired from her own life experiences. She observes herself transformed in her childhood photographs from a beautiful child to a homely one after the loss of her mother. She traces her reactions to her own mastectomy. Lambert conceives of beauty as wholeness or integrity, as opposed to a lot of parts. Is the whole person involved? "The way to deny a woman her integrity as a person is to see her body as a collection of parts" (p. 31).

Female Perversions

Lambert's statement is illustrated in the postmodern film *Female Perversions* (1997), which was based on Louise Kaplan's psychoanalytic text of the same name. (This is in itself a commentary on the current tendency to thrust into public view what was once kept private and hidden.) Tylim (1997) has described this as a fragmented, evocative film that draws the spectator into a voyeuristic journey down mysterious pathways toward the sight of the forbidden. As soon as some meaning or understanding is achieved, the scene shifts and the spectator is left to wonder what is happening.

> The alluring presence of women's bodies at different stages of undressing or dressing up with close-ups of lips or hips, buttocks or breasts, arms or legs, shoes or lingerie, are juxtaposed with slogans or brief quotations from Kaplan's original work. The spectator is being guided through the maze of female perversions with the assistance of mini-texts, printed words that divert the gaze from the body to the written word, from flesh to symbols. [p. 17]

The film itself is not pornographic, but the spectators I was with experienced considerable anxiety as they watched it. It presents extraordinary challenges to both the superego and ego of the spectator, who wants to look and does not want to look, who needs to form a cohesive narrative and yet is consistently unable to do so. This fragmentation of the story communicates in itself the very essence of perversion: there is no relief. Nothing is consummated. The gorgeous clothes and the beautiful bodies bring no satisfaction.

Lambert (1995) also addresses issues of beauty and ugliness in a wide range of literary works including Morrison's *The Bluest Eye*, Scott's *Ivanhoe*, Joyce's *Portrait of the Artist as a Young Man*, Nabokov's *Lolita*, and Richardson's *Clarissa*. She concludes that there is great pleasure to be had in being looked at, in looking, in clothing, and in curiosity, and she disagrees with Wolf's (1991) position in *The Beauty Myth* that our best and brightest women are victims of a conspiracy to starve themselves to death.

> Appearances not only do but *should* matter. . . . Beauty matters to me precisely *as a feminist issue*. It matters just because outward beauty is the expression of the inner self, because it is the leaser of identity.

I believe it is a very basic need for an adult, as for a child, to be loved *in the body*. [p. 16]

In *The Symptom of Beauty* (1994), Pacteau analyzed numerous works of art and literature in order to focus upon not the attribute of beauty but the act of attribution itself. She claimed that the word *beauty* and the very act of attributing beauty to someone is best understood as a generic term for what she posited as a number of different, mainly masculine, symptoms. The expression "beauty is in the eye of the beholder" puts the focus on the one who sees rather than the one being seen.

Other Films

In Chapter 5 I illustrated at some length three men who insisted that the only thing that matters about a woman is how she looks. A film that addresses this topic in a form of particular interest to psychoanalysts is the 1983 remake of Francois Truffaut's comedy *The Man who Loved Women*. Burt Reynolds plays a famous sculptor, a Casanova type, who seeks help from a psychoanalyst, played by Julie Andrews. At the beginning of the film he is seen running all over town chasing a disembodied pair of well-shaped female legs that had appeared passing by the window of his basement studio. In one session he reaches out from the analytic couch and (accidentally?) touches Andrews's leg. In another session on the couch, an earth tremor occurs. A mirrored door from a small refrigerator opens, and Reynolds can see, from his vantage point on the couch, Andrews's reflected legs, and under her dress. He is transformed and becomes a well man; they fall in love and have an affair. The shallow philanderer changes into a different, more complete human being after one good look at his female analyst! As I pointed out in Chapters 5, 6, and 7, the (fantasied and developmental) connections between looking and cure need a great deal more exploration.

Another interesting facet of the portrayal of psychoanalysis in film was described by Gabbard (1997), who examined films made between the 1930s and the 1990s and discovered some interesting depictions of female analysts. His study included the roles played by Ingrid Bergman in *Spellbound* and Barbra Streisand in *Prince of Tides*, in which a drab, serious female is eventually and inevitably conquered by the love of her male patient, which reverses their initial power relationship. As she is conquered by the male, she becomes more alive and more beautiful. In these films, the career of psychoanalyst was depicted as a pathological defense against the traditional female role. The female psychoanalyst could be transformed into a real woman only through the power of the love of her male patient. Gabbard cited Doane, who in her review of films of the 1940s also found a theme of women who neglected their appearance then being changed by men.

Barbra Streisand's films emphasize the role of the gaze, both male and female. She also has a great interest in the vicissitudes of beauty. She has spoken of her suffering over her own appearance, particularly her prominent nose. Her appearance with Robert Redford in *The Way We Were* was notable in large part because he was beautiful and she was homely. In *Funny Girl*, Streisand sang about the limited chances for girls who are not pretty to be on the stage. In *The Mirror Has Two Faces* she plays the plain, dowdy, intellectual daughter of a powerful beauty who is never without a man in her life. She meets, through a personal ad taken out for her by her sister, a fellow Columbia University professor, a handsome playboy who views her as a platonic friend. Nevertheless, he marries her in order to escape from a tormented sexual affair with a strikingly beautiful woman. While he is away for a few months, Streisand's character undertakes a makeover that eventually results in her husband's falling in love with her. Her films transmit the message that when a woman is plain, she will own the gaze. When she is beautiful, she will be looked *at*, and possess the power to attract a man. Her films concern themselves also with the notion of physical parity, that those of similar attractiveness fit together in love pairs (see Chapter 5).

Anna Karenina

Questions about the nature and meaning of beauty permeate Tolstoy's novel *Anna Karenina* (1874–76). According to Greenblatt (1998), Anna's beauty is described at first as a "natural, integrated aspect of herself which reveals her inner feelings. Yet as the novel progresses her beauty becomes an unnatural, separate part of herself which obscures these feelings" (p. 1). She is initially perceived as vital and animated: "She alone was noticeable—simple, natural, elegant and at the same time merry and animated" (p. 2). But— never believing that she is loved for her whole self—she begins to use her beauty to manipulate others. In her desire for Vronsky she begins to hide her emotions and her true feelings under the mask of her beauty, and eventually becomes unable to recognize herself: "'Who's that, she thought, gazing in the mirror at the feverish, scared face with the glittering eyes looking out at her'" (p. 3).

Anna refuses to become pregnant out of fear of deforming her body, and ironically dooms her relationship with Vronsky, who wanted her to have children. Greenblatt characterizes Anna as a hysterical woman who dislikes sex and does not experience a full sexual response, but who dresses in sexually intriguing ways in order to be alluring to men. According to Greenblatt, Tolstoy himself seemed charmed by his own character and her physical beauty, but in her gruesome suicide, Anna obliterates her beauty: "In her death, Anna mirrors what she feels inside: twisted, deformed, terrified" (p. 8).

CONCLUSION

The images and ideas of popular culture daily impact the psyches of psychoanalytic patients. Their identifications, their ways of getting love, their very notions of what is good and what is bad, of how they should look and be (and not look or be), are influenced by what they see in the movies and by what they read in books.

One of the hazards of conducting psychotherapy all day is the possibility of withdrawal from the popular culture. Our days are filled with authentic real-life dramas, and our evenings with professional meetings. We do not have much time available to participate in many aspects of the broader culture, and this in some ways allows us a degree of objectivity about it. Nevertheless, some participation is needed for thorough understanding, and understanding is needed if we are to grasp the world in which our patients live.

Vision in the Therapeutic Encounter

In this book I have meandered: from the evil eye and looks that kill to the mutual gaze of mother and child, to the mirror and its many meanings, and to voyeurism and the arts. I have presented a number of clinical examples that highlight the role of therapist as spectator, both reluctant and otherwise. In concluding his epic work, Jay (1993) wrote, "Vision and visuality in all their rich and contradictory variety can still provide us mere mortals with insights and perspectives, speculations and observations, enlightenments and illuminations, that even a god might envy" (p. 594). I hope here to have shed some light on the important role of vision and what it means in the therapeutic encounter, and to allow vision to assume its proper status in our profession as listening's twin.

References

Abraham, K. (1913). Restrictions and transformations of scopophilia in psycho-neurotics. In *Selected Papers on Psychoanalysis*, pp. 169–234. London: Hogarth, 1942.

Almansi, R. J. (1960). The face-breast equation. *Journal of the American Psychoanalytic Association* 8:43–70.

———— (1979). Scopophilia and object loss. *Psychoanalytic Quarterly* 48:601–619.

Aragno, A. (1997). *Symbolization: Proposing a Developmental Paradigm for a New Psychoanalytic Theory of Mind*. Madison, CT: International Universities Press.

Argyle, M., and Cook, M. (1976). *Gaze and Mutual Gaze*. Cambridge: Cambridge University Press.

Arlow, J. A. (1979). Metaphor and the psychoanalytic situation. *Psychoanalytic Quarterly* 48:363–385.

Aron, L., and Anderson, F. S., eds. (1998). *Relational Perspectives on the Body*. Hillsdale, NJ: Analytic Press.

Aronson, J. (1990). The use of the telephone as a transitional space in the treatment of a severely masochistic patient. In *Fantasy, Healing, and Growth*, ed. J. Sanville and J. Edward, pp. 163–178. Northvale, NJ: Jason Aronson.

————, ed. (1993). *Insights in the Dynamic Psychotherapy of Anorexia and Bulimia*. Northvale, NJ: Jason Aronson.

Bach, S. (1994). *The Language of Perversion and the Language of Love*. Northvale, NJ: Jason Aronson.

Balsam, R. (1996). The pregnant mother and the body image of the daughter. *Journal of the American Psychoanalytic Association* 44(suppl.):401–428.

Barglow, P., and Sadow, L. (1971). Visual perception: its development and maturation from birth to adulthood. *Journal of the American Psychoanalytic Association* 19:433–450.

Barzilai, S. (1995). Modes of reflexive recognition: Wallon's "origin du caractère" and Lacan's "mirror stage." *Psychoanalytic Study of the Child* 50:368–382. New Haven, CT: Yale University Press.

Bass, A. (1997). The problem of "concreteness." *Psychoanalytic Quarterly* 66:642–682.

Bataille, G. (1927). *Story of the Eye,* trans. J. Neugroschel. New York, 1982.

Beebe, B., and Lachmann, F. M. (1988). The contribution of mother–infant mutual influence to the origins of self and object representations. *Psychoanalytic Psychology* 5:305–337.

——— (1998). Co-constructing inner and relational processes. *Psychoanalytic Psychology* 15:480–516.

Beebe, B., and Stern, D. (1977). Engagement-disengagement and early object experience. In *Communicative Structures and Psychic Structures,* ed. N. Freedman and S. Grand, pp. 35–55. New York: Plenum.

Benjamin, W. (1963). The salon of 1846 and the heroism of modern life. In *Illuminations, Essays, and Reflections,* ed. H. Arendt. New York: Schocken.

——— (1983). *Charles Baudelaire: A Lyric Poet in the Era of High Capitalism.* London: Verson.

Berger, J. (1972). *Ways of Seeing.* Hardmondsworth: BBC (Penguin).

Berman, L. E. A. (1985). Rearview-mirror dreams. In *The Mirror: Psychoanalytic Perspectives,* ed. M. Bornstein, D. Silver, and W. Poland. *Psychoanalytic Inquiry* (special issue) 5(2):257–270.

Bernstein, D. (1990). Female genital anxieties: conflicts and typical mastery modes. *International Journal of Psycho-Analysis* 71:151–165.

Bion, W. R. (1958). On hallucination. *International Journal of Psycho-Analysis* 39:341–349.

Blos, P. (1962). *On Adolescence: A Psychoanalytic Interpretation.* New York: Free Press of Glencoe.

Blume, A. (1993). Andres Serrano. *BOMB,* pp. 36–41.

Bonaminio, V. (1999). *The struggle to integrate "foreign" sensations and alien affects: psychoanalytic material from an adolescent boy with gender identity confusion.* Panel on Adolescent Psychoanalysis, International Psychoanalytical Congress, Santiago, Chile, July.

Borbely, A. F. (1998). A psychoanalytic concept of metaphor. *International Journal of Psycho-Analysis* 79:923–936.

Bordo, S. (1999). *The Male Body: A New Look at Men in Public and in Private.* New York: Farrar, Straus, and Giroux.

Bornstein, M., Silver, D., and Poland, W., eds. (1985). *The Mirror: Psychoanalytic Perspectives* (special issue). *Psychoanalytic Inquiry* 5(2).

Bowlby, J. (1969). *Attachment and Loss,* vol. 1. New York: Basic Books.

Boxer, S. (1998). When verbal resists visual: Freud's defense against art. *The New York Times,* October 24, p. 11.

Bradlow, P., and Coen, S. J. (1984). Mirror masturbation. *Psychoanalytic Quarterly* 43:267–285.

Brooks, P. (1993). *Body Work: Aspects of Desire in Modern Narrative.* Cambridge, MA: Harvard University Press.

Broucek, F. (1991). *Shame and the Self.* New York: Guilford.

Bruch, H. (1978). *The Golden Cage: The Enigma of Anorexia Nervosa.* Cambridge, MA: Harvard University Press.

Brumberg, J. J. (1997). *The Body Project: An Intimate History of American Girls.* New York: Vintage.

Brunswick, R. M. (1928). A supplement to Freud's history of an infantile neurosis. *International Journal of Psycho-Analysis* 9:439–476.

Bucci, W. (1997). Discourse in good and troubled hours. *Journal of the American Psychoanalytic Association* 45:155–187.

Burka, J. B. (1996). The therapist's body in reality and fantasy. In *The Therapist as a Person,* ed. B. Gerson, pp. 255–275. Hillsdale, NJ: Analytic Press.

Busch, F. (1997). The patient's use of free association. *Journal of the American Psychoanalytic Association* 45:407–424.

Caper, R. (1994). What is a clinical fact? *International Journal of Psycho-Analysis* 75:903–913.

Chadwick, W., ed. (1998). *Mirror Images: Women, Surrealism, and Self-Representation.* Cambridge, MA: Massachusetts Institute of Technology Press.

Chused, J. F. (1997). *Male gender identity and sexuality.* Paper presented at International Psychoanalytic Association Congress, Barcelona, Spain, July.

Davidson, R., and Fox, N. (1982). Asymmetrical brain activity discriminates between positive versus negative affective stimuli in human infants. *Science* 218:1235–1237.

Davis, K. (1995). *Reshaping the Female Body: The Dilemma of Cosmetic Surgery.* New York and London: Routledge.

de Beauvoir, S. (1952). *The Second Sex.* New York: Knopf.

Demos, E. V. (1992). The early organization of the psyche. In *The Interface of Psychoanalysis and Psychology,* ed. J. W. Barron, M. N. Eagle, and D. L. Wolitzsky, pp. 200–232. Washington, DC: American Psychological Association.

Dio Bleichmar, E. (1995). The secret in the construction of female sexuality: the effects of the adult's sexual look upon the subjectivity of the girl. *Journal of Clinical Psychoanalysis* 4:335–342.

Doane, M. A. (1988–1989). Masquerade re-considered: further thoughts on the female spectator. *Discourse* 2(Fall/Winter):1.

Elkins, J. (1996). *The Object Stares Back: On the Nature of Seeing.* San Diego, CA: Harcourt Brace.

Elkisch, P. (1957). The psychological significance of the mirror. *Journal of the American Psychoanalytic Association* 5:235–244.

Elsaesser, T. (1995). Review of Zizek (1992). *International Journal of Psycho-Analysis* 76:632–636.

Emde, R. N. (1991). Positive emotions for psychoanalytic theory: surprises from infancy research and new directions. *Journal of the American Psychoanalytic Association* 39:5–44.

Etchegoyen, R. H. (1991). *The Fundamentals of Psychoanalytic Technique.* London: Karnac.

Etcoff, R. H. (1999). *Survival of the Prettiest: The Science of Beauty.* New York: Doubleday.

Faludi, S. (1991). *Backlash: The Undeclared War Against American Women.* New York: Crown.

Fantz, R. L. (1961). The origin of form perception. *Scientific American* 204:66–72.

Feldman, M. (1997). Projective identification: the analyst's involvement. *International Journal of Psycho-Analysis* 78:227–242.

Fenichel, O. (1945). *The Psychoanalytic Theory of Neurosis.* New York: Norton.

Fleming, J. (1975). Object constancy in the psychoanalysis of adults. *Journal of the American Psychoanalytic Association* 23:743–760.

Fogel, G. I. (1991). Perversity and the perverse: updating a psychoanalytic paradigm. In *Perversions and Near Perversions,* ed. G. I. Fogel, pp. 1 16. New Haven, CT: Yale University Press.

Fonagy, P., and Target, M. (1996). Playing with reality: I. Theory of mind and the normal development of psychic reality. *International Journal of Psycho-Analysis* 77:217–233.

Freedman, N., and Lavender, J. (1997). Receiving the patient's transference. *Journal of the American Psychoanalytic Association* 45:79–104.

Freud, S. (1900). The interpretation of dreams. *Standard Edition* 5:339–630.

——— (1901a). On dreams. *Standard Edition* 5:629–685.

——— (1901b). The psychopathology of everyday life. *Standard Edition* 6.

——— (1905a). Fragment of an analysis of a case of hysteria. *Standard Edition* 7:3–122.

——— (1905b). Three essays on the theory of sexuality. *Standard Edition* 7:125–248.

——— (1909). Notes upon a case of obsessional neurosis. *Standard Edition* 10:153–318.

——— (1910). The psycho-analytic view of psychological disturbance of vision. *Standard Edition* 11:209–218.

——— (1911). Psycho-analytic notes on an autobiographical account of a case of paranoia (dementia paranoides). *Standard Edition* 12:3–82.

——— (1912a). Recommendations to physicians practising psycho-analysis. *Standard Edition* 12:109–120.

——— (1912b). Totem and taboo. *Standard Edition* 13:1–161.

——— (1913). On beginning treatment. *Standard Edition* 12:122–144.

——— (1914). On narcissism: an introduction. *Standard Edition* 14:67–102.

——— (1915). Instincts and their vicissitudes. *Standard Edition* 14:111–140.

——— (1918). From the history of an infantile neurosis. *Standard Edition* 17:3–122.

——— (1919). The "uncanny." *Standard Edition* 17:219–256.

——— (1920). Beyond the pleasure principle. *Standard Edition* 18:3–64.

——— (1922). Medusa's head. *Standard Edition* 18:273–274.

——— (1923). The ego and the id. *Standard Edition* 19:3–66.

———— (1924). The economic problem of masochism. *Standard Edition* 19:157–170.

———— (1930). Civilization and its discontents. *Standard Edition* 21:9–148.

———— (1931). Female sexuality. *Standard Edition* 21:225–243.

Friday, N. (1996a). The age of beauty. *The New York Times Magazine,* May 19, p. 82.

———— (1996b). *The Power of Beauty.* New York: Harper Collins.

Gabbard, G. (1997). *Wayward women analysts of celluloid: cinematic mythology and psychoanalysis.* Presented at the Association for Psychoanalytic Medicine, New York, October.

Gamman, L., and Makinen, M. (1994). *Female Fetishism.* New York: New York University Press.

Gamman, L., and Marshment, M., eds. (1989). *The Female Gaze: Women as Viewers of Popular Myth Culture.* Seattle, WA: Real Comet Press.

Garbarino, S. (1993). Death through the eyes of a photographer. *Newsday,* February 12, pp. 81–82.

Gediman, H. K., and Lieberman, J. S. (1996). *The Many Faces of Deceit: Omissions, Lies, and Disguise in Psychotherapy.* Northvale, NJ: Jason Aronson.

Gedo, J. (1979). *Beyond Interpretation: Toward a Revised Theory for Psychoanalysis.* New York: International Universities Press.

———— (1995). Channels of communication and the analytic setup. *Psychoanalytic Inquiry* 15(2):406–412.

———— (1996). *The Language of Psychoanalysis.* Hillsdale, NJ: Analytic Press.

Gilman, S. L. (1995). *Picturing Health and Illness: Images of Identity and Difference.* Baltimore, MD: Johns Hopkins University Press.

———— (1998). *Creating Beauty to Cure the Soul: Race and Psychology in the Shaping of Cosmetic Surgery.* Durham, NC: Duke University Press.

Giovacchini, P., ed. (1972). The concrete and difficult patient. In *Tactics and Techniques in Psychoanalytic Therapy,* ed. P. Giovacchini, pp. 351–363. New York: Science House.

Goldberger, M. (1995a). The couch as defense and as potential for enactment. *Psychoanalytic Quarterly* 64:23–42.

———— (1995b). The importance of facial expressions in dreams. *International Journal of Psycho-Analysis* 76:591–593.

Gordon, M. (1998). *Spending.* New York: Scribner's.

Gould, L. (1996). Mommy dressing. *The New York Times Fashions of the Times,* August 25, p. 68.

Greenacre, P. (1947). Vision, headaches, and the halo. *Psychoanalytic Quarterly* 16:177–194.

———— (1953). Penis awe and its relation to penis envy. In *Emotional Growth,* vol. 1, pp. 31–49. New York: International Universities Press.

———— (1958). Early physical determinants in the sense of an identity. In *Emotional Growth,* vol. 1, pp. 113–127. New York: International Universities Press, 1971.

———— (1960). Considerations regarding the parent–infant relationship. In *Emotional Growth,* vol. 1, pp. 199–224. New York: International Universities Press, 1971.

Greenblatt, R. (1998). *Anna Karenina's Beauty.* Unpublished paper.

Greenspan, S. I. (1992). *Infancy and Early Childhood: The Practice of Clinical Assessment and Intervention with Emotional and Developmental Challenges.* Madison, CT: International Universities Press.

Greer, G. (1991). *The Change: Women, Aging, and the Menopause.* New York, Knopf.

———— (1999). *The Whole Woman.* New York: Knopf.

Grotstein, J. S. (1995). A reassessment of the couch in psychoanalysis. *Psychoanalytic Inquiry* 15(2):396–405.

Gunsberg, L., and Rose, E. (1998). Psychological effects of facial disfigurement. In *Aesthetic Facial Restoration,* ed. E. Rose, pp. 339–356. New York: Lippincott-Raven.

Haglund, P. E. (1996). A clear and equal gloss: reflections on the metaphor of the mirror. *Psychoanalytic Psychology* 13:225–245.

Hamburg, P. (1991). Interpretation and empathy: reading Lacan with Kohut. *International Journal of Psycho-Analysis* 72:347–362.

Hall, S. S. (1999). Bully in the mirror. *The New York Times Magazine,* August 22, p. 30.

Harrison, B. G. (1996). *An Accidental Autobiography.* Boston: Houghton Mifflin.

Haskell, M. (1987). *From Revenge to Rape: The Treatment of Women in the Movies,* 2nd ed. Chicago: University of Chicago Press.

Hersey, G. L. (1996). *The Evolution of Allure.* Cambridge, MA: Massachusetts Institute of Technology Press.

Hinshelwood, R. D. (1997). The elusive concept of "internal objects" (1934–1943): its role in the formation of the Klein group. *International Journal of Psycho-Analysis* 78:877–898.

Hopkins, P. (1999). *The evolution and dissolution of the self.* Case presented at the Institute for Psychoanalytic Training and Research, March.

Inderbitzen, L. P., and Levy, S. T. (1994). On grist for the mill: external reality as a defense. *Journal of the American Psychoanalytic Association* 42:763–788.

Irigaray, L. (1978). *Interview with M.-F. Hans and G. Lapauge, eds. Les femmes, la pornographie, et l'éroticism.* Paris.

Jacobs, T. (1999). On the question of self-disclosure by the analyst: error or advance in technique? *Psychoanalytic Quarterly* 68:159–183.

Jacobson, E. (1964). *The Self and the Object World.* New York: International Universities Press.

Jacobson, J. G. (1995). The analytic couch: Facilitation or sine qua non? *Psychoanalytic Inquiry* 15(2):304–313.

Jay, M. (1993). *Downcast Eyes: The Denigration of Vision in Twentieth Century French Thought.* Berkeley, CA: University of California Press.

Jullian, P. (1971). *Dreamers of Decadence: Symbolic Painters of the 1890's.* New York: Praeger.

Kaplan, E. H. (1997). Telepsychotherapy. *Journal of Psychotherapeutic Practice and Research* 6:227–237.

Kaplan, L. (1978). *Oneness and Separateness.* New York: Simon & Schuster.

——— (1991a). Women masquerading as women. In *Perversions and Near-Perversions in Clinical Practice,* ed. G. I. Fogel and W. A. Myers, pp. 127–152. New Haven, CT: Yale University Press.

——— (1991b). *The Female Perversions.* New York: Doubleday.

Kernberg, P. (1984). Reflections in the mirror: mother–child interaction, self-awareness, and self-recognition. In *Frontiers of Infant Psychiatry,* vol. 2, ed. J. Call, E. Galenson, and R. Tyson, pp. 101–110. New York: Basic Books.

Khan, M. (1971). To hear with eyes: clinical notes on body as subject and object. In *The Privacy of the Self,* pp. 234–250. New York: International Universities Press.

Kleeman, J. A. (1967). The peek-a-boo game. *Psychoanalytic Study of the Child* 22:239–273. New York: International Universities Press.

Klein, M. (1930). The importance of symbol formation in the development of the ego. *International Journal of Psycho-Analysis* 11:24–39.

Knafo, D. (in press a). *By Herself: Female Representation in Twentieth Century Art.*

———— (in press b). Out of the dolls' house: Barbie comes to life. *Psychoanalytische Blaetter.*

Kohut, H. (1971). *The Analysis of the Self.* New York: International Universities Press.

Koulomzin, M., Beebe, B., Jaffe, J., and Feldstein, S. (1993). Infant self-comfort, disorganized scanning, facial distress and bodily approach in face-to-face play at 4 months discriminate "A" vs. "B" attachment at one year. *Society for Research-in-Child Development* [Abstract issue] 446, March 25–28.

Kris, E. (1956). The recovery of childhood memories. *Psychoanalytic Study of the Child* 11:54–88. New York: International Universities Press.

Kuspit, D. (1998). *Freud and the visual arts.* Meeting of the International Institute of Object Relations Therapy, Washington, DC, October.

LaBelle, J. (1988). *Herself Beheld: The Literature of the Looking Glass.* Ithaca, NY: Cornell University Press.

Lacan, J. (1936). *The mirror stage as formation of the function of the I as revealed in psychoanalytic theory.* Paper presented at International Psychoanalytic Association Congress, Marienbad.

———— (1953). Some reflections on the ego. *International Journal of Psycho-Analysis,* 34:11–17.

———— (1953–54). Le seminaire: livre I. In *Les Ecrits Techniques de Freud,* ed. J. A. Miller. Paris: Editions du Seuil, 1975.

———— (1977). *Ecrits: A Selection,* trans. A. Sheridan. New York: W. W. Norton.

Lachmann, F. L. (1982). Narcissistic development. In *Early Female Development,* ed. D. Mendell, pp. 227–248. Jamaica, NY: Spectrum.

Lakoff, G., and Johnson, M. (1980). *Metaphors We Live By.* Chicago: University of Chicago Press.

———— (1999). *Philosophy in the Flesh.* New York: Basic Books.

Lambert, E. Z. (1995). *The Face of Love: Feminism and the Beauty Question.* Boston: Beacon.

Laplanche, J., and Pontalis, J.-B. (1973). *The Language of Psychoanalysis.* New York: W. W. Norton.

Lax, R. (1997). Some roots of persistent homosexual fantasy and the quest for father's love: conflicted parental identification in a male patient, fragment of an analysis. *Psychoanalytic Review* 84:843–863.

Lecours, S., and Bouchard, M. (1997). Dimensions of mentalisation. Outlining levels of psychic transformation. *International Journal of Psycho-Analysis* 78:855–875.

Lehmann, H. (1994). The gazing reaper. *Mirror* (Canada) October 20–27, p. 30.

Lemche, E. (1998). The development of the body image in the first three years. *Psychoanalysis and Contemporary Thought* 21:155–276.

Lerner, H. E. (1976). Parental mislabeling of female genitals as a determinant of penis envy and learning inhibitions in women. *Journal of the American Psychoanalytic Association* 24(5):269–284.

Levin, F. (1979). Metaphor, affect, and arousal: how interpretation might work. *Psychoanalytic Quarterly* 48:231–243.

Lewis, M., and Brooks-Gunn, J. (1979). *Social Cognition and the Acquisition of Self.* New York: Plenum.

Lichtenberg, J. D. (1983). *Psychoanalysis and Infant Research.* Hillsdale, NJ: Analytic Press.

——— (1985). Mirrors and mirroring: developmental experience. *Psychoanalytic Inquiry* 5(2):199–210.

——— (1995). Forty-five years of psychoanalytic experience on, behind, and without the couch. In *The Relevance of the Couch in Contemporary Psychoanalysis,* ed. G. Moriatis. *Psychoanalytic Inquiry* 15:290–293.

Lieberman, J. S. (1991a). *Technical, dynamic, and countertransference considerations with patients who lie.* Paper presented at the 37th International Psychoanalytic Association Congress, Buenos Aires, July.

——— (1991b). Issues in the psychoanalytic treatment of single women over 30. *Psychoanalytic Review* 78:177–198.

——— (1994). *Through an analyst's lens: Are Sally Mann's photos benign or abusive?* Paper presented at American Psychological Association, Division 39, Washington, DC, April.

Lindon, S. A. (1988). Psychoanalysis by telephone. *Bulletin of the Menninger Clinic* 52:521–528.

Mahler, M. S., Pine, F., and Bergman, A. (1975). *The Psychological Birth of the Human Infant.* New York: Basic Books.

Major, R. (1980). The voice behind the mirror. *International Review of Psychoanalysis* 7:459–468.

Makari, G. (1994). In the eye of the beholder. *Journal of the American Psychoanalytic Association* 42:549–580.

Malcolm, J. (1981). *Psychoanalysis: The Impossible Profession.* New York: Vintage, 1982.

Malcolm, R. R. (1988). The mirror: a perverse sexual phantasy in a woman seen as a defense against a psychotic breakdown. In *Melanie Klein Today,* vol. 1, ed. E. G. Spillius, pp. 115–137. London: New Library of Psychoanalysis, Routledge.

———— (1999). Interpretation: the past in the present. In *On Bearing Unbearable States of Mind,* pp. 38–52. New York and London: Routledge.

Mann, T. (1911). *Death in Venice.* New York: Vintage, 1954.

McDougall, J. (1989). *Theaters of the Body.* New York: W. W. Norton.

McGihan, C. L. D. (1996). The body's contribution to a female sense of self. *Journal of Analytic Social Work* 3:47–64.

Meissner, W. W. (1998). The self and the body: IV. The body on the couch. *Psychoanalysis and Contemporary Thought* 21:277–300.

Melnick, B. A. (1997). Metaphor and the theory of libidinal development. *International Journal of Psycho-Analysis* 78:997–1015.

Menninger, K. (1934). Polysurgery and polysurgical addiction. *Psychoanalytic Quarterly* 3:173–199.

Miles, M. R. (1994). Textual harassment: desire and the female body. In *The Good Body,* ed. M. G. Winkler and L. B. Cole, pp. 49–63. New Haven, CT: Yale University Press.

Mitrani, J. L. (1998). Unbearable ecstasy, reverence, and awe, and the perpetuation of an "aesthetic conflict." *Psychoanalytic Quarterly* 67:102–127.

Moore, A. M. (1994). The good woman: asceticism and responsibility from the perspectives of battered women. In *The Good Body,* ed. M. G. Winkler and L. B. Cole, pp. 36–48. New Haven, CT: Yale University Press.

Moore, S. (1994). Here's looking at you kid. In *The Female Gaze: Women as Viewers of Popular Culture,* ed. L. Gamman and M. Marshment, pp. 44–59. Seattle, WA: Real Comet Press.

Moriatis, G., ed. (1995). The couch as protective shield for the analyst. *Psychoanalytic Inquiry* 15:406–412.

Muller, J. P. (1985). Lacan's mirror stage. *Psychoanalytic Inquiry* 5(2):233–252.

Muller, J. P., and Richardson, W. J. (1982). *Lacan and Language: A Reader's Guide to Ecrits*. New York: International Universities Press.

Mulvey, L. (1975). Visual pleasure and the narrative cinema. In *Art and Modernism*, ed. B. Wallis, pp. 361–373. New York: New Museum of Contemporary Art.

O'Dell, K. (1998). *Contract with the Skin: Masochism, Performance Art, and the 1970's*. Minneapolis, MN: University of Minnesota Press.

Ogden, T. (1995). Analyzing forms of silence and deadness of the transference–countertransference. In *Reverie and Interpretation*, ed. T. Ogden. Northvale, NJ: Jason Aronson, 1997.

———— (1996a). The perverse subject of analysis. *Journal of the American Psychoanalytic Association* 44:1121–1146.

———— (1996b). Reconsidering three aspects of psychoanalytic technique. *International Journal of Psycho-Analysis* 77:883–900.

———— (1997). Reverie and metaphor: some thoughts on how I work as a psychoanalyst. *International Journal of Psycho-Analysis* 78:719–732.

Oliner, M. (1996). External reality: the elusive dimension of psychoanalysis. *Psychoanalytic Quarterly* 65:267–287.

Orbach, S. (1978). *Fat Is a Feminist Issue*. New York: Berkeley.

Ostow, M., ed. (1974). *Sexual Deviation: Psychoanalytic Insights*. New York: Quadrangle.

Pacteau, F. (1994). *The Symptom of Beauty*. London: Reaktion.

Paniagua, C. (1998). Acting-in revisited. *International Journal of Psycho-Analysis* 79:499–512.

Papousek, H., and Papousek, M. (1974). Mirror-image and self-recognition in young human infants. I: A new method of experimental analysis. *Developmental Psychobiology* 7:149–157.

———— (1977). Mother and the cognitive head start. In *Studies in Mother–Infant Interactions*, ed. H. R. Schaffer, pp. 63–85. New York: Academic Press.

Phillips, K. A. (1996). *The Broken Mirror*. New York: Oxford University Press.

Pines, M. (1984). Reflections on mirroring. *International Journal of Psycho-Analysis* 11:27–42.

———— (1985). Mirroring and child development. *Psychoanalytic Inquiry* 5(2):211–232.

Plotkin, F. (1997). *Age, gender, and erotic transference manifestations.* Paper presented at American Psychological Association, Division 39, Denver, CO, March.

Pollack, George (1989). *The Mourning–Liberation Process,* vol. 1. Madison, CT: International Universities Press.

Pollack, Griselda (1988). Modernity and the spaces of femininity. In *Vision and Difference,* pp. 50–90. London: Routledge.

Priel, B. (1985). On mirror-image anxiety. *Psychoanalytic Study of the Child* 40:183–196. New Haven, CT: Yale University Press.

Rapaport, D. (1960). On the psychoanalytic theory of motivation. In *Collected Papers,* pp. 853–915. New York: Basic Books.

Reed, G. (1994). *Transference Neurosis and Psychoanalytic Experience.* New Haven, CT: Yale University Press.

Reik, T. (1948). *Listening with the Third Ear.* New York: Farrar, Strauss.

Reiss, A. (1978). The mother's eye—for better and for worse. *Psychoanalytic Study of the Child* 33:381–409. New Haven, CT: Yale University Press.

———— (1988). The power of the eye in nature, nurture, and culture—a developmental view of mutual gaze. *Psychoanalytic Quarterly of the Child* 43:399–417. New Haven, CT: Yale University Press.

Renik, O. (1992). Use of the analyst as a fetish. *Psychoanalytic Quarterly* 61:542–563.

Richards, A. K. (1996). Ladies of fashion: pleasure, perversion, and paraphilia. *International Journal of Psycho-Analysis* 77:337–352.

———— (1998a). Woman as Medusa in "Basic Instinct." *Psychoanalytic Inquiry* 18:269–280.

———— (1998b). *The two faces of self-love, body narcissism, and relational narcissism.* Unpublished.

Riding, A. (1997). Dead but not forgotten. Body art. *The New York Times,* April 19.

Riviere, J. (1929). Womanliness as a masquerade. *International Journal of Psycho-Analysis* 10:303–313.

Rivlin, R., and Gravelle, K. (1984). *Deciphering the Senses: The Expanding World of Human Perception.* New York: Touchstone.

Rodin, J., Silverstein, L. R., and Striegel-Moore, R. (1985). Women and weight: a normative discontent. In *Psychology and Gender,* ed. T. B. Sandregger, pp.

267–307. Nebraska Symposium on Motivation. Lincoln, NE: University of Nebraska Press.

Ross, J. M. (1999). *Once more onto the couch.* Presented at New York Psychoanalytic Society, New York, January.

Rushdie, S. (1997). Crash. *New Yorker Magazine,* September 15, p. 68.

Sadow, L. (1995). Looking, listening, and the couch. *Psychoanalytic Inquiry* 15:386–395.

Sandler, A. M. (1963). Development of blind infants. *Psychoanalytic Study of the Child* 18:343–360. New York: International Universities Press.

Schafer, R. (1970). The psychoanalytic vision of reality. *International Journal of Psycho-Analysis* 51:279–297.

——— (1976). *A New Language for Psychoanalysis.* New Haven and London: Yale University Press.

Schjeldahl, P. (1993). Andres Serrano. *Village Voice,* February 16, p. 91.

Schneider, L. (1985). Mirrors in art. *Psychoanalytic Inquiry* 5(2):283–324.

Schore, A. N. (1991). Early superego development: the emergence of shame and narcissistic affect regulation in the practicing period. *Psychoanalysis and Contemporary Thought* 14:187–250.

——— (1997). Interdisciplinary developmental research as a source of clinical models. In *The Neurobiological and Developmental Basis for Psychotherapeutic Intervention,* ed. M. Moskowitz, C. Monk, C. Kaye, and S. Ellman, pp. 1–71. Northvale, NJ: Jason Aronson.

Schust-Briat, G. (1996). "Fertile eyes": considerations on visual phenomena in the analyst's mind at work. *Psychoanalytic Inquiry* 16:376–389.

Segal, H. (1978). On symbolism. *International Journal of Psycho-Analysis* 59:315–319.

——— (1991). *Dream, Phantasy, and Art.* London: Routledge.

Shengold, L. (1974). The metaphor of the mirror. *Journal of the American Psychoanalytic Association* 22:97–115.

Sifneos, P. E. (1975). Problems of psychotherapy in patients with alexithymic characteristics and physical disease. *Psychotherapy and Psychosomatics* 26:65–70.

Silver, D. (1985). Mirror in dreams: symbol of mother's face. *Psychoanalytic Inquiry* 5(2):253–256.

Silverman, M. (1987). Clinical material. *Psychoanalytic Inquiry* 7:147–166.

Sours, J. (1974). *Starving to Death in a Sea of Objects: The Anorexia Nervosa Syndrome.* New York: Jason Aronson.

Spitz, R. A. (1965). *The First Year of Life.* New York: International Universities Press.

Stannard, U. (1971). The mask of beauty. In *Women in Sexist Society: Studies in Power and Powerlessness,* ed. V. Gornick and B. K. Moran, pp. 118–132. New York: Basic Books.

Stern, D. (1977). *The First Relationship.* Cambridge, MA: Harvard University Press.

——— (1985). *The Interpersonal World of the Infant.* New York: Basic Books.

Stern, D., Sander, L., Nahum, J., et al. (1998). Non-interpretive mechanisms in psychoanalytic therapy: the "something more" than interpretation. *International Journal of Psycho-Analysis* 79:903–922.

Stimmel, B. (1995). The written dream: action, resistance, and revelation. *Psychoanalytic Quarterly* 65:658–671.

Sussman, E. (1996). In/of her time: Nan Goldin's photographs. In *Nan Goldin: I'll Be Your Mirror,* eds. N. Goldin, D. Armstrong, and H. Holzwarth, pp. 25–44. New York: Whitney Museum of American Art.

Thompson, J. K., Heinberg, L. J., Altabe, M., and Tantleff-Dunn, S. (1999). *Exacting Beauty: Theory, Assessment, and Treatment of Body Image Disturbance.* Washington, DC: American Psychological Association.

Traub-Werner, D. (1998). The erotization of the gaze. *Canadian Journal of Psychoanalysis* 6:35–49.

Trevarthan, C. (1993). The self born in intersubjectivity: the psychology of an infant communicating. In *The Perceived Self: Interpersonal; Sources of Self-Knowledge,* ed. U. Neisser, pp. 121–173. New York: Cambridge University Press.

Tyler, A. (1995). *Ladder of Years.* New York: Knopf.

Tylim, I. (1997). "Female perversions" or the woman who mistook her power for her lipstick. *Round Robin* 13:17.

——— (1998). *Body as Text, Text as Body. The Pillow Book.* Paper presented at the International Federation for Psychoanalytic Education, New York, November.

Tyson, P. (1986). Female psychological development. *The Annual of Psychoanalysis* 14:357–373.

Vygotsky, L. (1988). Thinking and speaking. In *The Collected Papers of L. S. Vygotsky,* vol. 1, ed. R. W. Rieber and A. S. Carton, pp. 39–288. New York: Plenum.

Wallon, H. (1921). La conscience et une conscience du moi. *Journal de Psychologie* 18:51–64.

——— (1931). Comment se développe chez l'enfant la notion du corps propre. *Journal de Psychologie* November–December: 705–748.

Weich, M. J. (Reporter) (1986). Clinical aspects of language. Scientific proceedings, panel reports. *Journal of the American Psychoanalytic Association* 34:687–698.

Weissman, S. M. (1977). Face to face: the role of vision and the smiling response. *Psychoanalytic Study of the Child* 32:421–450. New Haven, CT: Yale University Press.

Werner, H. (1948). *Comparative Psychology of Mental Development*. New York: International Universities Press.

Wilde, O. (1894). *Salome*. London: Creation Books, 1996.

Wilson, A., and Prillaman, J. L. (1997). Early development and disorders of internalization. In *The Neurobiological and Developmental Basis for Psychotherapeutic Intervention*, ed. M. Moskowitz, C. Monk, C. Kaye, and S. Ellman, pp. 189–233. Northvale, NJ: Jason Aronson.

Wilson, A., and Weinstein, L. (1992). Language and clinical process: psychoanalysis and Vygotskian psychology, part II. *Journal of the American Psychoanalytic Association* 40:725–759.

——— (1996). Transference and the ZPD. *Journal of the American Psychoanalytic Association* 44:167–200.

Wilson, C. P., Hogan, C. C., and Mintz, I. L., eds. (1984). *Fear of Being Fat: The Treatment of Anorexia Nervosa*. Northvale, NJ: Jason Aronson.

Winkler, M. G., and Cole, L. B., eds. (1994). *The Good Body: Asceticism in Contemporary Culture*. New Haven, CT: Yale University Press.

Winnicott, D. W. (1971). *Playing and Reality*. London: Tavistock/Routledge.

Witham-Levinstein, K. (1996). *Women and Sadomasochistic Tension in Film and Prime-Time Television Melodrama: An Application of Psychoanalytic Film Theory to Television*. Bethel, CT: Rutledge.

Wolf, E. (1995). Brief notes on using the couch. *Psychoanalytic Inquiry* 5(2):314–323.

Wolf, N. (1991). *The Beauty Myth: How Images of Beauty Are Used Against Women*. New York: William Morrow.

Wolfe, T. (1987). *The Bonfire of the Vanities*. New York: Farrar, Straus, & Giroux.

Wolff, P. H. (1965). Visual pursuit and attention in young infants. *Journal of the Academy of Child Psychiatry* 4:473–484.

Wolfflin, H. (1932). *Principles of Art History*, trans. M. D. Hottinger. Mineola, NY: Dover.

Wright, K. (1991). *Vision and Separation: Between Mother and Baby.* Northvale, NJ: Jason Aronson.

Wurtzel, E. (1998). *Bitch: In Praise of Difficult Women.* New York: Anchor/ Doubleday.

Young, S. (1989). Feminism and the politics of power: Whose gaze is it anyway? In *The Female Gaze: Women as Viewers of Popular Culture*, ed. L. Gamman and M. Marshment, pp. 173–188. Seattle, WA: Real Comet Press.

Zalusky, S. (1998). Telephone analysis. *Journal of the American Psychoanalytic Association* 46:1221–1242.

Zizek, S., ed. (1992). *A Triumph of the Eye Over the Gaze: Everything You Always Wanted to Know about Lacan But Were Afraid to Ask Hitchcock.* London: Verso.

Index

ABOUT THE AUTHOR

Janice S. Lieberman, Ph.D., is in the private practice of psycho-analysis and psychoanalytic therapy in New York City. She is a faculty member and a Training and Supervising Analyst of the Institute for Psychoanalytic Training and Research (IPTAR). A member of the American Psychoanalytic Association, she serves on the editorial board of *The American Psychoanalyst* and the Committee for Government Relations and Insurance (CGRI). She is a Training and Supervising Analyst of the International Psychoanalytical Association and a member of the North American New Groups Committee. Dr. Lieberman is co-author of *The Many Faces of Deceit: Omissions, Lies, and Disguise in Psychotherapy* (1996) and has published numerous articles and book reviews, many of which pertain to issues of gender and/or contemporary art, in the *Journal of the American Psychoanalytic Association, International Journal of Psychoanalysis, Psychoanalytic Review*, and *Psychoanalytic Books*. She has presented papers at the scientific meetings of the American Psychoanalytic Association, the International Psychoanalytical Association, Division 39, IPTAR, the New York Freudian Society, and other organizations. In her spare time she lectures at the Whitney Museum of American Art.